See 155 →

The Indian Economy
Poverty and Development

The Indian Economy
Poverty and Development

Pramit Chaudhuri

Crosby Lockwood Staples   London

Granada Publishing Limited
First published in Great Britain 1978 by
Crosby Lockwood Staples
Frogmore St Albans Hertfordshire AL2 2NF and
3 Upper James Street London W1R 4BP

ISBN 0 258 96911 3

Printed in India

Die Sattgefressenen
sprechen zu den Hungernden
Von den grossen Zeiten
die kommen werden

Those who have eaten their fill
speak to the hungry of the wonderful
times to come

Bertolt Brecht
Die das Fleisch Wegnehmen vom Tisch
Svendborger Gedichte, Brecht Gedichte IV
Suhrkamp Verlag, 1961

Preface

This book is intended primarily as an introduction to the problems of economic development in India. The information that is available to us is so vast that any reasonably detailed summary of it would have resulted in a book many hundred pages long. On balance, I have decided against writing such a book, choosing instead to present briefly such parts of the information as appear to me to be of the most critical importance. The student can read this book fairly quickly—although I am afraid that it has to be read with some care, because its arguments are sometimes rather involved—to obtain his general bearings. He can then pass on to the more specialized material that is documented in the bibliographical references. Attempts to tell the story of Indian development within the compass of a few pages raise problems of their own. One has to decide what to leave out and how the material that is included fits together. More important, one has to decide whether the developments are to be studied from the point of view of the experience of the economy as a whole or in the light of how those developments affect a particular part of society, such as the poor. The account that is presented is, therefore, a very personal view of Indian economic development in many ways. That personal point of view, I am fairly confident, can be defended both in terms of its analytical and empirical underpinnings. I have no pretensions to have offered any final resolutions of the many complicated problems that face us in the interpretation of recent economic phenomena in India. This book is no more than an exploratory essay, designed to raise certain questions in the reader's mind.

A few words need to be said about the contents of the book. It attempts to explain the past and not to predict the future. It has nothing to say, therefore, on such issues as the 'oil crisis', which cannot be seen as in any way a logical development of past forces operating within the economy and whose future impact is uncertain. The book also lays relatively less emphasis on external factors, such as problems of export policy or foreign aid. While I agree that such issues are not unimportant, I firmly believe that the basic explanation of the course of economic events in India in recent years has to be formulated in terms of forces and relationships that are internal to the economy. As this is a book written by an economist about economic development, it does require a certain amount of knowledge of economics to follow its arguments. One would not need a very extensive knowledge of economics to read this book (especially if one is charitable enough to give the author the benefit of the doubt at times) but one would need to know that little amount rather well. However, I have tried fairly hard to explain things in as simple terms as possible, without access to too many technical terms. It might help the reader to be told at this stage that what I have tried to present in this book is a 'structuralist' view of Indian economic development, in the sense that economists use that term.

The suggestion that I should attempt to write an introductory textbook on India came originally from Professor Michael Lipton. While the end product has turned out to be very different from what either of us then had in mind, I remain grateful to him for the initiative, and also for reading the manuscript with care and sympathy. It was also read by Dr Ashok Mitra, Dr Deepak Nayyar and by Rohini Nayyar. They have been the most understanding and constructive of critics. Parts of the manuscript were also read by Professor Amiya Bagchi and Robert Cassen. I remain grateful to them all. None of them is responsible for the views that are expressed in this book and the errors that it might contain. I should here also thank the publisher's reader, who read the book with much care and a degree of understanding of my point of view which was greater than I could have expected. If the basic thesis of the book has emerged with any degree of clarity at the end, much of the credit for that is his. My publishers are to be thanked for putting up patiently with many delays.

The first draft of the manuscript was typed by Anne Harland, Margaret Heywood and Phil Markwick; later amendments by Jan

Birbeck and Pat Cobbett. My thanks to them for their patience and promptness. I am also grateful to Sue Rowland for drawing the charts and to Jean Chaudhuri for help with some of the tables. It is a great pleasure to acknowledge my debt to the staff of the library of the Institute of Development Studies for their continuous help, over a long period of time, always given cheerfully and efficiently. Not only have they always provided what I asked for but have often gone out of their way to draw my attention to publications that I did not know existed.

The material relating to foreign aid used in this book arises out of a study that was financed by the Social Science Research Council. I should also thank the University of Sussex for a term's leave of absence to enable me to work on the book.

I am grateful to the following for permission to quote extracts from published material:

(i) The International Economic Association and Dr Ashok Mitra for material used in Table 5;
(ii) The Editor, International Monetary Fund Staff Papers, for material used in Table 27;
(iii) The Editor, *Sankhya (Indian Journal of Statistics)*, for material used in Table 40.

The detailed textual references are given in the footnotes and the bibliographical references.

I am grateful to the Suhrkamp Verlag, Frankfurt am-Main, for permission to quote the extract from Bertolt Brecht—*Svendborger Gedichte, Brecht Gedichte*, Band IV.

Readers should note that Madras and Tamil Nadu are the same, as are Mysore and Karnataka. Data relating to the Census of Agriculture 1970 and the 1971-72 land holding survey became available after the book was completed.

This writing of any book causes a certain amount of domestic upheaval. My family rode out the occasional pockets of turbulence with admirable fortitude.

PRAMIT CHAUDHURI
University of Sussex

Contents

PART 1

CHAPTER ONE

Assessment of Economic Performance

Over the last 25 years, the Indian economy has made only limited progress towards self-sustained economic growth. After 25 years of effort, a substantial number of Indians, which can be counted in millions, remain desperately poor and can look forward to more abject poverty. These two congruent statements, addressed to the same body of facts, ought to lead us to similar conclusions regarding the nature of the problems that India faces and to the policies she should pursue. However, the way a problem is formulated influences the way in which we approach, select and analyse the evidence. Quite often, it shapes the answer that emerges. Very seldom is this more true than in the context of the complex, contradictory and vast body of facts that faces an economist who attempts to describe and interpret the performance of the Indian economy over the last quarter of a century.

The performance of an economy can be looked at from a number of alternative points of view. Economic historians might study the behaviour of the Indian economy today, with reference to her recent past, wisely disbelieving in revolutions that have not yet happened. On that basis, economists of very different dispositions agree that the Indian economy has performed rather well after independence.[1] Although a knowledge of the economic and social structure that India inherited at the time of independence is essential to an understanding of more recent experience, I have not here attempted such a historical approach.[2] Another

[1]Compare, for example, the articles by Bagchi (1970), Raj (1965) and Weisskopf (1972).

[2]Good introductions to the historical performance of the economy are

popular viewpoint is that of the inter-country comparisons, whereby rise in output or employment in the Indian economy are compared to China, rates of fertilizer consumption to Taiwan and the impact of aid to a group of other countries. It is unquestionable that such comparative studies can sometimes yield illuminating insights into the problems of economic development facing India and that some valuable work has been done in this area.[3] I believe, however, that the problems raised by inter-country comparisons are seriously underestimated in much of the published literature, especially if operationally usable conclusions are to be based on them.[4] I have, therefore, kept a somewhat myopic vision fixed firmly on India hoping that I do not present a very distorted view of the reality.

The yardstick that I have adopted for assessing economic performance, at least as a starting point, is the avowed objectives of the system, as formulated and declaimed by the policy makers.[5] These are laid down in the various plan documents, together with other policy prescriptions, from the ambiguous legal language of the industrial policy resolutions of 1948 and 1956 to the unambiguous language of the political market-place, *Garibi Hatao*.[6] This can only be a starting point, a vague and unsatisfactory pointer on a map. It is almost a logical impossibility to state what objectives such an entity as 'the economy,' through its policy makers, pursues. Moreover, not all real objectives need be explicitly stated and not all that is avowed, is or is meant to

provided by Buchanan (1934) and Macpherson (1972); on the controversy over standards of living in the nineteenth century, see Morris *et al.* (1969); on the behaviour of agricultural production, see Blyn (1966); on industrial development in the twentieth century, see the definitive work by Bagchi (1972).

[3]See, for example, the two interesting papers by Raj (1967) and Weisskopf (1975).

[4]Some of the major problems are caused by differences in size and the structural characteristics of the economy, including the degree of 'openness' of the economy. The Chinese experience is probably the one case that is most directly comparable to India on these grounds. However, the usefulness of that comparison is vitiated by the fact that China has a completely different social and economic system.

[5]For a more detailed discussion of alternative assessment criteria in the Indian context, see Chaudhuri (1971).

[6]India, Planning Commission (1952) Ch. II, (1956) Ch. II, (1961) Ch. IV and (1969) Ch. 1.

be implemented. Words, by themselves, do not affect the allocation of either resources or rewards. However, rough and unsatisfactory though it is, I believe that the major objectives that the
Government of India followed during our period can be identified sufficiently clearly for us to make a start at assessing the
performance of the economy.

I shall discuss later on in the book to what extent various
objectives laid down in policy statements were attained during
1950-1974. Here, I am solely concerned with establishing the
general analytical framework within which I have chosen to set
out the basic facts of economic life in India during that period.
From that point of view the various plan objectives can be
grouped into three: those which are desirable from the point of
view of the economy as a whole, those which are of especial
benefit to certain sections of the economy and those which are
designed to alter in some way the structure of the economy.[7]
Though the emphasis laid on the various objectives may have
shifted from time to time, there is a remarkable consistency in
the ends the economy set itself throughout this period.[8] However, the attitude of the Government to the choice of instruments
that were to achieve these ends did undergo certain changes over
the years.[9]

Under the first group of objectives relating to the whole of the
economy is the basic one of increasing the level of national
income. This is expressed both in aggregative terms and in terms
of the level of income *per capita*, thus relating it to an implicit or
explicit objective as to the desirable rate of growth of population
over a period of time, as well as to such general concepts as the
standard of living of the populace. The national income target is
set both in terms of desirable rates of growth and of a target
period by which the objective is to be attained. As we shall see,
this target has turned out in practice to be a receding one. There

---

[7]This classification is admittedly a rough and ready one adopted for
purposes of exposition. In practice, a particular objective may have more
than one of these attributes.

[8]The reader may compare the various references cited in n.6 above.

[9]The sharpest change is probably shown by the Approach document to
the fifth five-year plan, India, Planning Commission (1973), Ch. I, where
the elimination of poverty is stressed more strongly than, say, in the second
or third five-year plans; see also Chapter 9 below.

is a clear realization that the need to maintain the continuity of growth is as important as the achievement of any such target. This objective is usually embodied in the concept of 'self-sustaining' growth and sometimes more concretely in terms of a terminal capital requirement. Added to the national income target is the overall employment target, enshrined like so many idols in this iconoclastic age in the Directive Principles to the Constitution as the right to work.[10] In the practical world of planners, this is seen less as a question of providing full employment, although that is obviously a *good thing*, as that of providing a given and sufficient number of jobs within a particular plan period, so as to make it possible to absorb a proportion of the backlog of unemployment and the increase in the labour force in that period. The approach to the problem of unemployment has changed considerably in recent years.

There is much discussion in the plan documents of the importance of resource mobilization in the process of development. In one sense, resource mobilization is a mean, because the attainment of growth depends on such mobilization. A shortfall on the resources front might result in the failure to attain the growth targets. In another sense, in a mixed economy inadequate resource mobilization manifests itself in internal and external instability. A relative stability in the price level and a viable balance of payments are both seen as basic objectives of the plans.[11]

The second set of objectives, those that are related to certain sections or groups within the economy, is headed by the distributional objective. There is recognition that the present degree of inequality in incomes is unacceptable and should be reduced. This is to be brought about not so much by a redistribution of existing incomes as by channelling increasingly to the low income groups the incremental benefits of growth. Although the need to do something for 'the poor' has always figured prominently in the plans, in later years and especially in the fifth plan attention has focused mainly on increasing the standard of living of the

---

[10]Tarlok Singh (1974), Ch. III.

[11]One should distinguish here between physical and financial resources. An economy acquires physical resources of certain kinds that it cannot adequately produce at home through imports. However, additional financial resources to domestic savings are only made available by the net import surplus.

very poor part of the population.[12]

Just as the population can be divided into rich and poor and special attention directed to the latter, so the country can be divided geographically into rich and poor states and regions. Not all parts of India were equally developed in 1950, however we chose to measure it, and the regional inequalities persist, some will say are even growing, in the 1970s. Reducing regional inequalities is also an objective of the planners.

From the first plan onwards, the documents recognize the importance of the agricultural sector to the growth of the economy.[13] It is important both as a sector from which the bulk of the population derives its livelihood and as a source of food and raw materials for the rest of the economy. The relationship between agriculture and industry is seen as one of complementarity. Industrial development comes in for attention, both as a supplier of essential non-agricultural goods and in the longer run as an alternative source of jobs to the growing agricultural population.[14]

A word needs to be said here about the role of the external sector as perceived by the planners. The planners see the issue of self-reliance primarily as one where the economy will not be reliant on a large and continuing net inflow of foreign resources.[15] As such, the objective is one of maintaining external balance and not one of self-reliance in an autarchic sense. Some would dispute this interpretation and I discuss the question briefly later in Chapter 9.[16]

[12]India, Planning Commission (1973), pp. 1-3.

[13]All the plan documents from the first plan onwards have stressed the importance of the agricultural sector to the growth of the economy and the wellbeing of its population. However, statements contained in plan documents are not always a reliable guide to the policy that is followed. The Government's policy towards the agricultural sector is discussed in Chapters 5 and 9 below.

[14]Strictly speaking, the rural population rather than the agricultural population, because not all people living in the rural sector derive their living from agriculture.

[15]An exception is Professor Mahalanobis's writings, where he stresses the need to build up India's supply of scientific and technical manpower. Mahalanobis (1963).

[16]See below p. 217f; not everyone would agree with this interpretation of the trade policy followed by in the Government of India. Among the aid administrators in donor countries there is a strong feeling that the Government's policy is *de facto* autarchic.

However, we need to make one distinction at this stage. The need to build up industrial capacity during the process of development is put very much in terms of the inability of the economy to meet its total requirements of certain categories of goods through imports rather than of seeking independence for some strategic reason. It is important to note in this context that there is very little discussion at this level on the development of indigenous sources of technology.

Coming to the last set of objectives, those that relate to the structure of the economy, it is useful to distinguish between the agricultural and the non-agricultural sectors. Within the first, the problem is seen very much in terms of redistribution of land ownership, the so-called 'land to the tiller' programme, and in the reformulation of the rights and terms of tenancy. That is to say, within the agricultural sector the problem is recognized to be one about the ownership and control over the use of existing resources, requiring at one end actual redistribution of the existing stock of wealth. In the non-agricultural context, the problem is that of the concentration of economic power, of big business or the *growth* of monopoly, and the remedy is to control the further expansion of what are called large industrial houses. In addition, there is an implicit concept of countervailing power in the policy to build up a large public sector industrial complex, that will make the economy less dependent for certain critically important inputs such as steel and machinery on the private sector. Put like this, the enemy appears to be within the gate; the national bourgeoisie rather than the international, on whose access to knowhow both the public and the private sector might have to depend.[17]

Put this way, the list of objectives appears to be unexceptionable, and comprehensive. However, a closer look reveals much to be dissatisfied about. To put it briefly at this stage, there are three major shortcomings of this set of objectives.[18] First, very few of the objectives are quantified or have a time-horizon attached to them, with the exception of national income targets. Secondly, there is no discussion of the feasibility or consistency of the set of objectives that has been chosen. This would hardly have been possible without a clear quantification of the objectives. Thirdly,

---

[17]This issue is further discussed in Chapter 6 below.
[18]For further discussion of the planning strategy, see Chapter 9 below.

as there is no serious recognition of problems of inconsistency between the objectives, there is naturally no discussion of trade-offs amongst them. Thus, when the second plan, in which the implicit strategy is most clearly formulated, talks about the conflict between present and future consumption, there are no orders of magnitude laid down and there is no discussion as to the acceptibility of such a trade-off. The exception is, perhaps, the fifth plan, which does attempt to offer alternative guidelines for the removal of poverty and the redistributional trade-offs required between the rich and poor. It also attempts to quantify certain balance of payments effects of alternative policies.[19] However, these efforts are vitiated by another major defect of Indian planning; that the quantitative bases of the plans are so vague and ambiguous, at least as revealed in the published documents, as to make it almost impossible for us to decide for ourselves whether a set of objectives was either feasible or consistent.[20] For these reasons, although the plans read well they are of limited use to us in the assessment of policy.

The statement of objectives, however, does suggest in our minds a set of questions, the answers to which will chart the direction in which the economy was moving and the pace at which it was doing so. The first and most important question must surely be, who needed to benefit most from the growth and development of the economy, who has benefited most and who will continue to benefit in the future? What has, in some sense, been the total quantum of benefits?[21] If growth, which measures this quantum, has been inadequate or less than hoped for, what have been the basic constraints belabouring the economy? Is it a failure to mobilize resources or a misallocation of such resources? Has our control over the environment, both physical and economic, improved over the years? Has it improved for the peasant on his farm as much or as little as for the Government in the control and regulation of the economy? In our attempts to find answers to some of these questions, however inadequate those answers might be, we may begin to gain an understanding of the problems and prospects

[19]India, Planning Commission (1973), Ch. VI.

[20]For a detailed and severe criticism of the methodological basis of the fifth plan, see Tendulkar (1974a).

[21]For a brief but clear discussion of the problems involved in using total output as a measure of benefit, see Stewart and Streeten (1971).

facing the Indian economy. Here it is important to establish firmly
in our minds the need to put some of these questions simultaneously at two levels, one more aggregative and abstract, the other
more particular and related to observable elements within the
economy. For example, in talking about the performance of
agriculture we shall have to look at growth of output, yields and
changes in techniques of production for the economy as a whole.
On the other hand, it will be pertinent to ask sometimes who
produces the foodgrains, who buys and sells, who goes without
when the harvest is poor, who eats it when additional grain is
imported. An economist might be said to expiate his original sin
by having to operate at both these levels of consciousness. It is
one of my basic themes that our view of the problems as well as
our interpretation of events changes according to the level at which
the questions are put.

As this point has coloured, some will say biased, my approach
to the problems of economic development in India and is a somewhat unconventional approach to evaluation of economic policy,
it needs a little elaboration. This is not the place to attempt a
complete exegesis of the economic literature on India. There is
quite clearly a certain polarity in the assessment of India's achieve-
ments by different observers. Thus economists like Lewis, Reddaway and Robinson, while critical of some aspects of policy, credit
the Government with a considerable degree of achievement and
attribute at least part of the failures to the enormous difficulties
facing the economy and the external shocks it has been subjected
to. On the other hand, others like Bagchi, Minhas, Patnaik and
Weisskopf are extremely critical of what has been achieved and
the policies that have been followed.[22] I think that at least part of
the disagreement derives from the fact that different groups of
observers implicitly attach greater weights to different sets of
objectives that the Government has attempted to pursue.[23] To

---

[22]For the optimists, see Lewis (1962), Reddaway (1962) and Robinson
(1970); for the pessimists, see Bagchi (1970), Chattopadhyay (1973), Prabhat
Patnaik (1975) and Weisskopf (1972) amongst the Marxians; Minhas (1974)
amongst the non-Marxians. Among those who are more concerned with
criticisms of strategy and techniques are Lipton (1968) and Tendulkar
(1974a).

[23]There are, of course, other more fundamental areas of disagreement,
relating to differences in the ideologies or politics of the observers.

anticipate my conclusions, I wish to argue that we are likely to interpret the experience more favourably if we focus attention on the first group of objectives that I have outlined above and less favourably if we concentrate attention on the distributional objectives. Unfortunately, I shall have to argue against taking the easy way out by postulating that redistribution has suddenly become more important than growth. Such a way of resolving the problems, quite apart from yielding dubious policy conclusions, fundamentally misconstrues the nature of the economic problem, at least in the Indian context. I shall also attempt to suggest, although it is beyond my capacity to prove this beyond reasonable doubt, that the last few years, say from 1970 onwards, have been years of regress; that an observer in 1969 might have had more grounds for being optimistic about the prospects facing the economy than he would now.

What sort of an economy is it, in relation to which we are to pose and attempt to answer some of these questions? Part of the description lies in the answers to some of those questions, because a dynamic economy evolves and changes structurally during the process of development. As a starting point, and without any pretence at being exhaustive, I think the following characteristics are the important ones to bear in mind.

First, there is the sheer size of the country. India ranks second in the world in terms of population, after China. In terms of land area, she ranks seventh.[24] The country is made up of regions that are extremely heterogeneous in terms of resources, climate, language and infrastructure, amongst others. This makes it difficult sometimes to talk about *the* Indian experience in any meaningful fashion. Indeed, part of the essence of the problem lies in the diversity of regional experience of economic growth in India. Moreover, the sheer expanse of the country and the number of people it embraces sometimes makes the problem of co-ordination and implementation of economic policy uniquely difficult. Quite apart from knowing what is the right thing to do, there is the problem of having to do it on a grand scale, if it is to have any overall impact. Again, while the size of the country makes it possible for it to command an unusually wide and varied resource base, that goes hand in hand with a huge potential appetite for

[24]India, Ministry of Finance, Pocketbook (1970), p. 197.

resources.[25] India's total demand for many key inputs, be they food or fertilizer or steel, is likely to be so substantial in relation to the volume of world trade in these commodities that it is unlikely she could meet substantial proportions of her own consumption except from domestic production. For this reason trade, while it is an important part of her economic life, is quantitatively a small proportion of the total volume of activity.[26]

Secondly, India has a federal constitutional structure, which is of relevance to us for two reasons. Certain areas of policy, such as land reform or agricultural taxation, are purviews of the state governments and set limits to the powers of the central government to manipulate these policy variables. Furthermore, even where certain areas are not marked off in this way, implementation of economic policy requires successful co-ordination of efforts between the centre and a large number of state governments.[27]

Thirdly, India is a mixed economy, with a growing public sector that still constitutes a relatively small proportion of the total volume of activities in the economy.[28] For this reason, the problem of planning for development in India is fundamentally different from that in centrally planned economies. This is true both in respect of strategies of development and in the capacity of the Government to implement a chosen strategy.[29] In a centrally planned economy the patterns of production and distribution can be differentiated quite substantially. In a mixed economy, at least in the larger, private sector, the production decisions are controlled by the pattern of ownership of the production resources.[30]

[25]Although India has a wide and varied resource base, including some of the largest world reserves of iron ore and (non-coking) coal, she also lacks certain key inputs such as oil, her production of which is very small, and non-ferrous metals like copper.

[26]For example, in 1972-73 the ratio of the total value of trade to net national product was of the order of 9.2 per cent; for a discussion of the relationship between size and degree of openness of the economy, see Kuznets (1966).

[27]I do not intend to suggest that there are only negative aspects of being a federal state; in other ways, India may well benefit from such a structure.

[28]On the relative size of the public sector, see Hazari and Ojha (1970).

[29]See pp. 161-3 and 218-20, below.

[30]Strictly speaking, by control over the use of resources. Although ownership and control often go together, they are not inseparable.

If the mixed economy is one where labour is relatively abundant in relation to land and capital, the wages of labour, including the rewards of poor agricultural households, tend to be driven towards levels of subsistence. The returns accruing to the owners of the scarce means of production tend to be high. The particular pattern of production can then be associated with a particular pattern of distribution of incomes. This in turn is reflected in the pattern of demand for goods and services originating within the economy. By definition, the subsistence demands of the poor tend to be directed towards a narrow group of essential products, which in India consists mostly of the products of the agricultural sector. The rest of the demand is directed towards the consumption patterns of the better-off owners of scarce resources, including in this definition human capital.

The subsequent pattern of potential profitability in turn reinforces the pattern of production. More important, perhaps, it also reinforces the pattern of investment within the economy, both from the supply and the demand side. It is worth stressing that this link between the pattern of production and the pattern of distribution cannot easily be severed in an underdeveloped economy like India, merely through the redistribution of money incomes. While I shall return to this point later, it is largely because of the existence of groups with highly unequal bargaining strength in the context of a high degree of excess demand for goods and services that reflect the limited, present productive capacity of the economy. Indeed, in such a poor country, it can be argued that the pattern of real consumption is largely determined by the pattern of production. The Government, if it does not or cannot affect the ownership of the means of production, or to the extent that it cannot do so, can only operate on this set of relationships through a system of incentives and disincentives. While it has choice over a more or less optimal set of such measures, it cannot directly control the extent to which the system would respond to such measures.

Lastly, as part of the pattern of ownership of resources, it is worth remembering that the economy inherited from the past an extremely varied, complex and interlaced pattern of ownership of land and land use. Land is *par excellence* the scarce means of production, on which the lives and livelihood of the majority of the population depends. The inherited pattern of ownership and use has a very important bearing on both the interpretation and amelioration of problems facing the economy.

It remains for us, in this chapter, to say something about the nature of the constraints facing the economy and of the decision-making process. The precise nature of the constraints, as I see them, will become clear in the course of the following chapters. What are constraints depends partly, but only partly, on what choices we feel are open to the Government.[31] Some economists have questioned the very possibility of economic development in India under a system of partially state-controlled capitalism. They lay down the requirement of a widely reverberating socialist revolution as a precondition of any development.

Rightly or wrongly, in this book, I have discarded such a revolutionary scenario. Not so much because I feel that such a development is undesirable as that it is unlikely to come about in the near future. I have, therefore, taken the rules of the game as they are and concerned myself with non-revolutionary situations and solutions. I have not, however, ruled out the possibility that rules that have been amended in principle may also be amended in practice. I refer, of course, to such things as implementation of land reform. Within this context, I shall concentrate on the operation of the following constraints: domestic resources, external resources, the supply of wage-goods, the nature of technology and the institutional patterns of rewards and disincentives. Whether explicit or not, most of the discussion in the literature has centred on one or more of these constraints.

I have from time to time talked about the planners or the policy makers. It is as well to make it clear what I mean by that. Broadly speaking, by the term policy makers I mean those groups of people, or better still interests, within the formal structure of government, who are responsible for the formulation and implementation of economic policy. As I have hinted above, the control they can exercise might be less than full in a mixed economy. In this context, it will be useful to distinguish between at least three groups: the planners proper or those who are responsible for the

[31]This statement is only partly true because there are some technological constraints that an economy may be subject to which are largely to be taken as given for any feasible set of policies. In my view, the role of these constraints is generally underplayed in the literature.

formulation of economic strategy, the various ministries who are actually responsible for embodying the plan into a set of policies[32] and the state governments who are responsible for the implementation of many, though not all, of those policies at the grass roots.[33] The policy makers are not a body of people who are neutral in some sense to the environment that faces them. They have a *Weltanschauung*, a particular view of the problem, and by the very choice they exercise over policies, react with the various conflicting groups of interest that make up the society.

In this context, it should be pointed out that the language of analysis employed in this book is the somewhat parochial language of economic analysis. The process of creation and distribution of wealth in society is in a very integral sense part of a political process. In this book, I have not attempted to explore the interrelationships between economic and political factors.[34] I have confined myself fairly closely to what would perhaps be regarded as a partial explanation of economic processes. I have tried to bear this limitation in mind, so as to guard myself to a certain extent against the distortions that such a fragmentary approach might create.

On a matter of terminology, I have frequently used the term 'wage-goods' in this book. By this category, I do not designate only those goods which are purchased by wage-labourers. I have used the term to mean the goods that are consumed by the poorer parts of the population. These goods are wage-goods, because they exchange against incomes that have been earned in exchange for labour services, in contrast to incomes that are a reward for

---

[32]It is a matter of considerable practical importance that in India, while the actual process of drawing up a plan is largely undertaken by the Planning Commission, in matters of fiscal policy and foreign exchange budgeting the initiative has tended to rest with the Ministry of Finance. It is true, of course, that there are various channels of co-operation and consultation between the different organizations concerned. For a detailed discussion of the planning process, see Hanson (1966); on the relationship between the plan and economic policies for its implementation, see Gadgil (1972).

[33]The degree of devolution at the state level varies widely over different areas of policy making. It is very large for such areas as land reform or agricultural taxation, very small for allocation of foreign aid.

[34]For a discussion of these issues, see Mitra (1977).

ownership of land or capital or the possession of higher education. In the Indian context, the former category also covers those small peasants who may nominally own some land but whose main livelihood derives from sharecropping or agricultural wage labour.

We can now briefly describe the scheme of the book. Chapter 2 offers an inventory of the resources the economy started with, while Chapter 3 attempts to describe how the economy has grown during the 25 years under consideration. That is to say it tries to assess how the growth objective and the employment objectives have been attained. Chapter 4 deals with questions of resource mobilization and internal and external stability. Chapters 5 and 6 discuss in some detail the performance of the two major sectors, agriculture and industry, in the context of problems that have arisen in those areas. Chapters 7 and 8 move away from a consideration of the economy as an aggregate and look at one part of it. This is the heart of the problem, the question of the state of the poor and what has happened to poverty in India during this period. The last three chapters assess critically the role of the state in the formulation and implementation of economic policy, both at the level of strategy and tactics.

CHAPTER TWO

Resource Base of the Economy, *circa* 1950

The pace and spread of development of an economy over a given period of time depends obviously on the resource base it starts from, for that base delineates the production frontier within which any feasible set of objectives lie. In a dynamic economy, the resource base itself expands with the accumulation of capital and technical progress, the rates of which are themselves measures of the degree of success of the chosen strategy. Needless to say, I do not propose to offer an exhaustive inventory of the resource base of the Indian economy at the beginning of our period. What I attempt here is very rough and ready, a sort of iron ration of basic facts to fit us out for an exploration of a well-traversed, but still bewildering terrain. For this purpose, we do not only need statistical information. We also need to know a little about the physical characteristics of the Indian economy.

A word needs to be said here about the quality of the statistical information that is available to us. For an underdeveloped country, India is surprisingly well served by its statistical data.[1] Enough information is available to us to ask many interesting questions, although not always enough to answer those questions decisively. A great deal of the information, too, falls within what a patient economist will regard as tolerable limits of error, given the sort of world we have to work in. However, there are important gaps in our knowledge. Where data exist, they are not always comprehensive or comparable over a period of time, because both definitions and coverage of the data tend to change in course of time. Some-

---

[1]For a review of sources and limitations of Indian statistics, see Rao (1972).

times the data assume an air of confidence which is entirely misleading. The reader will do well to take the information as indicating broad orders of magnitude rather than certitude.

It is also worth bearing in mind that India is a very large country of infinite variety of experience. What is true for Gujarat or Punjab is not always true for Orissa or Kerala. Indeed, as Daniel Thorner used to point out, what is true of a village within striking distance of Delhi might cease to be true in the distant hinterland.[2]

A survey of the resource base of the Indian economy can start along the time-honoured categories of labour, land and capital. The first two are primary factors of production, of which land, though not usable land, is in fixed supply.[3] However, as capital is a produced means of production, I shall also have to look at the productive capacity of the economy in 1950 and how it was distributed.

Labour

The population of India in 1951, at the decennial census, was 361 million and it had been growing during the two previous decades at an annual rate of approximately 1·3 per cent.[4] The crude birth rate was 39·9 per 1,000, which was on the low side for developing countries generally or south Asian countries in particular at that time; the death rate per 1,000 was 27·4, roughly the same as that for south Asia, and rather on the high side for developing countries as a whole.[5] In stark contrast to the overall death rate, the infant mortality rate stood at a range of 175-190 per 1,000

[2] The reader will find some very interesting discussion of this point in Beteille (1974).

[3] The amount of land that is actually cultivated depends on such things as the extent and duration of fallow, investment in land reclamation, the emergence of land-saving techniques etc. Boserup (1974) argues that land is less of a fixed factor than is often supposed. For India, it will be reasonable to assume that the supply of usable land is not likely to increase on account of any of the above factors at a rate that keeps pace with the growth of population.

[4] India, Ministry of Finance (Pocketbook 1970) for 1951 population; growth rate from India, Registrar General (1971).

[5] India, Registrar General (1971); on comparative figures, see IBRD (1973).

live births.[6] The average life expectancy at birth was 32 years, having itself increased considerably over the previous decades. The high rate of infant mortality is a factor of considerable importance to which I shall refer later on.[7]

Of the population of 361 million, 82·7 per cent was rural and 17·3 per cent lived in towns. The rural population lived in some 560,000 villages, roughly 86 per cent of these villages having populations of less than 1,000. Of the 3,057 towns, only eight had populations of over half a million.[8] Thus, we have the picture of a population, predominantly rural, that lived scattered over a total area of 3,268,000 square kilometres, in fairly small agglomerations.[9]

How did this population derive its living? The terms rural and urban are not directly synonymous with the terms agricultural and non-agricultural. There are people living in rural India who do not derive their livelihood from agriculture. Similarly there are urban dwellers whose source of income might derive from participation in some ways in agricultural activities. To establish the occupational pattern of the population, we have to turn to the population censuses and are immediately faced with a problem. That is, the occupational definitions in the census change from time to time and the figures are not directly comparable. However, work done by Krishnamurthy and others have made such comparisons possible.[10] From these, we can see that about 70 per cent of the male working population in 1951 were either cultivators or agricultural labourers and another 2 per cent was engaged in plantation work, forestry and fisheries. Only 10 per cent of the population worked in the manufacturing sector.[11] Thus, any questions addressed to incomes of the people is in a direct manner related to what happens in agriculture, leaving aside the fact that even for the others agriculture is the basic source of consumer goods

[6]India, Planning Commission (1961), p. 652.

[7]See pp. 230-1 below.

[8]For rural-urban population and size distribution of villages, see India, Central Statistical Organization, *Statistical Abstract of the Indian Union* (annual).

[9]India, Ministry of Finance, Pocketbook (1970).

[10]Krishnamurthy (1973) and (1974); see also India, Planning Commission, Dantwala Committee (1970).

[11]Krishnamurthy (1973).

and raw materials.

While the size of the population gives us an indication of the number of mouths to be fed, only that part of the population which makes up the work force can strictly be counted as a resource. Moreover, the part which in turn actually contributes to production depends on the participation rate of that labour force, as well as the precentage employed. Whereas the potential stock is measured by the participation rate of the population of working age, the extent to which society succeeds in utilizing that stock depends on the level of employment. Unfortunately, it is not possible to give very accurate estimates of these magnitudes for India, especially at the beginning of the period.

There are both conceptual problems and problems of measurement involved in such estimation. While I cannot here give an exhaustive account of the difficulties, the major issues can be briefly summarized.[12] In a poor and underdeveloped country, where much of the economic activity is based on the household, both in the agricultural and non-agricultural 'informal sector', and where the poverty of many households puts a premium on supplementing the major source of earning, children tend to enter the work force at an early age and there is no formal age of retirement. The concept of the work force as that proportion of the population lying between certain age limits, therefore, becomes more diffuse. The very nature and organization of household activities also makes it difficult to estimate participation rates. However, figures available indicate that roughly 57 per cent of the rural and 65 per cent of the urban population in 1955 was not part of the labour force.[13] This has to be taken in connection with the fact that roughly 38 per cent of the population in 1951 was below 15 years of age. It is extremely unlikely in the Indian context that children would not have entered the labour force until 15 years of age, outside a narrow range of families, and not too much should be read into any of these estimates. The broad conclusion that dependency ratios are used to emphasize, that is that in a rapidly growing population a substantial part of the

[12]See India, Planning Commission, Dantwala Committee (1970), Raj Krishna (1973), Raj (1959), Sen (1973), for discussion of some of the conceptual problems relating to the measurement of unemployment.

[13]India, Planning Commission, Dantwala Committee (1970), p. 34.

population consumes more than it adds to production, will not be altered by the precise numbers we pick.[14]

However, the major conceptual problems arise in the context of employment and unemployment. At the risk of considerable simplification, we might distinguish between two different kinds of difficulty. Some economists, while accepting that what we ought to try to measure is the *number of people* without jobs, would distinguish between useful and nominal employment. They are concerned with the issue of 'underemployment' and the possibility of the existence of 'surplus labour', especially in agriculture. While the theoretical debate on this issue is by no means settled, one of the most carefully worked out studies relating to India, which tries to take account of a number of specific conceptual and estimation problems raised in the controversy, finds that on average 17 per cent of the labour force in India was 'surplus', in the sense of being in excess of the required labour force within the existing pattern of organization of production. If we accepted this finding as approximately correct, we could put forward a working hypothesis that scarcity of labour was not likely to be a major constraint on the development of the economy.[15]

The second group of economists would question the use of numbers of the jobless as the sole criteria of employment. They point out, quite rightly, that the search for employment is incidental to the search for an adequate source of income in the first instance and for bettering one's condition in life thereafter. They would, therefore, distinguish between the employment, income and recognition aspects of employment and unemployment.[16] This has major implications for economic policy and I shall return to this problem later on in the book.[17] For the present, I shall pass over further discussion of the quantitative aspects of the supply of labour at the beginning of our period by

[14]The discussion on population growth and its consequences here, and elsewhere in the book, owes much to the paper by Cassen (1973).

[15]On the estimation of 'surplus' labour in India, see Mehra (1966); on the concept of 'surplus' labour and its critique, see Schultz (1964) and Myrdal (1968), appendix 6 and 16, Rudra (1973) and Sen (1966).

[16]For further discussion of these issues, see Raj Krishna (1973) and Sen (1973) and (1975).

[17]See pp. 221-2 below.

noting that we do not have reliable estimates of any three of these magnitudes. A word needs to be said, however, about the quality of the work force.

As is well known, the literacy rate in India in 1951 was very low. The overall literacy rate was 16.7 per cent, 24.9 per cent of the male and 7.9 per cent of the female population being classed as literate.[18] This was regarded as a matter of major concern for the nation and universal primary education was laid down as a basic objective.[19] While literacy as a component in the standard of living of a population must obviously rank very high, there is no simple known relationship between literacy and the efficiency of the labour force.[20] For some idea of the latter, we have to fall back upon more impressionistic but not necessarily less significant evidence. India at the time of independence had a well-developed educational system, with substantial numbers of people in receipt of secondary and higher education. Large numbers were employed in the administration of the country, some at high levels. There was a core of scientifically trained manpower and India had a very small but quite well-developed industrial labour force, not only in such traditionally pioneer industries as textiles but also in a small but efficient steel and engineering sector. In that sense, India is somewhat untypical amongst poor countries in having at the early stage of attempts at planned development an existing core of modern industry.[21]

Land

While 70 per cent of the population derived their livelihood from land-based activities, approximately 50 per cent of the net national product originated in agriculture.[22] The availability and

[18]India, Registrar General (1971), p. 37.

[19]Originally, 60 per cent primary literary was expected to be in force by 1955.

[20]The two or three studies that have been carried out in India relate to the educational attainments of farmers and the evidence they provide is contradictory. While Chaudhri (1968) offers evidence in favour of the hypothesis that educated farmers are more productive, Rudra (1969) suggests that the majority of big farmers are illiterate.

[21]On early industrialization, see Bagchi (1972), Buchanan (1934) and Morris (1965).

[22]See Table 11, p. 55 below and source cited therein.

quality of land as a resource are matters that lie at the core of the problem. Produce grows on land and land without moisture is so much dust. We cannot, therefore, talk of land without discussing the patterns of water availability over the country as a whole.

Although India has a very large surface area, only a part of it is available for cultivation. In 1951, returns were available for 284.3 million out of a total geographical area of 326.8 million hectares.[23] Of the reporting area, 14 per cent was under forests and another 17 per cent was listed as not available for cultivation, being either barren or put to non-agricultural use. Another 17 per cent was used for pasture and grazing and roughly 10 per cent consisted of fallow land, where the period of fallow was unequal. Much less than half, in effect some 118.7 million hectares, consisted of the net sown area, to which we can add another 11 per cent for area cropped more than once during the agricultural year.[24] Obviously, what land is available for agricultural use or what is necessarily fallow will continue to be matters of dispute.[25] The overall picture is hardly likely to be altered, that only about half the total geographical area was available as an input to agriculture and allied activities, to which another 10 or 15 per cent might have been added through more careful husbanding of resources. It is in this context that we have to interpret the information that India had a high density of population to land of about 120 per sq km. This relative scarcity of land to labour at the beginning of our period and the limited possibilities of increasing the supply of land in the face of increasing population are matters of utmost importance to bear in mind.

About 17.6 per cent of the net area sown of 118.7 million hectares was covered with assured sources of water by means of irrigation. About half of this came from canals and the other half from tanks and wells, the latter mostly shallow and *kutcha*, or unlined. The rest of the country relies heavily on the annual rainfall to supply water necessary for cultivation. Most of the rain is brought by the south-west monsoons during the summer months, which is the main growing season. For small parts of the

[23]India, Ministry of Agriculture (1968), pp. 40-1.
[24]*Op. cit.*, pp. 40-1.
[25]For a discussion, see Boserup (1974).

south, there is a second winter monsoon, which brings some rain. There are three attributes of the monsoons that we have to bear in mind. The monsoon rains are distributed very unevenly over the total area covered even during a 'normal' monsoon, the annual variability of the rainfall is large and the timing of the rains, which is of critical importance for many agricultural activities, is very uncertain, both between regions and for the same region from year to year.

On average, 73.7 per cent of the total annual precipitation occurs during June-September from the south-west monsoon, with another 15 per cent from autumn and winter rains. The latter is important because in many areas it makes possible the growth of a second crop. In parts of the south-western coast and the Himalayan regions, the average rainfall is over 80 inches per annum. The rest of the area is divided almost equally into three groups, with rainfall ranges between 80-40, 40-20 and less than 20 inches. The bulk of the total area experiences degrees of variability in rainfall, ranging from between 15 to 30 per cent, with parts of Rajasthan and Gujarat experiencing variabilities of higher than 30 per cent. It is true, however, that the probability of rainfall being in excess of 60 per cent of normal, that is, being either disastrous or diluvian, is quite small. However, even for areas which are classified as being areas of 40-80 inches of rainfall, there is a 50 to 75 per cent probability that it might be less than 20 inches in a particular year. To cap it all, areas of low rainfall are also areas where that rainfall is the most variable. People who need it most are also people who are the least certain of obtaining it; a time-honoured principle in the allocation of resources!

It is much more difficult to quantify the periodicity of rainfall in terms of the timing of precipitation. Little work has been done on this aspect of the problem. However, it is a matter of common knowledge that even in years when the total rainfall is adequate, rains often come too early or continue too late to make it possible to obtain an optimum yield of the harvest.[26] Moreover, what makes the matter worse is that there is no clearly observable pattern in the year-to-year distributions in these attributes of the

[26]Spate and Learmonth (1972), Ch. 2; on the importance of rainfall to Indian agriculture, see Mann, H. (1967); on variability and pattern of rainfall, Minhas and Vaidyanathan (1969).

monsoon. The probability of a good year following a similar one is as small as that of two concurrent bad years, although that has been known to happen.[27] There is another point which also has to be considered. That is that much of the soil is badly drained, so that in a sense too good a monsoon is a problem in as much as it leads to easy flooding. However, it remains true that as far as agricultural production goes, the major threat is raised by the spectre of drought and not of floods, although those might also cause much localized loss and suffering.

The uneven distribution of rainfall, together with differences in types of soil, has created highly differentiated regional cropping patterns. The bulk of agricultural production is devoted, not surprisingly in a poor country, to the production of foodgrains. Rice is the major crop and the basic source of food to the majority of Indians. Wheat comes next but not for the very poor, who have to rely on the cheaper but more nutritious millets. Of the cash crops, the most important ones are sugar cane, cotton, jute and oilseeds.[28] For foodgrains, the bulk of the rice acreage is in the three eastern states, Bihar, Orissa and West Bengal, and in Uttar Pradesh, Madhya Pradesh and parts of the south, especially Andhra Pradesh and Tamil Nadu. Wheat is grown mainly in Uttar Pradesh, Punjab and Madhya Pradesh, while the 'drier' millets, jowar and bajra, are confined to Mysore, Madhya Pradesh and Maharashtra for the former and Rajasthan and Gujarat for the latter. Acreage devoted to pulses, an important source of protein, is confined to Bihar, Madhya Pradesh, Maharashtra, Rajasthan and Uttar Pradesh. Oilseeds are grown largely in Andhra Pradesh, Gujarat and Maharashtra, cotton in the latter two, sugar cane in Uttar Pradesh and jute in West Bengal. Of the two major plantation crops, tea is grown largely in Assam and in the northern parts of West Bengal and coffee in Mysore.

The importance of the different states as sources of supply is broadly but not strictly similar to the distribution of acreage, owing to regional differences in yield. Thus, Tamil Nadu, while it has a smaller acreage devoted to rice than Madhya Pradesh, has a larger volume of production. The bulk of the wheat that is

[27]For example, during the drought of 1965-67; on the analytical implications of this pattern of variability, see Lipton (1967).

[28]Details of production, acreage sown and yield are given in India, Ministry of Agriculture (1969).

grown comes from Uttar Pradesh and Punjab. This regional specificity of the major crops and the fact that the same states figure prominently in the production of both foodgrains and cash crops will emerge as points of major significance when we come to discuss the effects of technical change on Indian agriculture.[29]

This discussion of land and patterns of land use leads on naturally to questions of the nature of technology, efficiency of the production system and to the ownership of land as a form of property. To these issues I shall briefly turn, beginning with the question of technology and efficiency as measured by yields. For the period we are talking about, i.e. the early 1950s, the agricultural sector was structurally sharply isolated from the rest of the economy. It used very little manufactured inputs, relying mainly on labour and plough cattle to carry on production. Although this somewhat primitive method resulted in low yields, and yields in India were low by international standards, it proved to be a blessing in one respect. Agricultural production was not much affected by what else went on in the economy. Good and bad years reflected bounties of nature and not of bureaucrats. Obviously the state of demand for food reflected on agricultural prosperity but it only affected those farmers who had a surplus of food to sell. Relatively speaking there were not so many of those, especially if we define 'surplus' in net terms, to exclude those who sold and bought back to balance the needs of consumption to the pattern of production. This structural independence of the economy is also a point to which I shall have to return a little later.[30]

Much argument has centred on the question whether the Indian peasant is efficient or not. I have already drawn attention to this debate in the context of the issue of surplus labour in Indian agriculture.[31] As that debate shows, the facts are not free from ambiguities. Perhaps it will be fair to say that while there is much evidence of adaptive behaviour on the part of the peasant, there is also evidence in the shape of particular agricultural practices related to water use etc. that points to a low level of organizational

---

[29]See pp. 124-6, 138-9 below.

[30]On peasant rationality, see Schultz (1964) and Hopper (1965); these views are criticized in Lipton (1968).

[31]See p. 21 above.

ability.[32] There is one aspect of resource use, however, that is worth serious attention. If we think for a moment not of *the* peasant but distinguish between those who own, or at least farm, small as opposed to large land areas, it is beyond reasonable doubt that the small farmer utilizes the scarce resource of land more efficiently than his opposite number. A large number of studies show that in the early 1950s at least, the yield per acre was higher on small than on large farms.[33]

Land is not only an impersonal factor of production in society. Where it is scarce in an agrarian economy, the rights to land and its use are major determinants both of distribution of income and associated privileges in society, as well as of levels of living. In 1951, some 17.8 per cent of the total agricultural population, some 43 million people, were classified as agricultural labourers or their dependants.[34] This is probably an underestimate, in so far as people who possess very small amounts of land and derive the bulk of their income from wages are liable to classify themselves formally as cultivators rather than labourers. In any case, most of these either owned no land or owned so little as to make it impossible to derive even the low level of living they could expect from cultivation of their own land. To look at it in a slightly different way, roughly 50 per cent of agricultural labour households owned no land. To which we can add a margin for those who owned only nominal amounts.[35]

Even among those who were fortunate enough to own some land, it was very unequally distributed. Table 1 gives the basic data relating to the distribution of landholdings in 1961-62. We shall later have to consider some of the welfare and policy implications of this pattern of distribution of land.[36] For the moment

[32]See, e.g. Kanwar (1969).

[33]There is a large volume of literature on this issue. For a review of the controversy, see Bhagwati and Chakravarty (1968), p. 40f and references cited therein; of special interest are Khusro (1964), Rao (1966). On the post-'green revolution' relationships, see Rudra, Majid and Talib (1969), Rudra (1969) and Utsa Patnaik (1971).

[34]India, Ministry of Labour and Employment (1960), p. 11.

[35]That is to say, those households who may own some land, and therefore be classified as 'cultivators', without owning sufficient to maintain themselves from working the land. Their major source of livelihood may be derived from hiring themselves out as agricultural labourers.

[36]See pp. 133-8 below.

the basic details need only be brought out. The data refer to households rather than individuals and typically, the poorer households tend to be larger in size.[37] The data also distinguish between ownership units and operational units, to take account of the fact that some area is leased in or out by households.

The important aspects of the pattern of distribution are as follows:

1. The top 3 per cent of households owned 28 per cent of the land; the top 8 per cent owned roughly 45 per cent. The lowest third owned less than 1 per cent. The bottom 80 per cent of households owned less than one-third of the total area, in units of less than 1 hectare or roughly $2\frac{1}{2}$ acres.

2. The distribution of operational units was slightly less unequal amongst households. The top 1 per cent operated 12 per cent, in units of over 20 acres. The cutoff point at 20 acres is entirely misleading, because farm sizes can be over 200-300 acres in some areas. It does show, however, at least as far as declared information is concerned, that the proportion of land area covered by very large farms was not very great.[38] The top 5 per cent of households operated roughly a little less than one-third of total area worked; the bottom 10 per cent operated only 0.3 per cent, the bottom 74 per cent operated less than one-third of total area in units of less than 1 hectare.

3. Although there were a great many households which owned and operated land in very small units, the total amount of land that was farmed in small units was very much less. Only 30 per cent of total area was farmed in units of less than 1 hectare.[39] This is, of course, only a different way of expressing the gross inequality of distribution of land but it has various implications for policy. It is, therefore, worth stressing.

4. The area distribution of land owned and operated is roughly similar, indicating the absence of substantial transfers of land use through leasing. However, a great many poorer households owned land that they did not operate, i.e. leased out. On the other hand, many more households operated farms of a size-range $\frac{1}{2}$ to 7 acres

[37]Vaidyanathan (1947).
[38]Khusro (1973), Ch. 9.
[39]See Table 1, p. 29.

TABLE 1
SIZE-DISTRIBUTION OF OPERATIONAL AND OWNERSHIP HOLDINGS IN INDIA 1961-62

Holding size (ha)	Operational holdings				Ownership holdings			
	Number of households ('000s)	(%)	Area ('000 ha)	(%)	Number of households ('000s)	(%)	Area ('000 ha)	(%)
below 0.20	4,843	9.7	464	0.3	19,005	29.7	701	0.5
0.20— 1.0	14,042	28.7	8,545	6.4	16,058	25.1	9,063	7.0
1.01— 3.0	17,356	35.5	31,261	23.6	16,991	26.5	30,831	24.0
3.01— 6.0	7,366	15.1	30,571	23.0	6,995	10.9	29,509	22.9
6.01—10.0	2,958	6.1	22,291	16.8	2,887	4.5	22,201	17.3
10.01—20.0	1,795	3.7	23,778	17.9	1,627	2.5	22,012	17.1
above 20.0	514	1.1	15,776	11.9	437	0.7	14,317	11.1
Total	48,874	100.0	132,686	100.0	64,000	100.0	128,634	100.0

SOURCE: India, Ministry of Food and Agriculture, *Indian Agriculture in Brief* (annual). (The data are derived from the National Sample Survey, 17th Round.)

than owned them; that is to say, they leased in land. But the total volume of land that changed hands in this process was quite small. People who own very little land have very little to hire out.

I need to mention here only one additional characteristic of the agrarian structure before going on to discuss the initial capital stock of the economy. That is, however, a vital break between those farmers who have a surplus to sell over their own subsistence and thus produce at the margin for the market, and those that produce either just enough for subsistence or less and thus appear at the margin as net buyers of foodgrains. Because the small farmer utilizes land more efficiently with the help of his labour, his share in total output is very much larger than his share of land. Roughly speaking, 50.9 per cent of total foodgrains output is produced on farms of below 10 acres. However, being small, they have little to spare beyond their needs. Large farms of over 25 acres, which produce only 22.8 per cent of total output, generate at the same time 32.5 per cent of the marketed surplus.[40]

It should be borne in mind that the comfortable feeling of security that the term 'ownership' suggests would be entirely misplaced in this context. Ownership is defined largely in terms of possession and a large part of the land so defined would be held under various forms of tenancy. The terms of tenancy varied immensely and were often highly uncertain and onerous. I shall have to return to this aspect of the problem in Chapter 5.

Capital

The rate of capital formation or investment and its counterpart, the rate of savings, have an important part to play in the analysis of recent economic development in India. It is, therefore, unfortunate that our knowledge of the quantitative magnitudes of these variables, as well as of the initial capital stock of the Indian economy at the beginning of the period, is highly approximate and uncertain. The problems of estimating the stock of capital at a point in time are well known.[41] In the Indian context, there are

[40]Dharm Narain (1961), Ch. 7.
[41]For a survey of the capital controversy, see Harcourt (1972).

also formidable problems of estimating the rate of investment in the economy. They are related partly to the structure of the economy; a large part of investment and savings goes on in small, dispersed, unorganized and partially monetized agricultural and other household sectors. In addition, there are also major gaps in the data required to make reliable estimates.[42] As our concern is mainly with the process of saving and investment rather than the stock of capital at a point in time, I shall defer any detailed discussion of the behaviour of these variables until later, when we come to look at the progress of the economy.[43] For the present, the picture I draw had best be taken as a highly approximate one.

The most recent study by Mukherjee puts the stock of reproducible capital in India at the beginning of 1950-51 at Rs 17,086 crores.[44] Of this, a little less than one-third was in agriculture, something like one-quarter in construction, and not more than 14-15 per cent in manufacturing, both large and small.[45] Although it is possible to divide these figures by the size of the work force and obtain ratios of capital per head, it is unlikely that such exercises will be very useful in our present state of knowledge, bearing in mind that our idea of the size of the work force itself is somewhat approximate. It is worth noting in passing, however, that agriculture, which had 70 per cent of the labour force, had only about 30 per cent of the reproducible capital.[46] It is possible to form more reliable estimates of the rate of investment, especially for more recent years. Even then, it is fairly clear that they tend to underestimate the rate of capital formation in agriculture. For 1950-51, there are a number of alternative estimates for both gross and net investment. A CSO estimate of gross fixed capital formation gives a figure of Rs 876 crores, with a ratio of gross investment to GNP of 9.3 per cent. Two alternative estimates of net investment by the Planning Commission and the Reserve Bank give values of Rs 410 and Rs 534 respectively.

---

[42]For a good discussion of the limitations of data in this field see Rudra (1972).

[43]See Ch. 4, p. 76f below.

[44]Mukherjee (1969). This is the standard work on the national income of India.

[45]Mukherjee (1969).

[46]The estimates for capital in agriculture exclude the value of land.

Net investment as a percentage of NNP works out at 4.1 and 5.3 per cent respectively. The initial rate of gross savings works out at around 9 per cent and the marginal rate of net savings at a little less than 14 per cent.[47]

Much use has been made of the concept of the capital/output ratio to suggest policy alternatives, especially in the context of channelling additional investible resources to agriculture.[48] As I shall hope to show, there is a strong case to be made out for more investment in agriculture, at least for part of our period.[49] However, I think that the case is probably not greatly strengthened by being formulated in terms of incremental capital-output ratios. The reasons for holding this view are partly methodological and they have been put forward with great clarity by Streeten.[50] They relate also to the way in which these ratios are derived in the various studies relating to India.[51] I shall not, therefore, dwell further on this issue.

Gross National Product and its Composition

Just as an economy starts with a certain stock of factors of production which embody its productive potential, so it inherits a structure of production at that point. We have noted earlier the large share of the labour force in agriculture.[52] In 1950-51, 53.8 per cent of net domestic product originated in agriculture, 20.3 per cent in

[47]Raj (1970).

[48]Ch. 5, p. 116f below, for a discussion of these problems.

[49]The case for more investment in agriculture has been most cogently argued by Lipton, in Streeten and Lipton (1968); for a discussion of these issues, see Ch. 5, p. 116f below.

[50]Streeten (1972); see also Myrdal (1968), Vol. III, Appendix 3, by Streeten.

[51]Apart from the methodological objections raised by Streeten, there are two practical ones relating to the Indian data. First, the prices used by economists like Shukla (1965) for evaluating the capital stock are collected from surveys conducted for different purposes and may not accurately reflect the productive value of the equipment. Secondly, both the average and marginal capital-output ratios are derived from the values of the aggregate stock of capital and total agricultural output at different dates and may not reflect operationally useful data that can be related to particular agricultural techniques.

[52]See p. 19 above.

mining and manufacturing and the rest in transport, communication and services, measured in real terms at 1960-61 prices.[53] Agriculture again dominates the picture as the single largest sector, making up over half the size of the economy. As Kuznets has noted in the general context of growth of economies, the share of agriculture in total production is lower than that for the labour force, indicating a lower than average productivity; itself a reflection of the lower share in accumulated capital.[54]

The volume of NNP in 1950-51, the total national cake so to speak, was Rs 650 crores, measured at 1960-61 prices. This yielded a *per capita* income level of Rs 269 in real terms, roughly equal to about $50 per year at then current rates of exchange.[55] This is what classifies India as a poor country, although there is much more to poverty than the *per capita* figure indicates.[56] I shall spend some time later discussing the nature of poverty in India, then and now. It is worth quoting at this stage an alternative measure of the average standard of living in a poor country that is probably less misleading in many ways. The *per capita* availability of foodgrains in India in 1950 was 394 grammes per day, consisting of 337.4 grammes of cereals and 57 grammes of pulses.

It was noted earlier that India is somewhat unusual amongst developing countries in having started off with a modern industrial base.[57] The size of it, in relation to the total volume of economic activity, was quite small. It is doubtful if, of the 20 per cent share in the net domestic product mentioned above, more than 6 or 8 per cent was in the so-called organized sector.[58] The rest was mostly in mining and small-scale industry, especially the latter. The organized sector was dominated by the textile industry which has a long history in India. According to the Census of Manufacturing 1951, which covers the larger enterprises, total

[53]Table 11, p. 55 below; see also Chaudhuri (1971), p. 34f.
[54]Kuznets (1966).
[55]See Table 8, p. 51 below.
[56]For a discussion of the nature of poverty in India, see Chs. 7 and 8 below and references cited therein,
[57]See p. 22 above.
[58]The organized sector or the large-scale sector consists of those establishments which employ more than 25 workers without power or more than 10 workers with power.

value added in manufacturing for that year was Rs 347.2 crs. Of
this 56.8 per cent orginated in cotton and jute manufactures, 6.6
in sugar, 8.4 in engineering, 7.6 in steel, 4.1 in chemicals and 2.1
in cement.[59] As a group, total food processing and tobacco came
second after textiles.[60] There was hardly any in capital goods
industry.

Textiles apart, the significance of the industrial sector at this
point did not lie so much in its capacity to supply India's requirements, meagre as they were. For that, India was mainly dependent on imports of manufactured goods, although tariff policy and
the War had stimulated to some extent the pace of industrialization.[61] It lay more in the unquantifiable advantages of the
familiarity of a small part of the population with industrial skills
and enterprise, which could serve as a nucleus of further development. Moreover, it provided the seed-bed for the development
of an indigenous industrial capitalist class, that industrial
bourgeoisie which today plays such an important part in the
current exegesis of development in India.[62]

The last structural characteristic of the Indian economy that
we should note is the relationship of trade to total economic
activity. At current prices, the ratio of the total volume of trade
to NNP in 1950-51 was 13 per cent. The export ratio was 6 per
cent.[63] The external sector in this period was not large, although it
was important as a source of the manufactured goods and raw
materials that India needed and as an outlet for her agricultural
exports. By composition, roughly 40 per cent of her imports consisted of industrial inputs, including oil, and about 20 per cent
consisted of machinery.[64] Apart from iron and steel, of which
India consumed only 1.3 million tonnes and imported about 25

[59]Mukherjee (1969).

[60]*Op. cit.*

[61]For the industrial development of India prior to the Second World
War, see Bagchi (1972) *passim*; although it is known that both the First
and the Second World Wars stimulated industrial development in India,
there are no studies of the effect of the latter upon the economy.

[62]The role of the industrial bourgeoisie is discussed in Bagchi (1970),
Chattopadhyay (1973) and Prabhat Patnaik (1975) from the Marxist point
of view. On a wider discussion of the relationship between class and
development, see Barrington Moore (1966).

[63]Calculated from India, Ministry of Finance, Survey (annual).

[64]India, Ministry of Finance, Pocketbook (1970), p. 112f.

per cent of her requirements, she was almost totally dependent on imports of machine tools and machinery.[65] Her exports were made up roughly as follows, as far as the major categories are concerned: cotton manufactures, 20 per cent; jute manufactures, 19 per cent; tea, 13 per cent; other products of agricultural origin, 24 per cent. Exports of other manufactured goods were negligible.[66]

Regional Pattern

I have mentioned earlier the regional diversity that India displays, which is not surprising in a country larger than Western Europe. I have also stressed the differences in climatic conditions, particularly in patterns of rainfall. In some ways, it is misleading to talk about *the* Indian experience, because that experience has been so varied between regions. It will make it easier to appreciate that point, if we triy to form an idea how diverse a picture India presented at the beginning.

In political terms, India is divided regionally into states under a federal structure of government.[67] Unfortunately, we do not have data relating to total output or income by states for the beginning of the period. Such data as are available for later periods are also not very reliable, although they might serve as bases of rough comparison. Moreover, we do not have figures for regional capital stocks. Subject to such limitations, it is possible to give some idea of differences in regional potential for economic development at the beginning of the period. As will be seen, the data are more suited to pointing out the bewildering variety rather than clear, well-defined patterns. Any selection out of the data that are available must be somewhat arbitrary. The information I have chosen to present is not comprehensive. It is best suited to illustrate the points that I wish to stress, because they appear to me to be the most important ones.[68]

[65]India, Ministry of Finance, Survey (1967-68), p. A64.

[66]India, Ministry of Finance, Pocketbook (1970), p. 112f.

[67]On a short introduction to the structure of government, see Morrist Jones (1967).

[68]There are no detailed studies of the patterns of regional development in India, although a great deal of information is available, especially about the agricultural sector and social indicators; see especially the following

TABLE 2

POPULATION, AREA, AGRICULTURAL LABOUR, FOODGRAINS OUTPUT AND LITERACY RATES: REGIONAL DISTRIBUTION, 1951

Area	Population 1951 (millions)	Population 1951 Per cent	Distribution of area 1951 Per cent	Agricultural labour, as percentage of total agricultural population 1951	Foodgrains output Ave. 1949-50 to 1951-52 ('000 tons)	Foodgrains output Per cent	Literacy rates 1951-52 Per cent
India	361.9	100.0	100.0	17.8	51,748	100.0	18.0
Andhra Pradesh	31.3	8.6	8.4	7.2	4,243	8.2	18.2
Assam	9.6	2.7	6.7	2.5	1,591	3.1	12.1
Bihar	38.8	10.7	5.2	25.8	4,751	9.2	21.2
Bombay	48.3	13.3	15.1	19.5	6,031	11.7	
Kerala	13.5	3.7	1.2	39.2	684	1.3	40.5
Madhya Pradesh	26.1	7.2	13.6	19.4	5,433	10.5	9.8
Madras	29.2	8.3	3.9	26.6	3,070	5.9	20.8
Mysore	19.4	5.4	5.9	14.7	2,528	4.9	19.3
Orissa	14.6	4.0	4.8	15.5	2,258	4.4	15.8
Punjab	16.1	4.4	3.7	4.5	3,336	6.4	15.2
Rajasthan	15.9	4.4	10.5	4.2	1,313	2.5	9.0
Uttar Pradesh	63.2	17.5	9.0	7.7	11,187	21.6	10.8
West Bengal	26.3	7.3	2.7	20.6	4,499	8.7	24.0

SOURCES: Cols. 1, 2, 3 and 7 India, Central Statistical Organization, *Statistical Abstract for India* (annual).
Col. 4 India, Ministry of Labour and Employment, Labour Bureau (1960).
Cols. 5 and 6 India, Ministry of Food and Agriculture, *Estimates of Area and Production of Principal Crops* (annual).

Table 2 gives the data on area, population and some attributes of the labour force, as well as total foodgrains production and literacy rates. Columns 2 and 3 give the distribution of population and area. It will be seen that the states are very unequal in size, whether we measure them in terms of space or people. Four states make up roughly 50 per cent of the area: the then undivided Bombay, Madhya Pradesh, Rajasthan and Uttar Pradesh. Three states contain roughly 40 per cent of the population: Bihar, Bombay and Uttar Pradesh. A comparison of the two columns brings out quite clearly the unequal incidence of population pressure on land, in a country that overall has a high density of population. The three most striking are Bihar, Kerala and Uttar Pradesh, which have a much larger share of population than of land area. As I have indicated above, overall density figures are very rough measures indeed of the pressure on land as a resource.[69] We have to be careful, therefore, on comparisons we draw. For example, the figures for Assam and Rajasthan are both misleading. One is very mountainous, the other is for large parts a desert.

A large part of our concern in this book is with the poor in India. As we shall see, agricultural labourers are among the poorest in the land and plenitude for the poor is measured in foodgrains. Columns 4 to 6 tell us a good deal in a shorthand manner about the incidence of poverty in different states. The proportion of agricultural labourers to the total agricultural population was well above the national average in four states, Kerala, Madras, Bihar and West Bengal, in that order. Bihar and Kerala are certainly amongst the poorest states in India, as is also Orissa. The distribution of foodgrains output also tells us something interesting about the regional pattern of production of basic foodstuffs. First, we can see that 45 per cent of foodgrains output was produced in three states: Bombay, Madhya Pradesh and Uttar Pradesh. Secondly, just as there are 'surplus' farmers, so there are 'surplus' states. A very rough idea of the latter phenomenon can be obtained by comparing column 2 to column 6. States like

---

publications: India, Planning Commission, PEO (1967), (1968) and (1970a). On agriculture, see Minhas and Vaidyanathan (1965), Mitra (1970), Parikh (1966), Rao (1965) and Vyas (1973), as also India, Ministry of Food and Agriculture (1968), (1970) Vols. I and II.

[69]See p. 23 above.

Punjab and Uttar Pradesh have a higher share of foodgrains output than of population, while Kerala and Rajasthan, for example,
have the opposite.

Some interesting conclusions can also be drawn from the figures
for literacy rates given in column 7. In spite of the widespread
use of this index as a measure of welfare, it is not an easy concept
to interpret. Formal literacy, once gained, can be lost and one
has to define the concept in terms of a certain minimum number
of contact years. This again causes problems in societies, like
India, where the dropout and wastage rates among primary
school children are very high.[70] Moreover, it is by no means
clear whether literacy should be taken as a form of consumption
or as a surrogate for 'skill', as so much embodied technical
knowledge. In my view, literacy remains an important concept of
welfare, however difficult it might be to measure accurately. It is
very closely related to a people's awareness of social injustice,
their ability to articulate such awareness and to attempt to eradi-
cate such injustice. It may not yield a measurable rate of return.
A high degree of literacy may, nevertheless, make for a better
world. Here, we should note the very high rate for Kerala, which
has often been remarked upon.[71] It is also significant that each
of the other three states which show a high rate contains a
primate city, Bombay, Calcutta and Madras. It is quite clear that
at this level we cannot draw any firm conclusions about the effects
of literacy rates on the efficiency of labour. Punjab, which is one
of the 'surplus' states and one of the most dynamic in terms of
agricultural growth, has a fairly low degree of literacy.

The agrarian economy dominates the rest. There has hardly
been a year when the economy has grown rapidly in the face of
agricultural stagnation. Table 3 presents us with some basic
features of the agrarian practices in different states. The first thing
to note is the wide variations in these practices amongst various
states, as well as differences in the yield per acre that they culmi-
nate in. Obviously the yield figures, being expressed in their
physical quantities, express a heterogeneous group of foodstuffs
and cannot be taken entirely at their face value. To do that
would be to assume that a kilo of wheat was 'worth' the same as

[70]Agricultural Economics Research Centre (1971).
[71]See, for example, Nair (1974).

a kilo of rice, which need not be the case either in terms of nutrition or market value.[72] However, for our purpose, the data do not misrepresent the situation. There were substantial differences in yield from land in the different states. There were, and there remain, substantial differences in yield between states for the same crop.[73]

TABLE 3
REGIONAL INDICATORS OF AGRICULTURAL PRODUCTION
AND PRACTICES, 1951-52

Area	Yield of food grains output Ave. 1949-50 to 1951-52 (kg/acre)	Net area sown as percentage of total area 1950-51	Net area irrigated as percentage of net area sown 1950-51	Double-cropped area as percentage of net area sown 1950-51
Andhra Pradesh	216	36.7	25.6*	8.9*
Assam	371	16.0	21.3*	16.2
Bihar	198	49.8	23.3	22.2
Kerala	365	48 1*		19.0
Madhya Pradesh	173	32.5	6.4	9.8
Madras	295	39.8	34.0	14.0
Mysore	169	49 8	7.7*	3.5*
Orissa	215	36.4	14.3*	7.8*
Punjab	243	55.5	45.3*	18.4
Rajasthan	101	33.6*	11.6*	9.4*
Uttar Pradesh	268	55.5	29.8	23.0
West Bengal	360	59.8	20.9	12.8
Gujarat	153	50.7*	5.6*	4.3*
Maharashtra	—	—	—	—

*Provisional.

SOURCES: Col. 1 India, Ministry of Food and Agriculture, *Estimates of Area and Production etc.* (annual).

Cols. 2, 3 and 4 India, Planning Commission, PEO (1967, 1968), Vol. 1.

[72]For a discussion of this factor, see Stewart and Streeten (1971) and Mahabub ul Haq (1963), Ch. 4.

[73]Regional yields for different crops are given in India, Ministry of Food and Agriculture, Estimates of Area and Production (annual).

A comparison of the figures for yield with the proportions of area sown or irrigated or double-cropped immediately leads to a difficulty. There are no significant correlations between yield and any of the other variables for the group of states. In a sense, the other variables tell us more about the differences in production structure in different states than in yield. This is not at all surprising. Just as the progress of the economy follows the progress of agriculture, so the latter follows the rains. The actual yields represent the bounties of nature rather than the ingenuity of man. That ingenuity is exhausted in the effort to stay alive against all odds, natural and man-made. There are no clear relationships between net area sown and net area irrigated or double-cropped for this period. We may, however, note two important characteristics. Areas that have high yields have relatively high proportions of area irrigated, although the actual percentage of area irrigated remains low, being less than half even in the Punjab. There are no areas that have a relatively high proportion of area double-cropped that do not have a high proportion of area irrigated, although the reverse is not always true, e.g. in Andhra.

CHAPTER THREE

The Growth of the Economy from 1950 to the early 1970s

In the previous chapter I attempted to describe in a highly selective and schematic fashion the resource base and economic structure that characterized the Indian economy at the beginning of our period. Behind an elegant statement of objectives of five-year development plans, it had an overriding ultimate objective. That was, quite simply, to raise to a tolerable level of existence, for now and for the future, a people, most of whom lived then in abject poverty. The rest of the book is mostly concerned with the question, how far this was achieved and what problems arose in the process. For that, we need first of all to describe the growth and progress of the economy over a period of some twenty-odd years.

As the information available is vast and complex, we need some framework for selection and an order of presentation. I begin with the stark and startling fact that the population the economy has to provide for has increased in this period by some 186 million and consider some aspects of that growth. Next, I look at the growth of the net national product and changes in its composition. Although the net national product is an imperfect index of development, and by itself can often be a very misleading indicator, it is an important one.[1] It tells us, so to speak, in a word, the most that is to be had by one or by all at any point in time or over a

[1] A short discussion of the problems of measurement and comparison of national problems relating particularly to poor countries are given in Rao (1953) and Seers (1952-53). On the inadequacy of the GNP measure as an index of development see Seers (1972) and the collection of articles in *Journal of Development Studies* (April 1972).

period of time. Nothing is to be gained by ignoring that imperative. From the point of view of society, two critical questions are
related to the distribution of the total product: the distribution
between present and future generations and between different
members of the present generation. In this chapter we shall look
at the behaviour of savings and investment as a preliminary to
the discussion of the first question, which is treated at length in
Chapter 4.

The rest of the present chapter will be concerned with details
of the growth of agricultural and industrial output and of the pattern of trade. The analysis of the pattern of agricultural and
industrial growth will be our concern in Chapters 5 and 6 respectively. The second question I shall defer to later chapters.[2]

Population and Employment

The population of India, which was 361 million at the time of the
1951 census, increased by 78 million to 439 million in 1961. In
1971 the total population was 547 million, 51.7 per cent of which
was male. The density of population had gone up from 120 to 182
per sq km, or by over 50 per cent in 20 years.[3] In spite of some
increase in cultivated acreage, it is evident that the man/land ratio
in agriculture had worsened, especially since the middle 1960s.[4]
Roughly 80 per cent of this population was rural, the situation
being more or less unchanged since 20 years ago. The literacy rate
had gone up from 16.7 to 29.3 per cent; the male literacy rate
stood at 39.5, the female rate at 18.4, although the latter had
increased at a faster rate.[5] Most Indians still live in villages and
they are still very far from the universal literacy that was held
forth as an objective.

Over the last two decades, the population had grown at a rate
of 2.16 per cent per annum for 1951-61 and 2.47 for 1961-71. Not
too much should be read into this apparent acceleration in the
rate of growth. The period involved is rather short and our knowledge of the demographic scene highly imperfect. While the former

[2]See Chs. 7 and 8 below.
[3]India, Registrar General (1971).
[4]For increase in acreage, see p. 112 below; for the analytical implications of a decline in the land/man ratio, see Cassen (1973).
[5]India, Registrar General (1971), p. 37.

rate was somewhat higher than had been expected, the latter was below the expected rate.[6] It is sufficient to note that the growth of population remains high and its implications for the future of a country the size of India ominous.

What factors lie behind these rates of growth? The census data for 1961 provide some indications. While the data for the 1971 census are not yet available, the sample registration system provides us with information for the late 1960s which is in some ways more reliable.[7] The crude birth rate for 1961 was 41.7 per thousand. The corresponding SRS figures for 1968 and 1969 were 39.0 and 38.8. Fifty per cent of live births occurred to mothers between the ages of 20 and 29, 35 per cent before the age of 25. It is clear that, in spite of the various family planning programmes, there has so far been no impact on the birth rate. The crude death rate has fallen from 27.4 per thousand for the whole country to 13.1 per thousand for urban and 19.1 for rural India.[8] It is clear that the broad pattern of growth, through a combination of a relatively high birth rate with a declining death rate, has remained unchanged. On the positive side, the average expectancy of life has risen considerably. In 1968-69, it was around 48 years, compared to 41 a decade before.[9] However, the infant mortality rate still remains high, having declined by some 30 per cent from the level of roughly 200 per thousand in 1951. In 1968 and 1969, the SRS rates were 136.8 and 139.9 respectively.

The SRS data also enable us to note some interesting features of population growth. We have noted above that the urban death rate was lower in the late 1960s than the rural one. This is true also of the birth rate and the infant mortality rate.[10] We can also note that there are very substantial differences in these rates between states. Thus, the infant mortality rate in rural India was below 80 for Kerala and Haryana, at the two extremes of the

[6]At the time of the formulation of the third five-year plan, the 1971 population was estimated at 555 million; India, Planning Commission (1961), p. 750.

[7]For an account of the sample registration system, see India, Registrar General (1972b); for the published data collected under the SRS, see the two references quoted in nn. 8 and 10 below.

[8]India, Registrar General (1972a).

[9]*Op. cit.*

[10]India, Registrar General (1971b) and (1972).

prosperity spectrum. Urban infant mortality rates were highest in Assam and Uttar Pradesh, 30 to 40 per cent lower in Punjab and Mysore.[11] The highest mortality occurred between the ages of 0-4 and over 50. More female children than male died between birth and the age of four, but they had a better chance of survival thereafter.

Much of the discussion of causes of mortality in India has concentrated on the epidemic diseases like smallpox and cholera. It is true that, historically, control of these diseases and of malaria has been a major influence on the decline of the death rate. However, in a normal year the major causes of death arise from very ordinary diseases like diarrhoea and bronchitis. By far the bulk of deaths in the first year of life, apart from pre-natal injuries and injuries sustained at birth, are caused by infections, diarrhoea and respiratory diseases. For mortality in general the major causes are waterborne and respiratory diseases.[12] In our discussion on standards of living, this is a point we shall have to return to.[13]

An increase in population goes hand in hand with an increase in the labour force. Unfortunately, owing to changes in definitions and coverage, it is not possible to give detailed comparisons of changes in the size and composition of the labour force. Thus, the 1961 and 1971 censuses give estimates of the labour force of 188.6 and 183.6 respectively, associated with total populations of 439 and 547 million. The absolute decline is associated with a fall in the size of the female labour force of about 25 million.[14] Now it is extremely improbable that the labour force could decline in absolute numbers in the face of an increase in total population of some 108 million. As pointed out by Krishnamurthy, the apparent decline is due to a change in the definition of the worker category. While not much reliance can be placed on the absolute numbers derived from the census, a little more can be said about the composition of the labour force. This is done on the basis of the readjusted data compiled by Krishnamurthy, which is confined to the male working population. For various reasons we would expect

[11]*Op. cit.*

[12]India, Registrar General (1971a); see also Wyon and Gordon (1971), Ch. 7.

[13]See below, pp. 230-1.

[14]India, Registrar General (1971), p. 29f.

the percentage engaged in the rural sector and in agricultural work to be higher for female workers.

The main point to emerge from Table 4 is the continuing importance of the rural agricultural sector as a provider of employment. As far as employment is an index, it shows up the low degree of structural change that has taken place in the economy over the last two decades. Indeed, instead of decreasing, the proportion of people classified as agricultural workers went up by about 2.5 per cent in the last decade, having declined by 1.5 per cent in the previous one.

TABLE 4

COMPOSITION OF MALE LABOUR FORCE BY SECTORS—1951, 1961 and 1971 (percentage)

Sector	*1951*	*1961*	*1971*
Agriculture	69.3	66.1	66.6
(i) Cultivators	51.9	50.4	45.0
(ii) Agricultural labourers	17.4	15.7	21.6
Plantations, forestry etc.	2.4	3.4	2.0
Mining and quarrying	0.5	0.5	0.6
Manufacturing	9.7	10.2	10.6
Trade and commerce	6.2	5.6	6.7
Transport, storage and communications	2.0	2.6	3.2
Other services	8.5	10.0	8.7
Total	100.0	100.0	100.0

SOURCE: Krishnamurthy (1974).

While the all-India position has remained virtually unchanged, there have been interesting variations in the different regions. Table 5 gives the percentage changes in population engaged in agriculture in different states between the census dates 1951-61 and 1961-71, together with changes in indexes of agricultural production for roughly corresponding periods. It is clear that the proportion of the population engaged in agriculture has varied greatly between the different states in each of the two periods, as well as for individual states between the two periods. There is also no significant correlation between growth of agricultural or foodgrains output and the share of population engaged in agriculture. However, the experience *in some states* may be of interest. Thus, for the period 1951-61, Krishnamurthy has noted a tendency of states with high rates of growth of output to show a declining share of agriculture in the labour force, e.g. in Punjab or Kerala.[15] Equally, states with low rates of growth of output showed a rise in the share of agricultural population. The tendency for states with low rates of growth of foodgrains output to show rises in the share of agricultural workers is noticeable for 1961-71 also, e.g. in Bihar, Kerala, Orissa, Uttar Pradesh and West Bengal. On the other hand, both Gujarat and Punjab, which show high rates of growth of both foodgrains and non-foodgrains output, increased their share of the labour force in agriculture. And Maharashtra and Mysore, which had falling foodgrains output and rising non-foodgrains output, showed a decline in the agricultural share of the labour force. It is unlikely that the basic conclusions will be altered by the fact that female labour is excluded from our data in Tables 4 and 5.

If there was so little change in the structural distribution of the labour force in India, what happened to the employment of that labour force? The data on employment and unemployment are the most unsatisfactory of all for India. There are no doubt serious methodological problems in defining 'employment' and 'unemployment' in the Indian context.[16] We have already referred to the difficulties of cognition in the case of household labour of various sorts.[17] We have also referred to the issue of 'surplus' labour in Indian agriculture. This can be looked at in slightly different ways, both of which relate to the role of labour as a factor of production. If we take a given quantum of output, we can define a part of the labour force as 'surplus' if the same output can be produced without them, after adjustment for seasonal and other factors. Or we can define a 'work-norm' and treat a given part of the work force as partially unemployed and hence forming a pool of labour, if their nominal employment is lower than the norm. From another

[15]Krishnamurthy (1974); the change in the share of the labour force in Gujarat, in the face of a rapid rise in output, is treated by Krishnamurthy as an exception. Similar relationships for Rajasthan, Madras and Mysore are explained in terms of changes in coverage and quality of data.

[16]See the references cited in n. 12, Ch. 2.

[17]Both Raj Krishna (1973) and Sen (1973) have pointed out that the concept of unemployment can be defined in a number of ways; see also India, Planning Commission, Dantwala Committee (1970).

TABLE 5
RATES OF GROWTH OF AGRICULTURAL OUTPUT AND
CHANGES IN THE SHARE OF AGRICULTURE IN THE
LABOUR FORCE BY STATES—1951-71
(Percentage per annum)

	1951-61 Changes in share of labour force in agriculture	1951-61 Rate of growth of agricultural output	1961-71 Changes in share of labour force in agriculture	1961-68 Rate of growth of foodgrains output
India	—1.3	3.57	2.5	2.36
Andhra Pradesh	—1.4	3.05	1.1	1.51
Assam	1.3	1.24	1.8	1.31
Bihar	8.7	2.42	6.1	—1.96
Gujarat	4.4	4.53	1.5	3.39
Kerala	—5.6	4.08	10.9	0.40
Madhya Pradesh	—1.9	4.07	2.3	—2.64
Madras	0.4	5.12	2.0	1.18
Maharashtra	—1.5	3.07	—1.0	—2.12
Mysore	0	4.36	—1.4	—1.47
Orissa	2.5	1.5	2.5	—0.12
Punjab	—3.7	5.14	3.7	3.88
Rajasthan	2.1	4.20	0	1.94
Uttar Pradesh	1.7	2.20	3.2	0.44
West Bengal	2.3	0.21	4.8	0.53

SOURCES: For cols. 1, 2, and 3, Krishnamurthy (1974); for col. 4, Mitra (1970).

point of view, given that in a mixed economy jobs are a means to earning an income for the bulk of the population, we can define the adequacy of employment in terms of the shortfall of actual earnings below some established minimum. To this we can add a third, which seems to me to be less significant from the social point of view in a poor country, that of people who are employed but are seeking better paid or more suitable jobs.[18] However, the fact

[18]The 'recognition' aspect of unemployment, as Sen calls it, is less significant only in the sense that a planning body might be justified in according a lower priority to finding better paid jobs to those already in employment, provided their present real wages are higher than some

that the problem of employment can be looked at in different ways does not rule out the possibility of estimating the various magnitudes involved. In the absence of any comprehensive information we have to fall back on somewhat impressionistic estimates collected from various sources.

Table 6 gives the Planning Commission estimates for the volume of unemployment existing at the beginning of each plan period, together with the employment created during each plan, measuring unemployment by the number of jobless, rather than people with inadequate incomes.[19] The facts speak for themselves. Until the middle 1960s, the growth of the economy failed to provide for the increase in the labour force during the plan period, let alone make any dent in the backlog of unemployment. Towards the end of that decade, total unemployment was expected to be around the 30 million mark, allowing for the fact that the rate of growth of population had originally been overestimated. For the early 1970s, Sen has provided us with some rough estimates of unemployment. According to his calculations, the number of unemployed defined as being 'surplus' to production requirements is a maximum of 42.4 million, and the numbers of jobless a minimum of some 20 million. Given the previous experience in job creation, the figures reveal an alarming prospect.[20]

TABLE 6
ESTIMATES OF VOLUME OF UNEMPLOYMENT AND
EMPLOYMENT GENERATED—1956-66 (MILLIONS)

	2nd Plan (1956-61)	3rd Plan (1961-66)	at 1966
Unemployment at beginning of plan	5.3	7.0	9.5
Addition to labour force	11.7	17.0	23.0
Total unemployment	17.0	24.0	32.5
Employment generated during plan	10.0	14.5	—

SOURCE: India, Planning Commission, PEO, Dantwala Committee (1970).

notional minimum compared to those who are unemployed. As can be seen, this is a matter of judgement and is not a clearcut distinction.

[19]India, Planning Commission, Dantwala Committee (1970), p. 7 f.
[20]Sen (1973).

While we do not possess reliable figures for total employment generated, data are available for employment in the public sector and for the modern, organized private sector. Broadly speaking, the latter cover mainly non-agricultural establishments employing 25 or more people working without power or 10 or more working with power. Thus, the figures exclude small-scale manufacturing, which has been a rapidly growing sector in the economy. They also exclude a large part of the services sector, although it might reasonably be objected that most of the employment provided here might be at very low wages and therefore open to objection on the 'income (adequacy) criteria' for measuring employment.[21] Table 7 gives the figures for employment in both public and private sectors for selected years. It will be seen that both in terms of total size and rates of growth the public sector is very much ahead of the private sector. Significantly, the rate of growth of employment in the private sector has declined steadily, while that in the public sector has picked up since the middle 1960s. It is worth noting that the biggest increases in public sector employment have occurred in trade and services and that the share of manufacturing, mining and power remained at around 10 per cent in 1974. While the major share of private sector employment is in manufacturing, the rate of growth of this component has been lower than that for total employment in the private sector.[22]

National Product and its Composition

Table 8 gives gross and net national product, at current and constant 1960-61 prices. Over the years 1950-51 to 1972-73, total real net national product doubled from Rs 9,530 crs to Rs 18,848 crs. At current prices it increased a little less than fourfold, from Rs 9,530 crs to Rs 38,573 crs. Until 1962-63, the real and money national product increased roughly in step, indicating an era of relatively stable, occasionally even falling prices. Since then the two series have steadily diverged, indicating the gathering pace of inflation. In 1965-66, when the net national product fell by 5 per cent, the rate of growth at current prices merely decelerated. In 1972-73, when the real income fell by 3.8 per cent, money

---

[21]See p. 47 above.
[22]India, Ministry of Finance, Survey (1973-74), p. 78f.

incomes actually rose at a somewhat faster rate than in the
previous year.

TABLE 7

EMPLOYMENT GENERATED IN THE PUBLIC AND THE
PRIVATE SECTOR—1961, 1966 and 1974
(In 00,000s)

	Public sector			Private sector		
	1961	1966	1974*	1961	1966	1974*
Plantations, forestry etc.	1.8	2.3	3.2	6.7	9.0	8.0
Mining and quarrying	1.3	1.6	6.1	5.5	5.1	1.4
Manufacturing	3.7	6.7	10.3	30.2	38.6	41.7
Construction	6.0	7.7	9.9	2.4	2.5	1.2
Electricity, gas, water	2.2	3.0	5.3	0.4	0.4	0.4
Trade and commerce	0.9	1.6	4.5	1.6	3.3	3.1
Transport and communications	17.2	20.9	23.4	0.8	1.2	0.8
Services	37.3	53.0	62.1	2.8	8.0	11.1
Total	70.4	93.8	124.8	50.4	68.1	67.7

*Provisional.

Employment figures as at March.

The 1974 figures are not strictly comparable with the earlier ones,
owing to small changes in coverage of area and sectors.

SOURCE: India, Ministry of Finance, *Economic Survey* (annual).

As we have noted, population increased by 186 million in this
period. A measure of the average standard of living is provided
by real income per head of population. From a level of Rs 269,
per capita income rose to a peak of Rs 335 in 1964-65. Thereafter,
it fell during the two drought years of 1965-67 and did not recover
that level until 1969-70. After some recovery in the early 1970s,
real incomes fell again so that the average Indian in 1972-73 was
slightly worse off than he had been eight years before. An
economy that started off some 20 years ago with brave hopes of
doubling standards of living in some 20-25 years, has generally
marked time, keeping alive a much larger population but not
achieving very much else.

It is well known that the level of activity in the Indian economy
tends to fluctuate from year to year and that has a great deal to

TABLE 8
NET NATIONAL PRODUCT, TOTAL AND
PER CAPITA—1950-51 to 1972-73

Year	Net national product (Rs crs)		Net national product per capita (Rs)	
	Current prices	1960-61 prices	Current prices	1960-61 prices
1950-51	9,530	9,650	266.5	269.0
1955-56	9,980	11,410	255.0	267.8
1960-61	13,279	13,279	306.0	306.0
1964-65	20,001	15,885	422.0	335.1
1965-66	20,636	15,082	425.5	311.0
1966-67	23,883	15,240	482.5	307.9
1967-68	28,102	16,494	555.4	326.0
1968-69	28,729	16,991	554.6	328.0
1969-70	31,770	18,092	600.6	342.0
1970-71*	34,776	19,033	637.3	351.8
1971-72*	36,535	19,367	660.7	350.2
1972-73*	39,573	19,077	700.4	337.6
1973-74*	49,148	20,034	851.8	347.2

Year	Net national product (1960-61=100)		Net national product per capita (1960-61=100)	
	Current prices	1960-61 prices	Current prices	1960-61 prices
1950-51	67.4	71.7	81.7	87.1
1955-56	70.6	84.8	78.2	94.2
1960-61	100.0	100.0	100.0	100.0
1964-65	150.8	119.8	138.1	109.7
1965-66	155.6	113.7	139.2	101.8
1966-67	180.1	114.9	157.9	100.8
1967-68	211.9	124.4	181.7	106.7
1968-69	216.6	128.1	181.5	107.3
1969-70	239.5	136.4	196.5	111.9
1970-71*	259.9	143.5	208.5	115.1
1971-72*	275.5	146.0	216.2	114.6
1972-73*	298.4	143.8	229.2	110.5
1973-74*	370.6	151.0	278.7	113.6

*Provisional, 1 crore = 10 million.
SOURCE: India, Ministry of Finance, *Economic Survey* (annual).

do, even today, with fluctuations in the harvest. We have noted this tendency already, in the experience of the years 1965-67 and 1972-73. What is equally clear is that the rate of growth of output has tended to fluctuate over longer periods of time, after the annual fluctuations in agricultural production have been evened out to an extent. This is brought out in Table 9, of which the first part gives the linear annual average rates of growth of net national product for the first three plans, as well as for the succeeding years. It can be seen that rate of growth fluctuated between 1 and 4 per cent. If one allows for growth of population at over 2 per cent per annum, very little is left for improvements in standards of living.

TABLE 9
LINEAR GROWTH RATES OF NET NATIONAL PRODUCT—
1950-51 to 1973-74

Year	Net national product at 1960-61 prices % per annum	Net national product per capita at 1960-61 prices % per annum
1951-52 to 1955-56	3.7	1.7
1956-57 to 1960-61	3.1	0.6
1961-62 to 1965-66	2.5	0.3
1966-67 to 1970-71	4.6	2.4
1971-72 to 1973-74	1.0	—1.2

Year	Net national product at 1960-61 prices 3-year moving averages % per annum	Year	% per annum
1960-61 to 1962-63	1.8	1966-67 to 1968-69	4.2
1961-62 to 1963-64	2.5	1967-68 to 1969-70	3.1
1962-63 to 1964-65	4.5	1968-69 to 1970-71	3.6
1963-64 to 1965-66	0.7	1969-70 to 1971-72	2.1
1964-65 to 1966-67	—1.3	1970-71 to 1972-73	0.2
1965-66 to 1967-68	3.4	1971-72 to 1973-74	0.7

SOURCE: Calculated from India, Ministry of Finance, *Economic Survey* (annual).

The picture given by rates of growth calculated between two points in time can in some ways be misleading. A very low base-year value yields a high rate of growth, while the total amount of increase in output can be quite small. This is clearly the case with the period 1966-71, the very high rate of growth for which, 4.6 per cent, is due in part to the low level of output obtained at the beginning of the period. As Table 8 shows, the level of net national product in 1966-67 was lower than that obtained in 1964-65, on account of the drought. Part of the distortions introduced by point rates of growth can be overcome by taking some sort of a moving average for the growth rate. This is done for the second part of Table 9, where we use a three-year moving average. This shows up the fluctuations in rates of growth during this period; it shows as well that the rates of growth have tended to be lower than is indicated by the earlier figures. Far more interesting is the clear evidence of a deceleration in the rate of growth of output that is so clearly visible during the post-drought years of the late 1960s and early 1970s. Throughout this period the economy had been slowly running down, so to speak, instead of making a recovery from the drought. It is true, however, that the year 1973-74 shows something of a recovery.

In our discussion of the nature of the development strategy followed by the Indian planners, we shall see that the rate of investment plays a key part. The essential point to bear in mind is that the planners expected the rate of investment in the economy to increase in course of time, until a given proportion of real output went into capital formation. Moreover, they expected a growing proportion of this rising level of investment to be financed out of domestic savings. The savings-investment relationship is explored at greater detail in the next chapter. We can look now at the proportion of net domestic product that went into investment and how this was financed out of domestic and foreign savings. The rate of investment in the economy never exceeded 13 per cent and has since stabilized at a lower level, below 10 per cent. This is a fact of profound significance in any analysis of development of the Indian economy. It is true that of this falling rate of investment, a larger share has been financed out of domestic savings. However, we shall see that that development is more due to an exogenous decline in foreign aid in the late 1960s than to any improvement in the domestic front.

As an economy grows, it also changes its structure. Broadly speaking there are two ways in which such structural changes can be measured. One is to look at the relative shares of the major sectors in the total product. The other is to look at the economy in the form of an input-output matrix and measure changes in the sets of input coefficients.

It has been known since the pioneering work of Kuznets on the quantitative aspects of economic growth that the share of agriculture in real output declines and that of, first manufacturing and then services, increases with growth of output.[23]

TABLE 10

NET INVESTMENT, DOMESTIC AND FOREIGN SAVINGS AS PERCENTAGE OF NET DOMESTIC PRODUCT—
1960-61 to 1973-74

Year	Net investment	Net domestic savings	Foreign savings
1960-61	12.0	8.9	3.1
1961-62	10.8	8.6	2.2
1962-63	12 0	9.6	2.4
1963-64	12 7	10.7	2.0
1964-65	12.0	9.8	2.2
1965-66	13.4	11.1	2.3
1966-67	12.2	9.0	3.2
1967-68	10.6	7.9	2.7
1968-69	9.5	8.4	1.1
1969-70	9.2	8.4	0.8
1970-7[1]	9.6	8.3	1.3
1971-72	9.6	8.2	1.4
1972-73	10.5	9.5	1.0
1973-74	11.1	10.2	0.9

SOURCE: India, Planning Commission, Vol. 1 (1971).

The data summarized in Table 11 tend to substantiate this finding for the Indian economy. Before interpreting the data, one needs to enter a word of caution. Sectoral comparisons on the basis of a set of base-year prices give a more or less accurate picture in later years, if the relative prices ruling at the later date correspond to the base-year ratios. While there were no large changes in relative prices between agriculture and industry up to the middle 1960s, we know that in recent years agricultural prices have risen much more sharply than other prices. To this extent a comparison between, say 1950 and 1970 might require more cautious interpretation. If we take the figures as they stand it appears at first sight that the Indian experience has been fairly typical, the share of agriculture having fallen between 1950-51 and 1972-73, those of the three other sectors having increased. It is

[23]Kuznets (1966) *passim*; Chenery (1960).

interesting to note that the increase in the share of manufacturing has been small. More interesting, perhaps, is the fact that since 1965-66 there has been very little structural change in the economy. The only noticeable change is the fall in the share of agriculture and the rise in the share of administration and defence.

TABLE 11

COMPOSITION OF NET DOMESTIC PRODUCT, BY SECTORS:
AT 1960-61 PRICES
(Per cent)

Sector	1950-51	1960-61	1965-66	1970-71	1972-73
Agriculture, forestry, fishery and mining	53.8	52.5	44.2	45.9	41.4
Manufacturing, construction, power, etc.	20.3	19.2	23.6	22.5	23.8
Commerce, transport, communications	13.7	18.3	20.8	19.7	21.2
Administration, defence, etc.	12.2	10.5	12.4	12.8	14.5
Net domestic product at factor cost	100.0	100.5	101.0	100.9	100.9
Net factor income from abroad	0.0	—0.5	—1 0	—0.9	—0.9
Net national product at factor cost	100.0	100.0	100.0	100.0	100.0

SOURCE: India, Ministry of Finance, *Economic Survey* (annual).

Although some data are available on input-output matrixes for India, they neither go back far enough nor are they reliable enough to make comparisons of changes in the input-output structure of the economy. The basic data relate to the work done in the early 1960s for the original fourth five-year plan (1966-71), although it had been worked upon and modified in various ways since. It is likely, though there are no hard facts, that technological relationships within the Indian economy changed during and after the industrial recession following the 1965-67 drought and the input coefficients used in the original matrix may be no longer applicable. They are, therefore, not very useful for making broad comparisons between major industry—or commodity—

groups over a period of time. However, a structural characteristic of the economy, first stressed by Manne and Rudra, is of considerable analytical significance. Writing in 1965, they noted that the agricultural sector had very low linkages with the rest of the economy, except via the final demands vector, forming as it were a closed sub-matrix.[24] Planning Commission figures for the same period also indicate that the agricultural sector *bought* very little of manufactured inputs.[25] We know, however, that in some ways, after the 'green revolution', the agricultural sector has become a larger consumer of manufactured inputs in the form of chemical fertilizers, pesticides, diesel oil, etc. It would be useful to bear this point in mind in studying the behaviour of agriculture.

Agricultural Production

Earlier in this chapter we have noted that in terms of proportion of both employment and output generated, the agricultural sector remains the major sector in the economy. As far as output is concerned, its relative size, if anything, underestimates its strategic significance to the economy. It is the major source of wage-goods, like the foodgrains on which the bulk of poor people's incomes are spent. It is the source of raw materials for the production of industrial goods like cotton and jute manufactures and of export crops like oilseeds, tea and coffee. The behaviour of agricultural production is a major element in the assessment of performance of the economy, reinforced by the fact that the agricultural sector is potentially an enormous market for the growing industrial sector. In this section we can look at the growth of agricultural production in India during this period, leaving until later any detailed explanations of that performance.[26]

There are two major components of agricultural production, foodgrains and non-foodgrains. The former makes up roughly two-thirds of total agricultural production.[27] The data relating to

[24]Manne and Rudra (1965).

[25]India, Planning Commission (1966), p. 13.

[26]See Ch. 5 below.

[27]The weights given to the various major components in the Index of Agricultural Production (average 1959-60 to 1961-62=100) are as follows: non-foodgrains=34.14; foodgrains=65.86, of which rice=34 80 and wheat= 8.36; other cereals=14.73; pulses=7.97; oilseeds=11.44; fibres=5.04.

total agricultural, foodgrains and non-foodgrains, production are summarized in Table 12 and Figures 1 and 2. They bring out quite clearly the two basic facts about agricultural production in India that require to be stressed: its overall rate of growth and its periodic fluctuations.[28] Figure 1, which is on a semi-log scale, brings out the point that with the exception of a spurt of growth in 1952-54 and a sharp fall in 1965-67, the growth of production shows no very sharp breaks in trend, although it would appear to have slowed down towards the second half of the period. This is largely due to a slower rate of growth of non-foodgrains production. Thus, between the periods 1952-53 to 1964-65 total agricultural foodgrains and non-foodgrains production grew at the

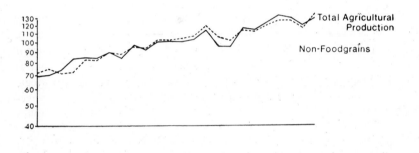

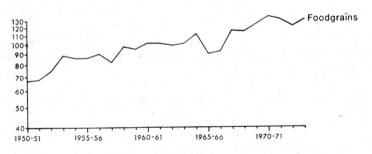

FIGURE 1

Index of foodgrains non-foodgrains and total agricultural production, 1950-51 to 1973-74. (Average 1959-60 to 1961-62=100: Semi-log scale)

[28]For a discussion of the behaviour of agricultural production see Rao (1965), Minhas and Vaidyanathan (1965), India, Ministry of Food and Agriculture (1968).

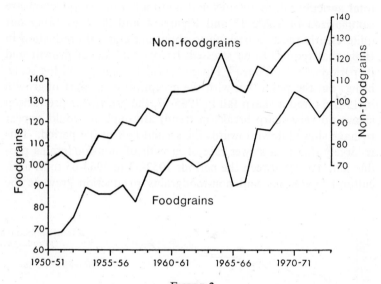

FIGURE 2
Index of total foodgrains and non-foodgrains production, 1950-51 to
1973-74. (Average 1959-60 to 1961-62=100)

following linear rates per annum: 3.42 per cent, 2.75 and 4.79 per
cent. The corresponding rates for the period 1964-66 to 1972-74
are 2.18 per cent for agricultural production and 2.73 and 1.25
per cent for foodgrains and non-foodgrains. While foodgrains
have grown at a more or less steady rate since the early 1950s, the
growth of non-foodgrains output has slowed down considerably
after the 1965-67 drought.[29]

These rates of growth are not, historically, particularly
low. They are much higher than those achieved in India during
the previous half-century and are roughly comparable to the
long-run rates of growth of agricultural production for countries such as Japan.[30] However, given the fact that the rate of
growth of the population has been over 2 per cent per annum, it

[29]See pp. 128-30 below.
[30]For rate of growth of agricultural production in India, see Blyn
(1966); on Japan, see Ohkawa and Rosovsky (1960) and Rosovsky (1968).

is clear that agricultural production, and especially food production, has barely managed to keep pace with this growth.

The general inadequacy of food production in the face of growing requirements is also borne out by the experience of the different states. During the 1950s, in 8 out of 14 major states, food production managed to keep ahead of population growth. The states which failed to do so were Assam, Gujarat, Orissa, Uttar Pradesh and West Bengal. Between 1960-61 and 1967-68, population increased faster than food production in twelve states, the only exceptions being Gujarat and Punjab. In seven states,

TABLE 12
INDEX OF AGRICULTURAL PRODUCTION: ALL CROPS, FOODGRAINS AND NON-FOODGRAINS
(1959-60 to 1961-62=100)

Year	Foodgrains (65.94)	Non-foodgrains (34.1)	All crops (100.0)
1950-51	67.4	72 2	68.9
1951-52	68.2	75.0	70.3
1952-53	75.4	71.1	74.1
1953-54	89.0	72.0	83.9
1954-55	85.7	82.6	84.8
1955-56	85.6	81.6	84 4
1956-57	89.5	89.6	89.5
1957-58	81.7	88.3	83.7
1958-59	97.0	95.6	96.6
1959-60	95.2	92.7	94.3
1960-61	102.1	103.8	102.7
1961-62	102.7	103.5	103.0
1962-63	99.4	105.4	101.4
1963-64	101.7	108.2	103.9
1964-65	112.0	120.9	115.0
1965-66	89.9	107.1	95.8
1966-67	91.9	103.7	95.9
1967-68	117.1	115.6	116.6
1968-69	115.7	113.2	114.8
1969-70	123.5	120.5	122.5
1970-71	133.9	126.6	131.4
1971-72	132.0	128.9	130.9
1972-73	121.2	119.4	120.6
1973-74	130.3	134.1	131.6

Figures from 1966-67 onwards provisional.
SOURCE: India, Ministry of Finance, *Economic Survey* (annual).

the balance between population growth and food production changed adversely between the decades, while only in Gujarat was there a change in the opposite direction.

As wage-goods, non-foodgrains are an imperfect substitute for foodgrains, although they are an alternative source of income and employment to the agricultural population and they are often higher-value crops than foodgrains. However, the problems created by a lagging food production were by no means countered by a more favourable climate of non-foodgrains production. We have already noted the overall low growth rate of non-foods production. Only in states like Gujarat did a high rate of non-foods production make up for a failure of food production to rise rapidly. Elsewhere, the states which showed a high rate of growth of non-foods production were almost always those which showed a rate of growth of food production higher than the national average. Generally speaking, food and non-food production pulled in the same direction. A sluggish performance of food production in India is not induced by the growth of commercial agriculture in this period.[31]

Figures for *per capita* availability of the basic foodstuffs reinforces this picture of a stagnant level of production of the basic wage-goods, not in absolute terms but in terms of the need to sustain a growing population and raise its low levels of consumption. We shall have to return to this point at greater length in our discussion of poverty. To summarize the main points, the *per capita* availability of cereals in 1974 was lower than in 1965, following a bumper 1964 harvest; that for pulses was as much as one-third lower. Comparing 1951 to 1974, the last year for which we have the information, the overall availability of cereals and pulses together was 448 grammes in 1974 and 395 grammes in 1951, an improvement of 13 per cent in 23 years. However, whereas the availability of cereals had increased by 22 per cent, that for pulses had declined by 34 per cent in this period.[32]

It could be objected that the total availability of foodgrains does not depend solely on domestic production. It can be added to through imports of food and it falls short of production by the

[31]Mitra (1970) for data up to 1970-71; see also Dharm Narain (1972) for the relationship between food crops and commercial crops.
[32]See Table 38, p. 187 below.

requirements of seed and of additions to stocks. We do not have very reliable estimates of total seed requirements of the economy or of total changes in stocks.[33] The available data are summarized in Table 13. It will be seen that broadly speaking, availability has been determined largely by domestic production, as one would expect for a large country like India. Imports have generally averaged 5 to 8 per cent of availability, although in particular years, the years of harvest failure, they have substantially ameliorated the overall scarcity. For example, in the drought years 1965-67, imports amounted to 12 to 14 per cent of net availability. It is also true that for the 1970s, the effects of shortfalls in domestic production have been cushioned to a very much smaller extent by imports, the contribution of imports being lower both in proportionate and absolute terms.

TABLE 13

DOMESTIC PRODUCTION, IMPORTS AND NET AVAILABILITY OF FOODGRAINS 1951-55 to 1971-74

Annual average	Net domestic production (million tonnes)	Imports (million tonnes)	Net availability (million tonnes)	Imports as percentage of net availability
1951-55	46.20	2.44	48.64	5.0
1956-60	53.29	3.45	56.74	6.1
1961-65	72.65	5.09	77.74	6.6
1966-70	76.15	6.44	82.59	7 8
1971-74	90.61	2.72	93.33	2.9

Net domestic production is obtained by allowing a margin of 12.5 per cent of gross production to cover seed and feed requirements and wastage. No allowance is made for changes in stocks in hands of traders.

SOURCE: India, Ministry of Finance, *Economic Survey* (annual).

The observed inadequate growth of food production has been reinforced by its short-run instability. This fact is well known and does not require lengthy substantiation. The situation is

---

[33]An allowance of 12.5 per cent is made for seed requirements, animal feed and wastage. The data also exclude changes in stocks of foodgrains with private traders, which might be substantial from year to year. The net availability figures are not, therefore, accurate measures of consumption. India, Ministry of Finance, Survey (1967-68) p. A.10.

brought home quite clearly in Figure 2, which marks out the poor harvest years in 1957-58, 1965-67 and 1972-73. It is worth stressing that even in such years not all states are affected similarly. Thus in 1965-67 the worst effects were felt in Andhra Pradesh, Bihar, Maharashtra, Mysore, Orissa, Rajasthan, Uttar Pradesh and West Bengal. In 1972-73 the states mainly affected were in western and central India. On the other hand, in 1968-70 Rajasthan suffered severely from a drought which did not affect total output equally. This indicates that against the background of a production problem there is superimposed the problem of the regional distribution of food products.[34]

The unequal regional incidence of poor harvests is attributable to two characteristics we have noted earlier, those of regional variations in rainfall and regional specialization of crop production. If rains fail in eastern India, they may not fail simultaneously elsewhere; if they fail in the east, it is rice production that is mainly affected. Similarly for wheat in Uttar Pradesh and millets in western India. The varying experience of different crops both in terms of rates of growth and periodic fluctuations is given in Figure 3. The following major points can be noted.

1. The 1950s were a period of moderate but fairly steady growth for a number of agricultural products but especially for non-food products such as sugar cane and oilseeds.

2. For foodcrops, there has been very little overall growth between the early 1960s and the early 1970s; the average level of production of two important food crops, millets and pulses, has been more or less unchanged, especially if we exclude a bumper jowar and bajra harvest in 1973-74; a point of major importance, to which I shall return in the discussion of the impact of the 'green revolution', is that since 1967-68 the only cereal crop that has shown a substantial acceleration in its rate of growth is wheat.[35]

3. The production of millets and pulses has not only grown little over the last decade but they have also been subject to sharper fluctuations in levels of production.

Production of any particular crop can be broken down into two

[34]For figures of regional production, yield and acreage, see India, Ministry of Food and Agriculture (1972-73).
[35]See p. 124 below; see also Srinivasan (1972).

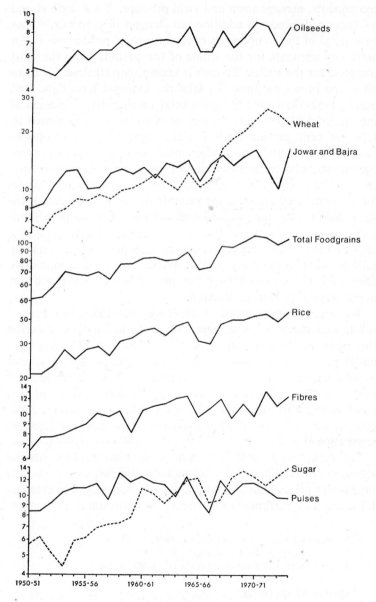

FIGURE 3

Production of selected agricultural commodities, 1950-51 to 1973-74.
(Million tones: Semi-log scale)

components, acreage sown and yield per acre. Total agricultural production depends, in addition, on changes in crop-mix.[36] Our knowledge of the components of the growth of production is not uniformly adequate for the whole of the period, being the most complete for the 1950s. Enough is known, nevertheless, for us to fill in the broad outlines. To take the national level data first, during 1952-53 to 1964-65 agricultural productivity increased at the rate of 1.91 per cent, whereas area under crops increased by 1.28 per cent per annum.[37] For the eight-year period 1964-65 to 1972-73, area under production increased by less than 1 per cent per annum, whereas productivity increased by a little over 2 per cent.[38] For foodgrains, corresponding increases were 1.02 and 0.94 for area and 1.60 and 3.42 for productivity in 1952-64 and 1964-72.[39] Non-foodgrains, which increased more rapidly than foodgrains up to the middle 1960s and since have increased less rapidly, increased the area under cultivation by 2.56 per cent and yield by 1.79 per cent in the early period. We do not have comparative figures for the second half of our period but we know the low overall rate of growth production.

We also have independent evidence that there has been a substantial switch of land from cash crops to foodgrains during this period.[40] Between the years 1964-66 and 1970-72 the area under production of three major cash crops, cotton, jute and sugar cane, actually declined, while that of oilseeds increased at a rate of less than 1 per cent. Although in each case there was some increase in yield, the rates were low, being around 2 per cent for oilseeds and cotton and less than 1 per cent for jute and sugar cane.[41]

All the figures point towards a major conclusion. Towards the second half of the period it became more difficult to increase the area under production and food and cash crops began to compete for land. To a certain extent increases in agricultural productivity

---

[36]Minhas and Vaidyanathan (1965) *passim.*
[37]India, Ministry of Food and Agriculture (1968).
[38]India, Ministry of Finance, Survey (1973-74), p. 59.
[39]See reference cited in n. 34 above.
[40]Dharm Narain (1972).
[41]The relative contributions to total agricultural production of increases in yield, acreage and crop-mix are discussed in Rao (1965) and Minhas and Vaidyanathan (1965).

enabled agricultural production to keep pace roughly with population growth but yields did not increase sufficiently to achieve very much more.

In the previous chapter, I had pointed to the regional diversity of the Indian economy, not only in matters of size or population density but also in terms of levels of output, incidence of poverty and level of literacy. A reduction in the levels of regional inequality was an objective of planning in India. The question naturally arises whether, during this period, there was any tendency towards an evening-out of such disparities in levels of development. Whether, that is to say, the poorer regions tended to grow at a faster rate relatively to the richer regions.

A general answer to this question is not easy to give. There are no regional aggregate output figures that can serve as a basis for comparison, beyond some data for state levels of income for 1961. Therefore, we have to fall back on a number of partial indicators of economic progress or development, such as foodgrains production, net value added in manufacturing or changes in levels of literacy. On the basis of such fragmentary evidence, we can say that there has been no systematic tendency towards a reduction in regional inequality. Rather the contrary is the case in India. Some relatively prosperous regions, such as Punjab or Gujarat, show much faster increases in, say, total foodgrains output or food output *per capita* than do some of the poorer regions, such as Andhra Pradesh, Bihar or Orissa.

Industrial Production

For statistical purposes, the data relating to industrial production can be divided into two groups, to cover organized and small-scale industries respectively. The Annual Survey of Industry data cover the former category, which is defined in terms of either 50 or more people with power or 100 or more people without power working under the establishment, on a censal basis. The small-scale sector is covered by a sample survey. The last published Annual Survey data relate to 1966, although some basic 1968 data are also available. More up-to-date data are published under the Monthly Statistics of Production of Selected Industries. These are the data we have used in this chapter. A basic limitation of the data that needs to concern us here is that for a number of industries only the large-scale organized sector is covered in the Monthly Statistics of Production. The result is that the level of production of small-scale industry, which covers roughly one-third of total industrial production, is under· represented. There is a great deal of casual evidence that during the 1960s especially, the small-scale sector expanded very rapidly. The published data underestimate the rate of growth of output of this sector for, quite possibly, the whole of this period.

Tables 14 and 15 give the indexes of industrial production for the period 1951 to 1972, by major industry groups. Although a series with a common base-period, i.e. 1960, is available for the whole of the period, a more useful classification for analytical purposes is only available for part of the period. We have, therefore, given the information for selected years up to the middle 1960s, together with a more detailed coverage for 1960-72.

TABLE 14
INDEX OF INDUSTRIAL PRODUCTION—1951, 1955 and 1965
(Base 1960 = 100)

Industry	Weight	1951	1955	1965
Mining	9.72	66.6	74.6	131.7
Manufacturing	84.91	54.6	73.8	153.8
Food Processing	12.09	66.9	75.9	122.2
Textiles	27.06	79.7	94.1	114.8
Chemicals	7.26	42.4	60.1	153.9
Petroleum	1.34	11.0	56.1	158.7
Basic Metals	7.38	46.5	53.3	180.1
Machinery	3.38	22.2	35.5	316.0
Transport Equipment	7.77	19.6	99.2	206.3

SOURCE: Reserve Bank of India, *Report on Currency and Finance* (annual).

For an underdeveloped country, India started off in 1950 with a small but significant industrial sector, all of it in the private sector. During the next 15 years the industrial sector increased rapidly, especially after 1957, when a balance of payments crisis led to the imposition of severe import controls.[42] Throughout

[42]Good short summaries of industrial development in India are provided by Medhora (1968) and Shirokov (1973).

TABLE 15
INDEX OF INDUSTRIAL PRODUCTION 1961-72
(Base 1960 = 100)

Year/weight	Total (100.0)	Basic industries (25.11)	Capital goods (11.76)	Intermediate goods (25.88)	Consumer goods	
					Non-durables (31.57)	Durables (5.68)
1961	112.7	112.7	118.0	105.8	105.8	110.8
1962	119.8	128.2	153.0	113.6	107.2	112.4
1963	129.7	146.5	170.0	122.9	108.7	119.6
1964	140.8	152.1	206.1	132.2	115.9	133.6
1965	164.3	164.3	244.2	140.1	120.5	166.5
1966	172.9	172.9	210.1	136.7	122.6	179.4
1967	176.5	176.5	205.3	139.7	114.9	185.6
1968	194.6	194.6	210.3	148.2	117.4	212.4
1969	212.0	212.0	214.0	154.4	128.3	239.7
1970	221.7	221.7	224.6	158.8	137.8	249.5
1971	233.8	233.8	224.3	160.4	140.2	268.0
1972	199.4	254.3	243.5	171.2	168.2	284.2

SOURCE: Reserve Bank of India, *Report on Currency and Finance* (annual).

this period, the traditional industries such as food processing and textiles grew less rapidly than the newer industries such as iron and steel, machinery production, petroleum and chemicals. Partly, of course, this difference in relative rates of growth is somewhat illusory. The latter industries started from a very small base and any given increase in volume or value of production then showed up as extremely high figures. However, there was during this period a considerable amount of real growth.

The reason why the newer industries grew more rapidly is twofold. As a matter of development policy, the Government began to invest very heavily in those industries in order to build up an industrial base. It was particularly concerned with building up a so-called 'heavy industry' or capital goods sector.[43] This, in turn, also required investment in what are strictly speaking intermediate goods industries, such as iron and steel. Indeed, in quantitative terms, the volume of investment in steel has dominated industrial investment proper, especially if we exclude investment in power generation. Investment in these industries created substantial amounts of new capacity and development expenditure

[43]On Government policy, see Chs. 9 and 10 below.

in general created the demand for these goods, especially until the middle 1960s.[44] This demand was strengthened by the introduction of a regime of import controls, which created a sheltered market for such products. This was due not so much to the levels of tariff protection as to the fact that throughout this period the economy generated a substantial volume of excess demand for these products, which made it relatively easy to expand sales—although, as we shall see later, capacity often ran ahead of demand or the supply of raw materials and thus resulted in high levels of excess capacity.

The experience of the period 1960-72 is more varied and interesting. The period can be divided roughly into two, 1960-65 and 1966-72. The three main features are highlighted by Tables 14, 15, 16 and can be briefly stated. First, in all sectors other than consumer non-durables, the rates of industrial growth have been much lower in the latter period than in the former. Secondly, the decline has been the most severe in the capital goods industries. A decline of 17 per cent in the rate of growth over a relatively short period is obviously not a statistical illusion. On the contrary, it is a matter of profound significance for develop-

TABLE 16
RATES OF GROWTH OF INDUSTRIAL PRODUCTION
(Base 1960=100)

	1960-65	1966-72
Total	8.98	4.47
Basic industries	10.45	6.66
Capital goods	19.53	2.49
Intermediate goods	7.02	3.81
Consumer non-durables	3.42	5.31
Consumer durables	10.72	7.97

SOURCE: Bose (1974).

ment policy, as will emerge later.[45] The drought years of 1965-67 and the recession which followed in its wake have dealt a body-blow to industrialization in India, from which it has yet to

[44]See also pp. 150-3 below.
[45]See pp. 150-2 below.

recover. Thirdly, while consumer durables took second place to capital goods and grew roughly at the same rate as basic industries such as iron and steel, after 1965 they have grown most rapidly of all industries. An eight per cent rate of growth during a period of relative stagnation—note the levels of total industrial production in 1968 and 1972—during which *per capita* income has remained more or less stagnant, is a significant fact.

One should, however, look also at the positive sides of industrial development in India. Leaving aside for the moment any detailed assessment of industrial growth in India, we can see from Table 17 that the Indian economy managed to achieve very significant increases in absolute volume of production of a large number of major industrial products. Over a relatively brief period of 25 years, it increased its production of iron ore eight times and of steel, automobiles and rail wagons five times, as is shown in Table 17. For other commodities such as machine

TABLE 17
PRODUCTION OF SELECTED INDUSTRIES—1950-51,
1960-61 and 1972-73

Industry	Unit		1950-51	1960-61	1972-73
Coal	million tonnes		32.8	55.7	79.3
Iron ore	,,	,,	3.0	11.0	24.0
Finished steel	,,	,,	1.04	2.39	5.02
Machine tools	Rs million		3	70	626
Cotton textile machinery	,,	,,	—	104	309
Sugar mills machinery	,,	,,	—	44	182
Automobiles	1,000 nos		16.5	55.0	89.4
Railway wagons	,,	,,	2.9	11.9	10.8
Power driven pumps	,,	,,	35	109	278
Diesel engines (stationary)	,,	.,	5.5	44.7	92.8
Power transformers	1,000 kVa		179	1,413	9,712
Nitrogenous fertilizers	1,000 tonnes		9	98	1,059
Cotton cloth	million metres		4,215	6,738	7,879
Refined petroleum products	million tonnes		0.2	5.8	17.9
Electricity generated	billion kWh		5.3	16.9	63.6

SOURCE: India, Ministry of Finance, *Economic Survey* (annual).

tools, diesel engines, power transformers or fertilizers, it obtained very substantial increases indeed. In terms of its own requirements, it also managed to achieve a high level of self-sufficiency in a number of important products, although in this the economy has certainly been helped, if that is the right word, by the relatively low rate of growth of overall activity. The decline in the importance of imports as a source of supply is brought out in Table 18. This industrial growth has also had a very important spin-off, in the development of a number of major new exports. This is shown in the next section.

TABLE 18

SHARE OF IMPORTS IN TOTAL ESTIMATED SUPPLIES—
SELECTED YEARS
(Per cent)

	1950-51	1955-56	1965-66	1972-73
Foodgrains	5.9	1.7	9.7	0.8
Raw cotton	27.8	12.3	10.9	6.7
Textile machinery	—	67.6	37.9	19.1
Machine tools	89.8	84.8	61.8	41.1
Iron and steel	25.2	39.9	16.7	19.6
Aluminium	72.8	68.5	25.6	1.0
Bicycles	62.5	22.4	neg	nil
Sewing machines	41.1	11.2	0.7	0.3
Ammonium sulphate	88.9	34.1	67.0	14.8
Man-made fibre and yarn	n.a.	20.7	6.0	5.4

SOURCE: Same as Table 17.

Imports and Exports

The external sector has dominated the discussion of Indian development performance, to the exclusion almost of all others except agriculture. Until 1965, it certainly claimed more attention than even the latter. Both long-and short-term strategy have also been greatly influenced by the balance of payments problem. Given the fact that it is quantitatively a very small part of the economy, this is indeed somewhat paradoxical.

The basic data relating to India's exports and imports are summarized in Figure 4 and Tables 19, 20 and 21. As we should be interested in the net inflows and outflows of foreign exchange rather than the domestic currency, the figures are given in terms of US dollars. This also avoids the spurious effect created by quoting rupee values, where a devaluation can set foreign exchange

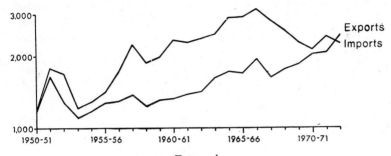

FIGURE 4

Total imports and exports, 1950 to 1972. ($ million: Semi-log scale)

earnings and aid receipts soaring; where in fact it reduces the purchasing power of the country over foreign resources.

To take exports first, the value of exports remained more or less stagnant during the whole of the 1950s and early 1960s, excluding the year of the Korean War boom. This point is well known and has been discussed in detail by Cohen, Patel and Singh, among others.[46] Briefly, this was partly due to the neglect of the Government, which took a highly pessimistic view of export prospects, in the belief that world demand for Indian exports was highly inelastic. In fact, the position was far more complicated. While it is true that some Indian exports suffered from demand constraints, supply difficulties, non-competitive prices and quality of products were all responsible for a dismal performance. Since 1966-67, following the devaluation of the rupee, exports have grown at a much faster rate, having increased by about 50 per cent in six years. The role that devaluation has had to play in this growth is uncertain and a matter of some controversy.[47] It is worth mentioning that the sharp increase in the last year is to a certain extent spurious, because it includes a substantial amount of exports to Bangla Desh, which might be more properly classified as commodity aid.

[46]Cohen (1964), Patel (1960) and Singh (1964); for more recent studies of Indian commercial policy and export performance, see Nayyar (1974) and Srinivasan (1974).

[47]For opposite views, cf. Srinivasan (1974) and Nayyar (1974).

Following a post-Korean War trough, Indian imports increased very rapidly until 1957, when there was a severe balance of payments crisis. This was caused partly as a result of a consumption

TABLE 19
TOTAL IMPORTS AND EXPORTS—1950-72
(million US $)

Year	Imports	Exports	Balance of trade
1950	1,173	1,178	+5
1951	1,794	1,646	—148
1952	1,696	1,299	—397
1953	1,208	1,116	— 92
1954	1,297	1,182	—115
1955	1,414	1,276	—138
1956	1,725	1,300	—425
1957	2,243	1,379	—864
1958	1,875	1,241	—634
1959	1,986	1,304	—682
1960	2,327	1,331	—996
1961	2,277	1,386	—891
1962	2,361	1,403	—958
1963	2,477	1,626	—851
1964	2,876	1,705	—1,171
1965	2,900	1,686	—1,241
1966	3,120	1,836	—1,284
1967	2,793	1,613	—1,180
1968	2,571	1,761	—810
1969	2,217	1,835	—382
1970	2,124	2,026	— 98
1971	2,406	2,051	—355
1972	2,230	2,408	+178

SOURCE: UNO *Yearbook of International Trade Statistics* (annual).

boom, partly of inventory accumulation and partly of a rising level of development expenditure within the economy. This ushered in a regime of strict import controls, which has stayed with us ever since, with changing degrees of liberalization.[48] After 1957, imports climbed steadily to a peak in 1966, growing at a faster rate than exports. The higher level of imports compared to exports, together with a higher rate of growth, resulted in continuous pressure on the balance of payments during this period.

[48]Srinivasan (1974), p. 21f.

TABLE 20
PRINCIPAL IMPORTS—SELECTED YEARS
(Million US $)

Commodity	1960-61	1967-68	1970-71
Cereals and cereal preparations	380.9	690.8	284.0
Intermediate goods of which:	1,034.5	1,068.5	1,188.6
fibres	212.7	140.4	168.9
petroleum products	145.4	99.7	181.2
fertilizer and chemicals	187.8	416.0	288.7
iron and steel	257.3	141.7	196.6
non-ferrous metals	99.3	118.5	159.5
Capital goods	747.6	689.5	525.1
Others	230.3	227.3	169.2
Total Imports	2,393.3	2,676.1	2,166.9

SOURCE: USAID, *Economic and Social Indicators: India*, New Delhi (1972).

TABLE 21
PRINCIPAL EXPORTS—SELECTED YEARS
(Million US $)

Commodity	1960-61	1967-68	1970-71
Jute manufactures	283.8	312.1	253.9
Cotton fabrics	120.8	87.1	100.4
Tea	259.5	240.2	197.7
Leather and leather manufactures	52.4	71.3	96.3
Oil cakes	30.0	60.7	73.9
Cashew kernels	39.7	57.3	69.5
Manganese ore	29.5	14.8	18.7
Iron ore	35.7	99.7	156.4
Iron and steel	11.6	69.2	105.6
Engineering goods	17.9	43.5	155.3
Chemicals and allied products	7.2	15.9	39.2
Total exports	1,386.4	1,598.0	2,046.9

SOURCE: USAID, *Economic and Social Indicators: India*, New Delhi (1972).

Since 1966, imports have shown a dramatic decline, thus considerably easing the pressure on the balance of payments and allowing India to accumulate some foreign reserves. It is unlikely that an increase in prices in the wake of devaluation is largely responsible for this decline in imports. The import unit value

index, after a sharp rise in 1966, has not increased over a period
of time, although it has stabilized at a level about 40 per cent
higher than the pre-devaluation period. It is more likely that
two other factors have been major contributors to the decline in
imports. One is the low level of overall economic activity and
industrial growth during this period, the other is the continuous
decline in net foreign aid, most of which goes to finance imports
from hard-currency areas. It has also to be borne in mind that
there has been a degree of import-substitution in Indian industries during this period. The overall import position remains
highly critical and uncertain, having worsened considerably since
1973, on account of the rise in oil prices and of the increased
rates of inflation in industrialized countries.

The composition of exports has changed significantly over
our period, most of the change coming after the middle 1960s,
with the emergence of a number of new exports. In most cases,
earnings from traditional exports have declined—this is true of
jute, cotton and tea—while for some others, such as cashew
kernels or leather goods, they have shown some increase. For
most of these products, India has failed to maintain her
relative share of the market, indicating that her exports suffer
not so much from demand constraints as from lack of competitiveness. Although it remains true that for some products such as
tea and jute, prospects for *increasing* earnings would remain small,
India should have been able at least to maintain her relative
share. The poor performance of traditional exports has been
offset by the rapid increase in a number of new manufactured
exports, and minerals. The most important among the former are
steel products and engineering goods, together with iron ore.
This trend is at least a positive contribution of industrialization to
development.[49]

The composition of imports is more predictable and has
remained more stable. Throughout this period India has imported very little consumer goods, with the exception of the most
basic, foodgrains. While in a year of good harvest, she has been
more or less self-sufficient in years of harvest failure, she has had
to import heavily in terms of the effect on her foreign exchange

---

[49]On Indian export performance until the middle 1960s, see Singh
(1964); thereafter see Nayyar (1974).

position. The fact that during part of this period she could obtain substantial amounts of food aid has also encouraged the Government to import food, to supplement consumption or to add to stocks. Apart from that, India has imported mainly intermediate and capital goods. It is worth noting that, while her imports of capital goods have declined, those of intermediate goods have not. This is true especially of fertilizer and steel imports, due in both cases to an inability to achieve a satisfactory level of capacity-utilization.

CHAPTER FOUR

Resource Mobilization, Stability and Self-Reliance

Investment occupies a central place in the formulation of planning strategies in India, if not always in their implementation.[1] A major part of investment is also expected to be concentrated in the public sector, because of the objective of bringing about a transformation of the economy according to the 'socialist pattern'.[2] Moreover, the Government is concerned with pursuing an investment-oriented growth policy, consistent with both internal and external stability, i.e. price and balance of payments stability. The success of such a strategy requires the maintenance of a certain balance between a number of macro-economic variables. This is necessary, not only to achieve an abstract or notional 'equilibrium' in the economy but to ensure that in a mixed economy, with different interest groups competing for resources, some basic investment targets are actually fulfilled in real terms.

Unfortunately, there has been a relative neglect of what, for the want of a better term, I shall call the macro-economics of development. This is true in the specific context of Indian problems, although economists like Bagchi and Raj are amongst the few who have stressed the significance of such problems.[3] It is also true of the general area of development economics.[4] In

[1] On the role of investment in the planning strategy, see below, pp. 215-21.

[2] See, for example, India, Planning Commission (1961), Ch. 1.

[3] Bagchi (1970); Raj (1967).

[6] See, for example, ILO (1970) or ILO (1971). This neglect is part of the theoretical literature on development. In the Indian context, see Tendulkar (1971).

part, the roots of this neglect lie in the discussion in the early 1950s of the relevance of Keynesian economics for development strategy.[5] However, starting from the quite legitimate conclusion that deficit financing is of limited usefulness in increasing output where the elasticities of supply are low, a quite erroneous conclusion has tended to be drawn that traditional macro-economics have little to contribute to an understanding of the problems of development. It is necessary, therefore, to spend a little time on an elementary theoretical digression.

The total value of public and private investment at constant prices must equal, in realized terms, the total of domestic savings, public and private, *plus* the net inflow of foreign resources. We shall call the latter 'aid', for purposes of simplification. This equalization can be brought about in two quite distinct ways. In the Kaldor world, investment generates its own savings.[6] Where investment is constrained by a supply of resources, a failure to achieve a given rate of total savings reflects a failure to divert resources from consumption to investment and leads to the non-fulfilment of investment targets. This can come about either through the inability to control domestic non-investment demand or the use of aid, directly or indirectly, to finance additional consumption.[7] Public investment must equal the difference between private savings and investment *plus* public savings *plus* aid. If private savings exceed private investment, the public sector has succeeded in acquiring a net draft on resources from the private sector. The opposite, of course, occurs if private investment exceeds private savings. Moreover, public investment can be divided into developmental and non-developmental investment, e.g. irrigation or defence hardware, so that even a given volume of real investment can have a smaller or larger impact on development, irrespective of how safe the world can be made for the poor who are confined to poverty. It follows, therefore, that the ability to carry out a core investment plan such as is implied

[5]For an early statement of this approach see Rao (1952); see also Chelliah (1960), Ch. II.

[6]Kaldor (1955-56); for further development of the Kaldor argument, see Passinetti (1961-62).

[7]There is a large and growing literature on the impact of aid on recipient countries; see *inter alia* Griffin (1970), Papanek (1972), Rahman (1968) and Weisskopf (1972).

in Indian development strategy depends both on the internal priorities within the Government budget, as well as on the success of budgetary and other policies in extracting a net surplus of domestic savings or in attracting foreign savings.

The economy as a whole cannot invest more than it has saved or borrowed from abroad. However, it is possible for a particular sector to try to obtain a larger share of resources through the use of the credit mechanism. We can illustrate this point with reference to the public sector, because it has the power to increase the supply of money within the economy. The private sector can also behave in a similar fashion if it can acquire a larger share of credit. If public sector investment exceeds the total of net private savings,[8] *plus* aid, by an amount larger than its own savings, this implies that government current expenditure is in excess of its revenue in terms of taxation *plus* the surpluses of public sector enterprises. This overall deficit can be financed through net borrowings from the private sector or an increase in the supply of money. As we have already taken account of net private savings, either method implies an excess of purchasing power within the economy over the available supply of goods at constant prices.

It is this excess demand, originating in this case within the public sector, that should be characterized by the term 'deficit finance'. What matters in this context is that the public sector is attempting to obtain a larger share of resources than the private sector is willing or can be persuaded to forgo. There is no simple distinction to be made here between increases in the supply of money and other forms of borrowing from the private sector, in so far as it does not come out of a reduction in current expenditure of the private sector. For both factors operate by altering the structure of asset-holdings within the private sector and its effects on the structure of interest rates, although it is true as a limiting case that there might sometimes be a more direct causal link between money supply and expenditure.[9]

---

[8]Net, that is, of private sector investment.

[9]There is a vast and growing literature on the theoretical and empirical aspects of the monetary controversy. A good introduction in Laidler (1969). A number of useful articles are reproduced in Walters (1973). Most of the work relates to developed countries with well-developed monetary institutions.

If excess demand is generated within the economy in this manner, there are four ways in which the economy can adjust to it. First, by lowering investment targets, either within the public or the private sector. This will lead to a lower rate of growth than previously expected. Secondly, excess demand may tend to cause internal instability, by causing prices to rise. In both these cases, how successful such an adjustment process would be, that is to say whether a lower rate of growth will give stability or whether inflation will be shortlived, cannot be determined on the basis of *a priori* reasoning. The final outcome depends on how particular expenditure plans are adjusted in the light of non-fulfilment of expectations. Thirdly, there might be instability in the external sector, a worsening of the balance of payments allowing additional net resources to be drawn in from abroad. Fourthly, the economy may devise various means of containing excess demand, such as rationing, various forms of licensing, delays, queues and patronage. This theoretical digression into the macro-economics of development provides a useful framework for the analysis of Indian economic performance.

We have noted earlier that the rate of investment reached a peak level of 13.4 per cent of net domestic product in 1965-66. After a period of decline, it appears to have stabilized at a little under 10 per cent.[10] Although domestic savings and foreign aid have both fallen over the same period, the former has declined less, so that a larger proportion of the lower level of investment is now financed out of domestic savings. The rate of investment reached target level at the end of the third plan, when it was 13.4 as against a planned level of 11.5 per cent.[11] But this was at current prices and we simply do not know enough about the structure of relative prices within the economy to say what this would have meant in terms of fulfilling real targets.[12] Instead of rising from that level, by the early 1970s the rate had fallen seriously below target. For example, the fourth plan aimed at a target rate of 14.5 per cent by 1973-74, which will imply an

[10]See Table 10, p. 54.
[11]India, Planning Commission (1961), p. 91.
[12]We do know, however, that large numbers of specific investment targets for particular types of capacity were not reached; see, for example, Medhora (1968).

increase of 50 per cent in the rate of investment.[13] Similarly, both the average and the marginal savings rates have fallen below the expected rate.[14] Indeed, K.N. Raj has argued that the official data underestimate the volume of gross savings at the beginning of the period and therefore overestimate the marginal propensity to save in the economy.[15]

Table 22 throws some interesting light on the savings behaviour of the economy. It will be seen that in absolute terms total domestic savings have doubled in 11 years, while private savings have increased by 1.5 times in that period. In contrast, net public savings have actually fallen from an average of Rs 464 crores to Rs 375 crores. The inability of total savings to rise faster is to a large measure caused by the failure of the public sector to generate a higher level of net savings. Moreover, the net draft of the public sector on the private sector for a flow of resources has also increased. While the excess of private savings over investment has risen from Rs 440 crores to Rs 1,210 crores, the shortfall of public savings over investment has increased from Rs 830 crores to Rs 1,210 crores, the balance between the two being bridged by foreign-aid receipts of the public sector.

In so far as the savings data are reliable (and they have shortcomings) they do not on the face of it stand up to the interpretation that throughout this period the public sector has been a net supplier of resources to the private sector. However, this ability of the public sector to generate a net inflow of resources from the private sector has not provided the foundations of either a high rate of capital formation or an expansion of public sector control over the productive resource base of the economy. It is not the kind of transformation of the economy that Preobrazhensky had in mind.[16] The answer to this riddle would appear to lie in the pattern of public expenditure that has

[13]India, Planning Commission (1969), p. 32.

[14]Raj (1970).

[15]Raj (1970).

[16]Preobrazhensky was concerned with the problem that, in the early stages of socialist development, the socialized industrial sector would be too small to generate a sufficiently large investible surplus *internally*. It had to obtain such a surplus from the backward and non-socialized agricultural sector. Preobrazhensky (1965), esp. Ch. II.

emerged, as we shall see below.[17]

TABLE 22

NET INVESMENT, DOMESTIC AND FOREIGN SAVINGS—
1960-61 TO 1971-72 CURRENT PRICES

(Rs crores)

Year *Average value*	*Net invest- ment* *Public* *Private* *Total*			*Domestic savings* *Public* *Private* *Total*			*Foreign savings*
	Public	*Private*	*Total*	*Public*	*Private*	*Total*	
1960-61 to 1963-64	1,294	632	1,926	464	1,072	1,536	391
1964-65 to 1967-68	1,857	1,172	3,029	561	1,821	2,382	647
1968-69 to 1971-72	2,017	1,428	3,444	375	2,638	3,013	432

1 crore = 10 million

SOURCE: Estimated from source cited. Table 10.

The bulk of private saving comeing from the household sector, corporate savings being a small proportion of total private savings. Both in 1960-61 and 1968-69, household savings made up about 86 per cent of private savings, the ratio having been as high as 95 per cent in 1965-66.[18] The bulk of this saving is done by relatively better-off households. According to a recent survey carried out by the National Council of Applied Economic Research, 74.5 per cent of rural and 63.3 per cent of all urban households below income levels of Rs 3,000 per year either saved nothing or dissaved. The top 1 per cent of all households ascounted for 37.4 per cent of all household savings in 1967-68, the year of the survey. While the relationship differed between the urban and the rural sectors and was not a continuous one, by and large the richer households saved a larger proportion of their incomes.[19] There are no detailed studies of corporate savings behaviour but it is likely that the low rate of growth of corporate savings is in part a reflection of the low rate of growth of industrial production. On the other hand, it is possible that for a variety of reasons profits in organized industry and in the informal sector may be under-reported.

The basic data relating to the patterns of resource mobiliza-

[17]See p. 87 below.
[18]USAID (1972), p. 20.
[19]NCAER (1972), p. 79f.

TABLE 23
PLAN OUTLAY AND ITS FINANCE—1951-69

	1951-56 Rs crs	%	1956-61 Rs crs	%	1961-66 Rs crs	%	1966-69 Rs crs	%
Plan outlay	1,960	100.0	4,672	100.0	8,577	100.0	6,756	100.0
Domestic budgetary resources	1,438	73.4	2,669	57.0	5,021	58.5	3,648	54.0
Current surpluses	754	38.5	1,230	26.3	2,882	33.6	1,622	24.0
Internal borrowings	684	34.9	1,439	30.7	2,139	24.9	2,026	30.0
Deficit finance	333	17.0	954	20.4	1,133	13.2	682	10.1
External resources	189	9.6	1,049	22.5	2,423	28.3	2,426	35.9

1 crore = 10 million
SOURCE: Reserve Bank of India, *Report on Currency and Finance* (annual).

TABLE 24
TOTAL BUDGETARY EXPENDITURE OF CENTRAL
AND STATE GOVERNMENTS AND ITS FINANCE—
1969-70 TO 1973-74
(Rs crores)

	1969-70	1970-71	1971-72	1972-73	1973-74	Percentage 1969-70	com-position to 1973-74
Total outlay	7,375	8,352	10,068	11,256	12,398	100.0	
Development	4,166	4,716	5,710	6,695	6,825	56.9	
Non-development	3,209	3,636	4,358	4,561	5,573	43.1	
Domestic budgetary resources	6,758	7,546	8,819	10,104	11,099	89.7	
Current surpluses	5,533	6,064	7,009	8,075	8,913	72.0	
Internal borrowings	1,225	1,482	1,810	2,029	2,186	17.7	
Deficit finance	43	424	738	852	790	5.8	
External resources	574	382	378	286	509	4.3	

1 crore = 10 million
SOURCE: India, Ministry of Finance, *Economic Survey* (annual).

tion and resource use in the public sector are given in Tables 23 and 24. There are no clear trends that we can observe for the period as a whole, the pattern of resource mobilization having undergone fairly large shifts from period to period. We can note, however, that at best less than 40 per cent of plan outlay was financed out of current government revenues. A substantial proportion, especially during the third and the annual plans of 1966-69, was financed out of external resources, i.e. foreign aid.[20] A large proportion, varying from around 40 to 50 per cent, was financed out of borrowings and money creation.

Here it has to be borne in mind that while accounting conventions list only the net borrowings from the Reserve Bank of India as deficit finance, a part at least of the borrowings from the private sector is inflationary in the sense of creating excess demand.[21] While the total of internal borrowings plus deficit finance, as narrowly defined, has fallen from 52 to 38 per cent from 1951-56 to 1961-66, this proportion had since risen to 46.5 per cent. Moreover, the 1969-74 figures are estimates. In reality, the volume of internal borrowing during the latter period was Rs 8,732 crores, as opposed to the estimated Rs 6,185 crores, while deficit finance reached a level of Rs 2,847 crores, as opposed to the estimated Rs 1,203 crores.[22] The main lesson is quite clear from these figures. Especially since the middle 1960s, the Government has failed significantly to mobilize sufficient resources to finance its plan expenditure and has resorted heavily to borrowing from the private and banking sectors, thus adding to the pressure of excess demand within the economy.

This conclusion is borne out by the data relating to increases in money supply given in Table 25. It will be seen that throughout this period the money supply has increased at a growing rate, until in 1972-73 it increased in a single year by roughly 64 per cent of the increase for the whole of 1966-70. It is equally clear, with perhaps 1966-70 being something of an exception owing partly to factors originating in the external sector, that the basic source of increase has been the borrowing requirements of the public rather than the private sector.[23] This raises the obvious

[20]India, Ministry of Finance, Pocketbook (1970).

[21]The part which is not financed out of a reduction in expenditure by the private sector. For a shorting discussion of the Indian procedure, see Chelliah (1960), p. 149f.

[22]Calculated from Reserve Bank of India, *Report on Currency and Finance* (annual).

[23]The industrial recession following on after 1967 helped to improve the Indian balance of payments by reducing the demand for imports, thus enabling the country to build up its foreign exchange reserves. India also benefited along with other countries from the creation of SDRs in 1970, her share being SDR 326.2 million, at 31 August 1974.

and controversial issue of the relationship of this increase to inflation in the Indian economy, a point to which I shall return below. At this moment, the point that needs to be made is the systematic failure of the Government to mobilize sufficient amounts of current resources for the purpose of financing development expenditure, even where there was an excess supply of savings from within the private sector.

TABLE 25
CHANGES IN MONEY SUPPLY AND ITS MAJOR SOURCES
(Rs crores)

	1951-56	1956-61	1961-66	1966-70	1970-71	1971-72
Money Supply	196	704	1,661	1,856	751	998
Currency	166	527	936	974	371	439
Bank deposits	30	177	725	881	380	559
Sources of Change in Money Supply						
Net bank credit to Government sector	298	1,384	1,321	917	510	1,182
Net bank credit to private sector	105	23	642	786	390	121
Net foreign assets of banking sector	—96	—664	—107	516	—28	60

1 crore = 10 million
SOURCE: Reserve Bank of India, *Report on Currency and Finance* (annual).

There is a fairly widespread belief in India that the failure of the Government to mobilize resources is due largely to its failure to use its powers of taxation effectively. The data for selected years are summarized in Table 26. Between 1950-51 and 1972-73, total Government revenue increased about elevenfold, the bulk of the increase coming from tax revenues. Interestingly enough, earnings from income tax increased least in proportionate terms, the high increases coming from Corporation tax and excise duties. Although earnings from taxes on wealth and the revenue surpluses of public sector undertakings have increased substantially in relation to their initial levels, they together provide a very small amount of total revenue.

TABLE 26

COMPOSITION OF CENTRAL GOVERNMENT REVENUE

(Rs crores)

	1950-51	1955-56	1960-61	1965-66	1970-71	1972-73
Taxes on Income and Expenditure	126	113	192	454	484	668
Of which:						
Income tax (net)	85	76	80	149	114	110
(gross)	(133)	(131)	(167)	(272)	(473)	(602)
Corporation tax	41	37	111	305	370	558
Taxes on property	4	3	14	20	27	58
Wealth tax	—	—	9	14	18	47
Indirect taxes	228	296	525	1,311	1,668	2,746
Customs duties (net)	157	167	170	539	423	810
Excise (net)	68	129	341	752	1,203	1,862
(gross)	(68)	(145)	(416)	(898)	(1,524)	(2,428)
Total tax Revenue	358	412	730	1,785	2,201	3,472
Total non-tax Revenue	49	70	147	536	842	1,101
Surplus of public undertakings	23	29	53	79	124	173
Total Revenue	406	481	877	2,321	3,293	4,573

1 crore = 10 million

SOURCE: Reserve Bank of India, *Report on Currency and Finance* (annual).

A more detailed study of India's tax efforts has been carried out by Chelliah for the period 1953-55 to 1966-68, which broadly spans our period. It indicates[24] that relative to the tax performance of other developing countries, Indian tax effort has not been particularly poor. Between 1953-55 and 1966-68, the tax/income ratio in India rose from 6.3 to 11.6 per cent. The marginal tax rate, i.e. the ratio of additional tax revenue to income, works out at 15.1 per cent for the period, which is significantly below countries like Brazil or Morocco with rates of over 20 per cent but better than Pakistan, Kenya or Sri Lanka. If one takes account of *per capita* income levels, the Indian comparative performance looks somewhat better, because although the income distribution is unequal in India, it is unlikely that it is

[24]Chelliah (1971). Chelliah's results areu pdated in Chelliah, Bass and Kelly (1975). Our basic conclusions remain unaltered however.

significantly more so than in Pakistan, Kenya or Brazil. The elasticity of total tax revenue for India for this period is 2.4, which is high by the standards of poor countries.

This overall view, however, hides a somewhat mixed performance. We know from the report of the Committee of Enquiry into Direct Taxation that there is very substantial evasion and non-payment of taxes, amounting in 1968-69 to no less than Rs 1,400 crores.[25] Whatever increased resources the Government has collected, it would have been able to gather in substantially more resources and thus reduce the degree of excess demand and the increase in money supply if it had paid more attention to widespread tax evasion. Moreover, the purpose of taxation is not solely to mobilize resources but also to achieve them in a more rather than less equitable manner.

It is with reference to this latter factor that the Indian tax effort gives serious cause for concern. Table 27 gives the change in the composition of tax revenue for 1953-55 and 1966-68. We can note that the share of direct taxes, the progressive element in the tax structure, has declined sharply while that of indirect taxes, especially various taxes on production such as excise duties, has risen. It is also known that a substantial part of the latter comes from a broad range of basic consumer goods and not from luxuries, which are consumed by the relatively rich, but which do not offer a wide enough base to provide a large volume of revenue. According to Chelliah, 58 per cent of the increase in total tax revenue came from these taxes, 18 per cent from income tax and 16 per cent from import and export duties.[26] If we take into account both the regressive nature of the Indian type of indirect taxes and the allocative effects of high levels of indirect taxes, the Indian tax effort leaves much to be desired. The conclusion is inescapable that caught between the strong vested interests of the relatively rich who can evade paying taxes and the Government's expenditure needs, it has turned increasingly to taxes on basic consumer goods and their components, thus adding most to the fiscal burdens of those least able to bear it.

This somewhat gloomy diagnosis of the Government's tax effort is reinforced by a look at certain aspects of the pattern of

[25]India, Ministry of Finance, Wanchoo Committee (1971), p. 6f.
[26]Chelliah (1971).

Government expenditure. I have pointed out in Chapter 3 that the largest increases in employment in the public sector have come, not in manufacturing but in the categories of administration.[27] Between 1964-65 and 1972-73, the proportion of plan expenditure to total Government expenditure, taking the central and state governments together, fell from about 43 to 32 per cent, while its level rose from Rs 2,031 crores to Rs 3,676 crores. Non-development expenditure rose at the same time from Rs 1,815 crores to Rs 4,844 crores. The level of defence expenditure doubled from around Rs 800 crores to Rs 1,600 crores, according to published official figures.[28] In terms of proportions, it rose from 8 to 17 per cent of government expenditure, dropping back to around 14 per cent in 1972-73.

TABLE 27
PERCENTAGE COMPOSITION OF TAX REVENUE—
1953-55 AND 1966-68

	1953-55		*1966-68*	
Total Direct Taxes		41.2		29.1
Taxes on Income	25.1		19.8	
Taxes on Property	16.0		9.3	
Total Indirect Taxes		58.8		70.7
Taxes on Trade	25.0		17.8	
Taxes on Production, Excise etc.	33.8		53.0	
Total Taxes		100.0		100.0

SOURCE: Chelliah (1971).

Lest too much significance is read into this later decline, it is worth pointing out that it indicates, almost certainly, the very heavy drafts made upon the Government to finance various kinds of relief expenditure in relation to famines and on the up keep of Bangla Desh refugees. While no one should detract from this entirely desirable shift in emphasis on humanitarian grounds, it does raise more serious questions of Government strategy that we shall have to return to. Suffice it to record here that the 'other

[27]See p. 44 above.
[28]India, Ministry of Finance, Survey (1967-68) p.A 28 and (1972-73), p. 72; see also Chakravarty (1971) on the significance of defence expenditure.

expenditure' category, which includes various relief items, rose to form 14 per cent of total expenditure in 1972-73, from the earlier level of 9 per cent before the 1965-67 drought.[29] As we shall see, the increase in Government borrowing, the change in the composition of Government expenditure and the limited increase in the surpluses of public sector enterprises are related aspects of the economic strategy, if that is indeed the right word, as it has evolved particularly since 1965.[30]

As I have stated above, the failure to mobilize the desired volume of surplus may have several effects on the economy.[31] These are the failure to achieve the desired rate of growth, a rise in the price level, a worsening balance of payments situation, and attempts to contain excess demand for resources through various forms of direct Governmental controls. I shall review very briefly the operations of the first three methods of coping with disequilibrium, leaving the last until we come to a discussion of Government policy in Chapters 9 and 10.

The fact that the rate of growth of the Indian economy has been below target for all periods other than the first plan period, is well known and needs no labouring. During the first plan, the economy achieved a rate of growth of net national product of 3.7 per cent in real terms, as opposed to a planned rate of 2.5 per cent. During the second plan, the corresponding rates were 3.5 and 5.0 per cent; during the third plan, 2.8 and 6.0 per cent. Not only did the economy fail to reach the target but it fell short by an increasing margin.[32] For more recent years, the actual rate of growth during 1969-73 has been around 2.5 per cent, against a planned rate of 5.5 per cent for 1969-74.[33] Indeed as performance consistently falls short of expectations, the planners show a sublime indifference to such mundane considerations as the reality of experience. For it is well known that targets maketh plans, in the rarefied world of planners

Figure 5 plots the net national product at current and constant 1960-61 prices, expressed as indexes with 1960-61 = 100. They are plotted on a semi-log scale and bring out in a dramatic fashion the

[29]India, Ministry of Finance, Survey (1967-68) and (1972-73).
[30]See pp. 248-9 below.
[31]See p. 79 above
[32]Chaudhuri (1971), p. 29f.
[33]India, Planning Commission (1969), p.30.

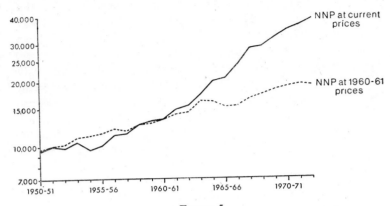

FIGURE 5

Net national product at current and 1960-61 prices, 1950-51 to
1972-73. (Rs crores: Semi-log scale)

behaviour of the overall level of prices in the Indian economy.
Until about 1962-63, the two series show roughly similar rates of
growth, indicating that the overall level of prices remained fairly
stable during this period. Thereafter, the two series diverge con-
tinuously, until in the early 1970s money incomes show rapid
increases in the face of an almost stagnant level of real output.
The fact that the Indian economy managed in the early years to
maintain relatively stable prices with a modest amount of growth
and that it has since been subject to continuous inflation with an
even poorer growth performance is a matter of the most profound
economic and social significance.

This overall picture is substantiated, if we look at the behaviour of some of the more specific price indexes. In doing so, we
have to consider two rather distinct phenomena. One is the
behaviour of the absolute level of prices and the other is the
changes in relative prices. In looking at the latter, I shall confine
myself to two questions which are the most important. One is to
what extent particular sections of the population have been affected by inflation. The other is the question of the relationship of
agricultural prices to the prices of manufactured goods.

Tables 28 and 29 give the indexes of wholesale prices for the
two periods 1952-53 to 1963-64 and 1961-62 to 1973-74, for all
commodities as well as the major commodity groups, e.g. food-

grains, manufactures and industrial raw materials. During the first years of our period, up to the early 1960s, the overall index rose by about 27 per cent or a little under 3 per cent per year. If we include the year 1963-64, when food prices especially rose rapidly, the picture changes a little. It does not change very dramatically and the rate of inflation still works out at a little over 3 per cent. Moreover, foodgrains prices, the price which is important for the majority of the population, especially those of the poor who are net purchasers of foodgrains, show a remarkable degree of stability, although it is true that in some years food prices have always risen steeply due to poor harvests. For people who exist on the penumbra of subsistence, the fact that food prices were stable contributed greatly to their welfare.

If we look at the 1960s and early 1970s, how very different the picture is. In a comparable ten-year period, the overall index rose by 88 per cent. Between 1971-72 and 1973-74 alone, it rose by 35 per cent. Moreover, over the whole period prices of agricultural products rose more rapidly than the overall index and the prices of foodgrains rose the most rapidly. Between 1961-62 and 1973-74 food prices trebled, having risen by 38 per cent in the latter two years. In contrast, the prices of finished manufactured goods have risen less, even though they too have doubled. Prices of industrial raw materials, which are heavily weighted by inputs of agricultural origins such as fibres, oilseeds and sugar cane, have naturally kept pace with the overall rise in agricultural prices.[34]

In addition, while in the early years the prices of agricultural and non-agricultural goods rose more or less in step, the relative price ratio has changed substantially in favour of agriculture during the later period.[35] This comes out most clearly if we compare the relative prices of industrial and agricultural goods between 1960-61 and the late 1960s. In this period, the agricultural 'terms of trade' moved in favour of agriculture by about

---

[34]The weights of the various components in the Index of Wholesale Prices (1961-62 = 100): agricultural commodities = 33.2; food articles = 41.3, of which foodgrains = 14.8; industrial raw materials = 12.1; intermediate manufactures = 5.7; finished manufactures = 23.7; machinery, etc. = 7.9.

[35]See p. 119 below for discussion of agricultural terms of trade; see also Thamarajakshi (1969).

TABLE 28

INDEX OF WHOLESALE PRICES—SELECTED YEARS
(Base 1952-53 = 100)

	All Commodities	Foodgrains	Manufactures	Industrial Raw Materials
1952-53	100.0	100.0	100.0	100.0
1955-56	99.2	86.1	102.9	110.6
1959-60	118.7	100.2	141.0	132.0
1962-63	127.4	102.2	129.5	135.3
1963-64	139.0	123.6	133.0	146.1

SOURCE: Reserve Bank of India, *Report on Currency and Finance* (annual).

TABLE 29

INDEX OF WHOLESALE PRICES—1961-62 TO 1973-74
(Base 1961-62 = 100)

Year	All Commodities	Agricultural Commodities	Foodgrains	Total Manufactures	Industrial Raw Materials
Weights	100.0	33.2	14.8	29.4	12.1
1961-62	100	100	100	100	100
1962-63	104	102	105	103	98
1963-64	110	108	115	105	100
1964-65	122	131	146	109	116
1965-66	132	142	154	118	133
1966-67	150	167	183	128	158
1967-68	167	188	228	131	156
1968-69	165	179	201	134	157
1969-70	172	195	208	144	180
1970-71	181	201	207	155	197
1971-72	188	200	215	167	191
1972-73	207	220	248	177	204
1973-74	254	281	296	206	299

SOURCE: Reserve Bank of India, *Report on Currency and Finance* (annual).

20 per cent.[36] It is true, however, that we can get quite different figures for changes in the terms of trade according to which years we chose for comparison, because agricultural prices especially

[36]India, Ministry of Finance, *Survey* (1973-74), p. 90.

are subject to strong short-run fluctuations. Therefore, we have to be careful in basing our arguments too casually on the behaviour of relative prices.[37]

On one aspect of price changes, there can be no reasonable doubt. While the population as a whole have suffered through inflation, the poor, defined in any reasonable terms, have suffered most. The figures are given in Table 30, which shows that the price index for one of the poorest sections of the economy, the agricultural labourers, has risen more than those for other working class groups. While prices for consumer goods paid by non-manual and manual workers have risen by around 60 per cent in seven or eight years, those paid by agricultural labourers have doubled. This point is also substantiated by prices of individual commodities, which show the largest rises in prices of basic consumer goods that have a large weight in the consumption of the poor.[38] This is a strange and sobering conclusion to come to about an economy whose main avowed concern is the alleviation of poverty.

TABLE 30

PRICE INDEX FOR VARIOUS CONSUMER GROUPS

Consumer Price Index for Agricultural Labourers		*Consumer Price Index for Urban Non-Manual Workers*		*Working Class Consumer Price Index*	
Year	*Index*	*Year*	*Index*	*Year*	*Index*
1960-61	100	1960	100	1961	100
1967-68	206	1967	157	1967	166

SOURCE: India, Department of Labour and Employment, *Pocketbook of Labour Statistics* (annual).

There are two useful studies of price behaviour in India, one by K.N. Raj for the period 1949-66 and a more recent one by Chakravarty and Maiti for 1952 up to the present.[39] They both

[37]However, the overall conclusion must stand that during the last few years prices of agricultural produce have tended to rise faster than non-agricultural prices.

[38]Bardhan (1970); this tendency has been noted by a number of other economists.

[39]Raj (1966), Chakravarty and Maiti (1974); see also the comments on Raj's article by Harris (1970).

look at the two questions, one of the changes in the general level of prices, the other of the relative prices of foodgrains to other prices. They both come to remarkably similar conclusions about the determinants of changes in price levels. In the earlier study, Raj finds that aggregate price behaviour can be fairly accurately 'forecast' for 1949-62 on the basis of the balance between aggregate demand and supply, assuming a constant marginal propensity to consume. Changes in money supply are not introduced as an explanatory variable, although Raj does find that Government consumption is a major component of aggregate demand in the economy. For relative prices, Raj uses a similar model, introducing a constant expenditure elasticity of demand for foodgrains to substitute for the constant marginal propensity to consume. The actual behaviour of the relative price can again be fairly accurately predicted on the basis of such a 'model'. For years of heavy foodgrains imports, Raj finds that such imports have tended to reduce food prices, a point to bear in mind when we come to discuss the effects of food aid on the economy. Interestingly, changes in prices can be explained without considering changes in the speculative hoardings of foodgrains.

In the more recent study, Chakravarty and Maiti explain the changes in the relative price of cireals to prices of manufactured goods in terms of the demand for food from the non-agricultural sector and the *per capita* availability of foodgrains. For the period 1952-70, their findings can be summarized as follows:

$$P_t = 206.20 + 0.3278Y_t - 9.5736Q_t - 12.0931Q_t - 1 + 0.4630P_t - 1 - 1.2189R_t - 1$$

t.s.   (7.78)   (7.78)   (—479)   (—5.77)   (3.57)   (—2.15)

               $R_2 = 0.9151$ $DW = 2.35$

where Y = *per capita* non-agricultural incomes
           P = relative price of cereals to manufactured goods prices
           Q = *per capita* availabilityof foodgrains
           R = procurement as percentage of cereal output.

They find that there is a strong and significant inverse relationship between *per capita* availability and relative prices, indicating that supply factors have been important in the determination of food prices. They also find that demand for foodgrains has a strong positive effect on prices. Here again, changes in stocks held by traders are not required as an explanatory variable to explain changes in food prices, a point worth stressing in view of the Government's insistence on this factor as against the more fundamental forces of supply and final demand. Speculation in foodgrains differs from other forms of speculation in an important respect, in the sense that there are no repurchases by speculators. Non-seasonal speculation in foodgrains can, therefore, only operate successfully if there is both an expectation of a secular rise in prices, as well as the fulfilment of that expectation. While this point is not conclusive evidence that speculation has no part to play, it does indicate that it acts probably more as an accelerator than a progenitor of inflation. Discussing in more general terms the behaviour of the aggregate price level during 1971-73, they find that the rising level of non-developmental government expenditure has been a major source of excess demand and that there has been a high rate of expansion in the money supply and in credit to account for the speeding up of the rate of inflation in these two years.[40]

An alternative manner in which an economy can come to terms with excess demand for resources is to allow its balance of payments to worsen, thus enabling it to increase the absorption of resources over available domestic supply.[41] We saw in the previous chapter that throughout our period the Indian balance of trade has been negative, although the size of the trade deficit has decreased since 1968. The balance on service account has also been negative, so that during the whole of this period India has maintained a net import surplus on current account.[42] This measures the net inflow of foreign resources into the economy during this period. This flow has been financed through a net capital inflow from abroad. The flow of private investment into India has been small and some would argue that it has indeed been negative.[43] In any case its relative magnitude is small, compared to the major source of foreign borrowing, official intergovernmental

[40]Chakravarty and Maiti (1974).

[41]The relationship is given by $B = A - Y$, where $B =$ the import surplus, $A =$ domestic absorption and $Y =$ domestic production; see Alexander (1952).

[42]India, Ministry of Finance, Survey (annual), statistical appendix.

[43]Chandra (1973).

capital transfers in the form of foreign aid.

Without doing much violence to reality, the role of foreign capital in resource mobilization can thus be discussed in the form of the role of foreign aid in Indian economic development. It is to this that I shall now turn. Although this topic has been a great source of controversy in India, the basic quantitative magnitudes of the phenomena are not easy to come by. I shall, therefore, spend a little time going over the question, although it may sometimes take us away from the narrower question of resource mobilization. In any case, foreign capital has come to play a highly important role in Indian development strategy, especially since 1957. It has, indeed, dominated the form that strategy has taken. The issue of foreign aid cannot be discussed as if it has played an entirely passive role in bridging a resource gap created by an otherwise inward looking strategy. Not only has the availability of aid played a strategic role in the economy, it can even be said to have created the resource gap which it has in turn bridged through external finance.[44]

The question of the role of foreign aid in economic development has various interrelated aspects. For the present I shall confine myself to the issues, broadly speaking, of the role of aid in the supply and mobilization of resources. Elsewhere I shall try to look at two further questions, the impact of aid on the development of industrial structure in India and its relationship to the economic strategy of the Government.[45] In the narrow context of resource mobilization, the issues can be grouped under two heads: how much aid has India received or what has been the magnitude of foreign resource inflow into the economy, and what has been its relationship to the savings and foreign exchange gaps engendered during the process of development.

Foreign aid adds to the net supply of resources available to the economy. The amount of real resources that are transferred depends not upon the nominal amount of aid that flows in but upon its equivalent in terms of net purchasing power over foreign resources. In order to derive the latter, a number of corrections have to be made to the nominal amounts of aid flows. The

---

[44]See, for example, Bagchi (1970), Chandra (1973) and Raj (1967).

[45]Part of the data on which the following section is based is contained in Chaudhuri (1974).

major corrections that have to be made are as follows. First, the
amount of resources transferred depends upon the volume of aid
utilized during any period rather than on the amount authorized,
which is more an index of intent on the part of donors and of
potential supply on the part of the recipient. Secondly, we have
to distinguish between net and gross aid. In so far as aid is in the
form of loans, these have to be repaid and the amount of foreign
exchange that is made additionally available to the economy at
any period depends upon the net amount. In this context, we
have to distinguish between grants and loans in the total flow.
Moreover, we have to look at the terms on which aid is given, for
how much aid is truly aid, that is to say resources made available
on concessional terms, depends upon the terms of aid, which can
be said to constitute the so-called 'grant element' in aid.[46]
Thirdly, it is now widely recognized that the practice of aid-tying
may considerably reduce the purchasing power of aid received.
We have to try to make some adjustment to the nominal figures
for the incremental costs of tied aid.[47] Fourthly, in so far as prices
of commodities that are purchased with aid in the donor countries
are subject to inflation, the same volume of foreign currency buys
less in real terms and we have to take account of the rate of
inflation in donor countries.

In what follows, I have tried to indicate in rough outline how
much difference is made to the nominal flow of aid to India on
account of each of these factors. At the beginning, however, a
very simple point has to be made which is sometimes ignored. A
great deal of Indian aid statistics is given in terms of its rupee
values. Owing to a substantial devaluation of the rupee in 1966-67,
the later figures would show a spurious increase in aid received
which is obviously not matched by any increase in the foreign
purchasing power of aid.[48] While I have given figures for the total
volume of aid received in terms of its dollar value, so as to give a

[46]On the definition and measurement of the 'grant-element', see
Chaudhuri (1974) and Ohlin (1966).
[47]For a theoretical discussion of the issue of aid-tying, see Bhagwati
(1967); for one of the earliest attempts to measure the cost of aid-tying, see
Haq (1967).
[48]The Indian rupee was devalued in June 1966, from a rate of Rs 4.8 to
Rs 7.5 to the US dollar. It is not clear how the problem of devaluation
has been dealt with by Chandra (1973), where the rupee figures are used.

more accurate picture, for the lack of sufficient detailed information I have had to rely on the rupee values for calculations of the
distribution of aid between loans and grants or between sectors,
as well as for its overall impact upon the economy. In what
follows, it will be pertinent to bear this point in mind.[49] Moreover, the bulk of the work on which the calculations are based
relates to the period up to 1969-70. I have given the overall
figures for aid received during the later years separately. As for
the rest, none of the basic conclusions is significantly altered by
the omission of the last three or four years.

Table 31 gives the total value of loans and grants utilized by
India during the whole of our period, together with the amounts
of interest and capital repayments. It will be seen that during
1951-73, India received very substantial amounts of foreign loans,
although in *per capita* terms she received very much smaller
amounts than many other poor countries. The gross amount of
aid received reached a peak during the period of the third plan;
the same is true of net aid. Although the total for gross aid received in rupee terms is higher for 1966-70, it is distorted by the
fact, which we have already mentioned, that the 1966-67 devaluation shows a spurious rise in the total volume of aid received.
Measured at pre-devaluation rates, the amounts of *loans* received
during 1966-70 works out at Rs 1,769.3 crores, as opposed to the
figure of Rs 2,808.4 crores shown in Table 31. The bulk of
the non-food aid received was received in the form of
loans, the proportion of grants being low and declining during
the whole of this period. In part, this reflects a conscious policy
decision by the Government not to relay on grants for political
reasons, although it is highly questionable that her reliance on
loans has to any extent reduced the 'leverage' of donors upon
Indian economic policy to any significant extent. Especially during
the second plan but well into the end of the 1960s, she also
received substantial amounts of food aid, mainly in the form of

---

[49]It is not unreasonable to assume that the composition of aid from
different donors and among different sectors is less influenced by the overall
devaluation of the rupee. This is an approximation even for the period
before the devaluation of the dollar in 1971, because the values of the
currencies of the major donor countries have changed their relative parities
from time to time and an 'aid dollar' is not always fully convertible.

PL 480 imports from the United States against rupee payments. After the Indo-Pakistani war of 1965, the bulk of this food aid had to be paid for in hard currencies and thus has ceased to have much attribute of aid attached to it.

TABLE 31

GROSS AND NET AID UTILIZED—1951-52 to 1972-73

(Rs crores)

	1951-52 to 1955-65	1956-57 to 1960-61	1961-62 to 1965-66	1966-67 to 1969-70	1970-71 to 1972-73
Non-Food Aid					
Loans	126.4	724.8	1,908.5	2,808.4	1,980.5
Grants	70.2	160.7	336.9	249.1	106.0
Food Aid	5.1	544.8	853.2	881.6	205.2
Total Gross Aid	201.7	1,430.3	3,170.6	3,939.1	2,291.7
Net of Debt Service	23.8	119.4	542.6	1,395.0	1,436.7
Total Net Aid	177.9	1,310.9	2,628.0	2,544.1	855.0

1 crore = 10 million

SOURCE: Chaudhuri (1974).

In net terms, after interest and amortization of loans, India has received very much less with the years, this decline having become most pronounced in recent years. This is largely due to the accumulation of past debt-servicing obligations, together with a decline in the flow of gross aid since the middle 1960s. For all practical purposes this decline in fresh commitments by donors is independent of any Indian policy decision consciously to do without aid, however much policy makers have decried in public the reliance on continued aid flows. The fact that we have noticed before that during this period India financed a larger proportion of a declining rate of investment through domestic savings is a reflection of this autonomous fall in foreign aid. To argue otherwise is to carry making of virtue out of necessity to a ridiculous limit.

A more accurate picture of the true volumes of nominal aid received is given by the dollar value of aid received during 1958-59 to 1971-72 in Table 32. It establishes quite clearly that the flow of net aid reached a peak as early as 1965-66 and has since been declining rapidly. Indeed, in 1971-72 India received considerably less net aid than she did during 1958-59. The persistence

TABLE 32

GROSS AND NET AID UTILIZED—1958-59 TO 1971-72

(US $ million)

	1958-59	1959-60	1960-61	1961-62	1962-63	1963-64	1964-65	1965-66	1966-67	1967-68	1968-69	1969-70	1970-71	1971-72
Gross and Less Debt Service	720	617	863	714	941	1,253	1,516	1,617	1,511	1,598	1,259	1,188	1,096	1,123
	37	60	122	191	182	213	258	315	365	444	500	550	600	626
Net Aid	683	557	741	523	759	1,040	1,258	1,302	1,146	1,154	759	638	496	497

SOURCE: Chaudhuri (1974).

of the idea that India has been receiving very large amounts of foreign resource transfer through aid during the whole period of economic turmoil she has passed through during the 1960s and has somehow been squandering it on acts of profligacy, casts more light on the psychopathology of the aid relationship than it does on an understanding of economic events in India.

The point that India has received considerably less net aid than is popularly supposed might be countered with the argument that the benefit of aid is not only to be measured in terms of the volume received but is also reflected in the concessional elements of aid as a form of subsidized capital flow. We can, therefore, ask the question, how favourable have been the terms of aid to India. We have already seen that most of the aid to India has taken the form of loans, not grants. The terms of loans vary enormously, both between donors and over periods of time. A standard measure of concessionality of aid that is commonly used is the so-called 'grant element'. Although there are conceptual problems in using this measure for some forms of normative analyses in a dynamic context, we can nevertheless use it as an index of concessionality.

India has received aid from the following major donors: Britain, West Germany, the United States, Russia, the World Bank and its associate, the International Development Agency. For 1966-67, the typical 'grnat element' fell within two broad ranges, around 20 to 28 per cent and from 50 to as high as 84 per cent for IDA loans alone. By 1971, the terms of aid had softened considerably; there has indeed been a fairly continuous softening of terms since the middle of the 1960s, and most major donors' terms yield grant elements of between 60 and 84 per cent, with the IDA again heading the list. Against this, however, some donors like Japan and France, who are important but not dominant, have given aid with 'grant elements' as low as 10 or 20 per cent even in the later year.[50] Thus, given that a 100 per cent 'grant element' makes a loan virtually a grant, anything from only one-quarter to four-fifths of gross aid in the form of loans can be regarded as truly concessional. While the data I have presented do not enable one to draw very firm conclusions, it will be fairly safe to infer that the low volume of aid to India has not been countered by over-generous terms on which such aid has been given. We have further to bear in mind that while most aid from major donors is tied, having costs that I indicate below, all repayment is in convertible currencies, which further reduces the net benefits obtained through aid transfers.[51]

It might be objected that we are leaving out of account a major component of total aid—food aid. Is not food in short supply, is it not a basic consumer good and has not the availability to the Indian consumers of cheap food been of considerable benefit? Especially as much of this has been obtained against payment in Indian rupees and not in hard currencies?

Much of this is true, but the matter is a little more complex than at first appears. The impact of food aid on the Indian economy is a matter of considerable importance and cannot be discussed here at any great length. However, the basic issues are as follows. First, the food obtained through aid has not been as cheap as at first appears, in terms of its foreign exchange cost. The price of foodgrains—for India this has been mainly wheat—is higher in the United States than its world price. At least, this is true for our period. As the United States has been the major source of this aid, the cost of purchase has been higher than it would have if, and it is a big if, India had free foreign exchange to buy in world markets. During this period, the world supply of foodgrains was easier than it has since become, with the overall supply diminishing rapidly in relation to demand. Moreover, the freight cost of imported food had to be paid for in foreign exchange, and because it had to be imported in American ships freight costs were much higher than charter rates. This, too, imposed an added foreign exchange cost on the economy.

Given that the shadow price of food in India can be taken to be higher than its market price, food aid even under these conditions must have conferred some added benefit. It has, however, been argued by some that PL 480 food imports did not add to the net availability of foodgrains in India during this period. They merely substituted imported food for domestic production and achieved this effect by depressing the relative prices of foodgrains,

---

[51]The aid received from the East European countries has been repayable in terms of rupees since 1959 and does not suffer from this particular disadvantage. See Chaudhuri (1975), Datar (1972) and Nayyar (1975).

thus discouraging domestic production.[52]

Although one cannot answer the question here, one can at least get the problem straight. Food aid could have helped India in two quite distinct ways. One question is that given harvests fail and cause a food shortage in certain years, does the availability of imported foodgrains help the economy? This it clearly does and has done in the case of India, especially if we do not lose sight of the fact that when food is in short supply, it is neither the rich nor the intellectuals who go without. The second question is somewhat different. If the supply of wage-goods is a 'constraint' as I shall argue later that it has been in India, does the supply of imported food ease this constraint by increasing total supply? The strategic impact of food aid on development rests upon the answer to this question and not upon the first one, whether it is good to keep the less rich alive by feeding them during poor harvests. The issue of the wage-goods constraint cannot, in turn, be solved by showing that imported food increased the total supply of food available in a particular period. For nobody has seriously argued that PL 480 imports reduced domestic supply by a greater amount, thus reducing the net supply of foodgrains. The argument that has been advanced is that the availability of imported food has helped to reduce the price of foodgrains relative to other agricultural commodities and has thus reduced the rate of growth of domestic supply by reducing incentives.

This problem still awaits a rigorous answer. However, it is difficult to avoid the conclusion that the price of wheat was kept relatively low by imported wheat and this discouraged the growth of production of wheat. And as wheat does not largely compete as a major food crop with either rice or millets in major producing areas for the latter, it is quite likely that the net availability of domestic food production was adversely affected. Thus, the effect on the wage-goods constraint of imported food was partially offset by its adverse effect on domestic production or rather its rate of growth. However, it is equally clear that such an effect was largely the result of Government food policy of keeping down prices

[52]On the effects of food aid on relative prices, see Mann, J. (1967) and Raj (1966), as well as Rath and Patvardhan (1967). For a critique of food aid policy, see Chandra (1973).

in urban areas rather than of foodgrains imports as such.[53]

We can now return to the question of the extent to which the practice of aid-tying has reduced the amount of foreign resources transferred through aid. For this purpose we have to distinguish between project and non-project aid. For project aid, there are no detailed studies available that relate to India, although Mahabub ul Haq, Eshag and others who have worked on other countries have found uniformly that tied project aid leads to considerable degrees of over-pricing of equipment and thus reduces the benefits accruing to the recipients.[54] For non-project aid, I have carried out some sample studies which are discussed in detail elsewhere. There is also a valuable study by Nirmal Chandra, based on the same sources of trade statistics.[55] Chandra finds that the costs of tied aid for non-project aid is of the order of 19 per cent, indicating that the actual amount of foreign resources transferred through such aid is about one-fifth less than its nominal amount. Our study, which is based on a wider sample, indicates that although the degree of over-pricing varies considerably, at a *conservative* estimate the *average* degree of over-pricing can be as high as 30 per cent. That is to say, only two-thirds of the nominal value accrues as foreign resources to the recipient country.

This leaves us with the last correction that has to be made to the nominal aid figures to derive its rough purchasing power equivalent. This is due to the fact that aid is spent on donor country imports and domestic inflation in donor countries reduces the real value of the foreign exchange transferred through aid. Fortunately, the 1960s were a period of relatively low rates of inflation in most donor countries. The overall increase in prices in these countries did not exceed 30 per cent between, say, 1958 and 1970. This gives an annual rate of inflation of a little less than 3 per cent. While this is very modest by current standards, it does indicate that over the years India, along with other net

[53]That the Government used food imports in this way has been argued by K. Bardhan (1966).

[54]On costs of aid-tying to recipient countries, see Eshag (1968) and Haq (1967).

[55]The references are to Chandra (1973) and Chaudhuri (1974); both studies use the import statistics contained in the *Monthly Statistics of the Foreign Trade of India*, published by the Directorate General of Commercial Intelligence and Statistics.

purchasers of manufactured goods and industrial raw materials from rich countries, suffered appreciably from inflation in donor countries.[56]

We have so far been considering the strictly arithmetical question of how much foreign resources India actually obtained through foreign aid during this period. We find that for the various reasons mentioned above, she obtained a very much smaller additional command over foreign resources than the nominal figure of gross aid indicates. Unfortunately, it is not easy and it would be very misleading to come up with a portmanteau figure of the correct amount, on the basis of the data that are available to us. I shall, therefore, leave that question to the reader's judgement and turn to the effects of this resource flow on the economy. First, however, we need to form some idea of the quantitative importance of foreign aid to the economy during this period. This is provided in Table 33.

Table 33 gives the data relating to non-food aid and the relative magnitudes should be taken as indicating orders of magnitude rather than precise measurements. As they relate to nominal amounts of aid, the figures might overstate the relative importance of aid to the economy. On the other hand, they exclude food aid and grants, which together are quite a significant proportion of total foreign aid. By and large the figures are roughly of the correct orders of magnitude. It can be seen quite easily that as a proportion of net national product, aid is extremely small.

TABLE 33
RELATIVE MAGNITUDES OF AID UTILIZED TO
SELECTED ECONOMIC INDICATORS

Total Aid Utilized as percentage of	1950-51 to 1955-56	1956-57 to 1960-61	1961-62 to 1965-66	1966-67 to 1969-70
1. Net National Product	0.4	1.4	2.3	2.7
2. Net Investment	5.9	13.0	17.2	23.6
3. Total Plan Outlay	10.0	19.1	23.5	33.1
4. Total Imports	5.4	18.2	32.4	40.6
5. Balance of Trade	33.4	48.5	84.1	132.6

SOURCE: Chaudhuri (1974).

[56]Chaudhuri (1974).

To conduct a discussion of Indian economic development largely in terms of aid relationships, as there is sometimes a tendency to do, is to let a very small tail wag the dog. However, aid is more important as a source of investible funds or the 'surplus', although even here the bulk of investment has been financed out of domestic resources.[57] It is, however, of considerable interest that the proportion of investment financed out of aid increased steadily until 1969-70, indicating a mounting failure of the economy to mobilize adequate domestic resorces. As we have seen earlier, the position has altered significantly in the last few years and aid has fallen both as a proportion of net national product and of investment. From Table 33 it is quite clear that the major importance of aid lies in its provision of budgetary resources to the Government and as a source of finance for imports. Aid has been quantitatively a more important source of foreign exchange than of total investible resources.

The controversy about aid and its relationship to Indian economic development has concentrated on two major issues, at least at the macro-economic level. It has been argued that aid has not added significantly to the supply of total savings within the economy, because it has tended to be substituted for domestic resources rather than to supplement them.[58] That is to say, aid is negatively correlated with domestic savings. It has also been argued that the mechanism through which this has worked is in part the budgetary mechanism. As foreign aid is channelled through the central government budget, it puts the Government in fund, so to speak, and enables it to avoid politically unattractive policies for mobilizing resources through higher taxation. In this sense, aid flows should be negatively correlated with a budget surplus. In what follows, I summarize the results of some attempts to test these relationships at an aggregative level.

The relationships to be tested were of the following forms:

$$(1) \quad \frac{St}{Yt} = a + b \left(\frac{At}{Yt} \right)$$

$$(2) \quad Bt = a + b \, (At)$$

[57] See Table 10 above, p. 54.
[58] See the references cited in n. 7 above.

In addition we have tested for an additional relationship,

(3) $It = a(Yt) + b(At)$

where

Y = Net national product
I = Investment
S = Domestic savings
A = Aid utilized
B = Budget deficit

For savings, the two relationships tested for gross and net aid give the following results:

(1a) $\dfrac{S}{Y} = 0.094 + 0.221 \left(\dfrac{A}{Y} \right)$ for gross aid

t.s. (4.33)   (0.36)
$R^2 = 0.016$ $DW = 1.17$

(1b) $\dfrac{S}{Y} = 0.082 + 0.736 \left(\dfrac{A}{Y} \right)$ for net aid

t.s.   (5.22)   (1.25)
$R^2 = 0.163$ $DW = 1.48$

Neither of the two results is significant at the 5 per cent level. The 'best' result is obtained with net aid but yields a relationship which is significant only at the 20 per cent level. The substitution of the net import surplus for net aid does yield a negative correlation between aid and the savings ratio but it is not significant and is weak. As far as we can judge, there is no evidence that aid has had much of an effect on the savings ratio, one way or another. Given that the bulk of the savings is from domestic sources and is influenced by a number of other factors, this is not altogether a surprising conclusion to come to.

Next we can look at the relationship between foreign aid and the budget deficit, bearing in mind that we should expect to find as a strong statement for the case that the flow of aid either increases the deficit or reduces the surplus. We find that

(2) $B = 269.870 - 0.234\ A$ for gross aid
t.s. (0.31)   (−2.13)
$R^2 = 0.363$ $DW = 1.68$

The observed relationship is significant at the 10 per cent level, indicating that aid might have had some effect in *reducing* the budget deficit. However, the relationship is not a strong one, having an R^2 of 0.36 only. Moreover, the Durbin-Watson statistic indicates that the null hypothesis cannot be rejected in this case. The position is not significantly altered by substituting net aid for gross aid or the inclusion or non-inclusion of food aid.

We now turn to the effect of aid on the level of investment. We give the 'best' results below, which are obtained by using figures for gross aid, with or without food aid. The substitution of net aid for gross gives equally high values for R^2 and results that are significant at the 5 per cent level. In these cases, however, the DW statistics are above the limit and the null hypothesis cannot be rejected.

$$(3a) \quad I=9012.877 + 0.028Y + 1.482\,A \qquad \text{for gross aid}$$

$$t.s. \quad (3.70) \qquad (1.38) \qquad (3.11)$$

$$R^2=0.914 \qquad DW=1.36$$

The constant and aid terms are both significant at the 5 per cent level, and the DW statistic is within the limits, so that the null hypothesis can be rejected.

$$(3b) \quad I=11449.908 - 0.007Y + 3.149\,A \qquad \text{for gross aid}$$
$$\text{minus food aid}$$

$$t.s. \quad (4.22) \qquad (-0.22) \qquad (3.08)$$

$$R^2=0.937 \qquad DW=1.47$$

The constant and the aid terms are both significant at the 5 per cent level; the Y-coefficient is not significant and the DW statistic is within the limits, so that the null hypothesis can be rejected.

At this highly aggregated level, therefore, we can say that we find no evidence that aid has either reduced the savings ratio or has enabled the Government to run a higher budget deficit or a smaller surplus. The evidence is entirely inconclusive. We do find fairly strong evidence, however, that aid has had a fairly strong positive effect on the level of investment within the economy. A greater volume of aid has a fairly strong effect on the level of investment, the coefficient roughly doubling in value if the food aid component, which goes directly into consumption, is left out, giving us an aid 'multiplier' of around 1.5 to 3. This is not inconsistent with figures for import contents of investment projects, as far as can be judged from a casual study of various project reports.

As a working hypothesis, and no more, I would like to suggest that these preliminary results give a fairly accurate picture of the role that foreign aid has played in the economy. Aid has not been large enough to have had a considerable impact on the level of 'surplus' generated by the economy. Equally, while it has been a major source of budgetary funds, it has not been by any means the most important. This is borne out by the data in Tables 23 and 24. Aid has, however, been a major source of imports and has added substantially to the size of the import surplus that the economy has been able to finance. Partly through project-tying and partly through the operations of the licensing machinery, a large proportion of aid-financed imports has been channelled to investment projects. By financing the import content of such projects, aid has enabled the economy to maintain a higher level of investment. Aid, in India, has largely financed the foreign exchange gap rather than the savings gap. This conclusion is reinforced if we bear in mind that the investment series largely measures investment in the public sector and the large-scale private manufacturing sector, where the import content of investment is typically high. I must, however, enter two words of caution at this stage. First, to say that aid has financed investment is to say nothing about the composition of that investment. Secondly, we cannot also draw the conclusion that a lesser availability of aid would necessarily have reduced the level of investment. For to say that would be to argue that no alternative strategic options were open to the Government even in the context of a fairly medium-term situation, which is not a view that I share.

After this somewhat lengthy digression on aid, it might be helpful to summarize the basic conclusions of this chapter. The Government's efforts to mobilize resources for development from within the economy have been inadequate to the development requirements of the economy. The problem of inadequate resource mobilization has been reinforced by the changes in the composition of Government expenditure and in the methods chosen by the Government to finance its expenditure. Owing to these developments, a net draft of resources from the private sector has not by itself helped the Government to bridge the resource gap, particularly as the overall savings rate of the economy has not been much higher than 9 per cent. The shortfall in resources has been balanced partly by lowering the growth rate and the rate of investment in the economy. An excess demand for resources has spent itself partly in a high and growing rate of inflation. It has been bridged partly by allowing the economy to run a balance of payments deficit. This deficit has been financed largely by the flow of foreign aid, although the actual amounts received have been much smaller than the nomimal amounts, owing to a variety of reasons. Foreign aid does not appear to have had a significant effect on domestic savings or on public savings or dissavings. It appears, however, to have enabled the economy to maintain a higher level of investment than it would have otherwise achieved by financing the import content of such investment.

However, the approach to the study of the economic impact of aid in terms of aggregate national income categories, such as savings or investment or import capacity, is somewhat unsatisfactory. If the immediate object of aid is to either increase the total volume of resources or make available some particularly scarce resource that has no adequate domestic substitute, e.g. imported inputs, the question should also be asked, who would benefit from the additional output that such aid would have made possible?

There are two fundamental questions that are easy to pose, if rather more difficult to answer. The first is that, in so far as aid transfers purchasing power over resources, to whom does the additional purchasing power accrue? What proportion of it is passed on to the relatively poorer sections of the population in the form of additional employment or real wages? Secondly, what form is taken by the additional output that is generated, taking account of indirect effects of aid upon the economy? Does it take the form of additional capital goods that lead to an increase in future output capacity? Does it add to immediate consumption in the form of additional outputs of wage-goods, through an increase in the supply of the necessary inputs, such as irrigation water or fertilizers? Or does it add to the output capacity for producing luxury or semi-luxury items that are largely consumed by a narrow section of the relatively rich people? An answer to such questions is complicated by the fact that the final net effects of aid can be different from its immediate direct effects. It does appear from the evidence that not a very large part of aid went directly into the production of luxury consumer goods. However, neither did a very large proportion go towards increasing the capacity of the economy to produce more wage-goods.

CHAPTER FIVE

Problems of Change in Agriculture

A great deal of work has been done over the last two decades on the problems of Indian agriculture, far more than can be adequately summarized in a short space. Broadly speaking, the literature covers two distinct yet related areas. Part of it deals with the nature of the agricultural economy. It covers such questions as rationality of peasant behaviour, incentives implications of alternative patterns of tenure, the existence of 'surplus' labour in agriculture, relationship of size of holdings to labour use and productivity and responsiveness of production and marketed surpluses to changes in price. I shall not go into the discussion of these problems directly, confining myself instead to the second set of issues.[1] These relate to the performance and prospects of Indian agriculture and the policy implications that are raised by alternative interpretations of such phenomena. Naturally, where the two areas impinge on each other, structural characteristics will have to be brought into the discussion.

Here, more than in any other area of dispute, it is important to emphasize the limitation of our sources of information on which any analysis is based. There are two major limitations that will suffice to start with. First, much of our information about

[1]For a discussion of some of these characteristics, see Bhagwati and Chakravarty (1969); see also the following readings: Chaudhuri (1972), Khusro (1968-73), Indian Society of Agricultural Economics (1966) and (1972); on surplus labour, see Mehra (1966); Rudra (1973); on the size-productivity debate, see Bardhan (1974), Khusro (1964), Mazumdar (1963), Rao (1966) and Sen (1962); on price-response see Bardhan and Bardhan (1971), Dharm Narain (1965), Krishnan (1965), Raj Krishna (1963); on institutional factors, see Bhaduri (1973).

important relationships in the agricultural sector is 'dated' and relates to surveys that were carried out some time ago. Thus, the data collected from farm management surveys go back mostly to the early 1950s.[2] The NSS data of distribution of landholdings do not extend beyond the early or the middle 1960s.[3] As much of the debate is about structural change within the agricultural sector, its results are bound to be inconclusive unless data are available relating to a terminal year that can be used for comparison. Secondly, in almost all major areas of dispute, different researchers have come up with different sets of findings. That this is so will become clear later on in this chapter. This particular problem which arises partly from differences in assumptions or methods of analysis followed by different people, is common to all applied work. More important, however, it reflects the vast heterogeneity of the agricultural sector itself. There is now a great deal of evidence that the response of agriculture to a similar set of stimuli varies considerably between different regions and for different crops; also, the technical conditions that govern the production of different crops show considerable variations. This makes it difficult to generalize the results obtained from some specific piece of work on to an all-India level.

To these two problems, one must add another that is of particular relevance to any discussion of the 'green revolution'. Throughout this period population was increasing at a rate of over 2 per cent per annum, constantly pressing on the margin of cultivation of traditional agriculture. In any evaluation of the effects of the 'green revolution', we have to bear in mind that we are comparing an actual historical phenomenon to a hypothetical state, to what the response of traditional agriculture would have been to the growing pressure of population on land.[4]

The basic features of agricultural growth have been described in Chapter 3.[5] It was noted there that growth has been both limited and uneven over crops, space and time. In relation to the

[2]Bharadwaj (1974).

[3]The latest available NSS results relate to the 17th round and are for 1961-62.

The term traditional agriculture is used in this chapter to mean pre-'green revolution' practices. The use of the latter term, however, does not imply an acceptance of the reality of the revolution.

[5]See pp. 56-65 above.

rate of growth of population, production of wage-goods such as foodgrains has been inadequate, leading over the whole period to a small decline in *per capita* availability from a barely adequate level.[6] Moreover, the rate of growth of production showed some decline after the middle of the 1960s for a number of major crops, with the major exception of wheat. On the credit side, while a large part of the increase in production had come in the first half of our period from expansion of acreage, the latter half has seen substantial increases in productivity per acre. It is worth remembering also that some commodities which figure as important in the budgets of the poor, such as the so-called 'inferior' grains and pulses, have shown both a relatively low rate of growth and sharper fluctuations. Some of these characteristics are summarized for our reference in Table 34 below.

TABLE 34
AGRICULTURAL PRODUCTION, AREA, YIELD

Year	Area	Production	Yield/Hectare
A. (1949-50 = 100)			
1950-51	99.9	95.6	95.7
1960-61	120.8	142.2	117.7
B. (Average 1959-60/1961-62 = 100)			
1960-61	100.0	100.0	100.0
1970-71	106.7	126.8	120.5

Figures for Area and Production in part B are three-year moving averages.
SOURCE: A. India, Ministry of Finance, Pocketbook (1970), p. 46.
         B. India, Ministry of Finance, Survey (1973-74), p. 59.

Three major debates have taken place against the backdrop of this pattern of agricultural growth, each concerned with attempts to explain the relatively poor performance of the agricultural sector. The first of these originated in the so-called 'urban bias' controversy, attributing the low rate of growth of agricultural output to the low priority accorded to the agricultural sector by the planners, in the allocation of resources.[7] The second concerns

[6]See Table 38, p. 187 below.
[7]Lipton (1968); see also p. 113 f. below.

the question whether the major constraint on agricultural development was a technological constraint rather than a resource constraint and to what extent such a constraint has now been severed through a process of technological change. This is the debate that ranges round the economic and social effects of the 'green revolution'.[8] The third plays down both the resource and the technological constraints to some extent and emphasizes the institutional characteristics of the agrarian economy and the need for institutional reform.[9]

I shall attempt to deal with each of these controversies in turn; in the course of what must inevitably be a sketchy treatment of very involved and wide-ranging discussions, I shall have to concentrate on what seem to me to be the main issues, ignoring some of the finer points of the debate. It must be said at the outset that the classification I have adopted relates to the problems and not to the contribution made by individual economists. Obviously, economists who have been debating the effects of the 'green revolution' have had important things to say about tenurial reform, just as much of the discussion on institutional change has arisen in the context of the allocative and institutional implications of such reform. Moreover, circumstances affecting agriculture and Government policy towards agriculture have not remained unchanged throughout our period. Views held by individuals, quite properly, have changed, explanations and analysis that made sense at one time might have been overtaken by events; equally, heterodox opinions have become commonplace. In the discussion that follows, I shall be less concerned with the question of who was right than with the problems that have been associated with agricultural change in India.

Intersectoral Allocation of Resources

I shall start with the question whether the relatively low rate of growth of agricultural production in India can be attributed to the agricultural sector's receiving too low a share of investible resources. Put simply, given the technological possibilities of traditional, pre-'green revolution' agriculture, did agriculture

[8]For references to the literature, see n. 30 below.
[9]Joshi (1971), Warriner (1969).

fail to produce output in adequate measure because it was denied an adequate supply of the necessary inputs? In discussing this question, I shall use the term 'investible resources' somewhat loosely, to embrace not only capital inputs that are directly supplied to agriculture but also fertilizers or skilled manpower, which would require investment elsewhere for their production. In a mixed economy, the physical availability of inputs do not automatically lead to their utilization. The latter depends on the relative profitability of alternative forms of activity. I shall, therefore, also have to consider the problems of incentives and disincentives in Indian agriculture.

I have argued throughout this book that a good deal of Indian economic performance is to be explained in terms of the inability of the Government to maintain an adequate rate of investment *and* an adequate rate of increase in wage-goods production. It is obvious that I would regard the agricultural sector, which produces the bulk of these commodities, as a major contender for investible funds. However, the view I have adopted is that prior to the discovery of the high-yielding varieties, more investment in agriculture would not necessarily have produced more output.

As this view will be controversial, it would be best to set out fairly clearly what precisely is implied in my holding this position. First, agricultural production in India is organized in a particular manner. This organization is characterized by extreme inequality in the distribution of landholdings, which in turn is correlated with the ownership of other productive assets, although not in some simple relationship of proportionality. This creates an environment in which a small number of large, rich farmers occupy a particularly strong bargaining position in that society. They have the power to appropriate to themselves any scarce resources that are made available. I shall accept for the moment, that in talking about the supply of resources to agriculture, I am not considering simultaneously the possibility of the Government working to introduce significant changes in these production relationships. As I have indicated elsewhere, there is ample evidence that this is a perfectly reasonable view to hold.[10] This being so, we have to accept for the sake of the argument that

[10]For a discussion on land reform, see below p. 142f.

additional resources will not have been distributed in an unbiased fashion between all farming households.

Secondly, I am assuming that any additional resources that were made available would have had to be utilized within the limits set by available technology and would not themselves have led to a significant technological breakthrough. It might be objected that this way of posing the problem is too restrictive, in that it precludes a major channel through which investment can lead to an increase in output. It has to be pointed out, however, that the time-scale over which investment in research and development will yield more output is quite different from that which obtains when more resources are invested in production of more inputs for a known technology.

Some economists have argued that the reason why agricultural output did not expand more rapidly during, say 1950-64, is that planners allocated *too low a share* of total resources to agriculture. During this period, the percentage of resources allocated to agriculture varied between 12 and 15 per cent or 18 and 37 per cent, according to whether irrigation is included in the allocation or left out. This was certainly lower than the share allocated to industry. It is argued that the marginal capital/output ration being lower in agriculture, as is shown by such data as exist, agriculture's share should have been higher relative to industry's.[11] How much higher, however, would depend on subtler comparisons of the second derivatives. While this is a serious argument that one should consider, it does leave some questions unanswered. Whatever its relative share, between the second and the third plan period the absolute share of agriculture at current prices increased by some 65 per cent.[12] Given that the marginal capital/output ratio was relatively low, one would have expected a much higher increase in agricultural output than in fact obtained, even allowing for the rise in prices.[13]

The reason why even such resources as were made available failed to make a pronounced impact lies in the way the money was spent, as much as in the amount that was made available.

[11]On marginal capital/output ratio in agriculture see Lipton (1969); India, Planning Commission (1952), p. 19.

[12]India, Planning Commission (1961), p. 59.

[13]In the same period, agricultural output increased by 20 per cent, approximately.

Economic policy makers failed, first, to identify what were the critical constraints on the growth of agricultural output. This was also related in part to the unwillingness of the Government to interfere with the fundamental production relations in agriculture. For example, it had been known for a long time that the availability of water through assured systems of irrigation was important for any sustained increase in agricultural production.[14] It is not that investment was not made in the provision of irrigation. In fact, very substantial amounts were spent, but on large-scale, multipurpose major irrigation schemes, which were costly and the benefits from which were bound to be more localized than those from cheaper minor irrigation projects, spread out more widely over the countryside. Moreover, the fact the benefits from major irrigation could only accrue to those farmers who could dig the feeder channels, and then in proportion to their landholdings, tended to concentrate the additional benefits from such irrigation projects on the larger farmers. The reason why in many areas such feeder channels were not dug must be at least in part that the rates of return from such investment were deemed by the larger farmers to be not sufficiently high.

At the risk of some simplification, it would be true to say that for a long time the Government held to the view that the main constraints on the growth of agricultural output lay neither in the lack of a more productive technology nor in a scarcity of traditional inputs. It lay, rather, in the lack of diffusion of knowledge of existing technology and practices. Hence the stress on community development and on extension network, those ill-conceived instruments of social change.[15] It is not very likely that more resources devoted to such tinkerings with the agrarian economy would have borne more fruit. Obviously, more minor irrigation, more fertilizers and more of other inputs would have done so. But that would have required something more than an increase in in the supply of additional resources. It would have required a very fundamental change in the Government's overall strategy towards agricultural development, away from general solutions and towards a keener perception of the nature of the technologi-

[14]See, for example, H. Mann (1967).
[15]For a summary discussion of the effectiveness of these programmes see Brown (1971).

cal and structural constraints facing the agrarian economy.

Any discussion of availability or non-availability of resources must be related to the question of incentives and disincentives facing Indian agriculture during this period. Lack of suitable incentives might lead to non-utilization of even existing resources. Before I attempt to deal with this question, we must branch off a little to review a controversy which besaddles both the resource allocation and the incentives questions. This is the issue of the relative overtaxation or undertaxation of agriculture as opposed to industry.

The amount of resources that are available to a sector for its own use has to be measured net of any taxes that are paid by the sector, while any subsidies that are received have to be added on. The question of the share of agriculture in total resources has, therefore, to take into account the relative tax burden imposed on Indian agriculture.

The pioneer work in this field was done by Ashok Mitra but in a different context.[16] He was concerned to show that from the point of view of resource mobilization, the agricultural sector was being undertaxed. He showed that the share of agriculture in tax revenue was lower than its share in national output. He argued that while average agricultural incomes were lower than non-agricultural incomes, indicating a lower taxable capacity, there was yet considerable inequality within the agricultural sector, indicating a potential taxable capacity that was not being utilized by the Government.

This approach has been further refined and elaborated by Ved Gandhi, Lipton and Shetty.[17] In the process, the emphasis has shifted a little from the question of mobilization of resources to that of intersectoral fiscal equity. While Gandhi has developed the thesis that agriculture has been relatively undertaxed, Lipton and Shetty have argued the opposite, basing their conclusions on a number of criticisms of Gandhi's methodology. All three studies are based on such considerations as the differences in average *per capita* incomes in the two sectors, agriculture and non-agriculture or rural and urban; price differentials; differences in the degree of inequality in intersectoral incomes as measured

---

[16]Mitra (1963).
[17]Gandhi (1966); Lipton (1969); Shetty (1971).

by the Lorenz coefficients, and allowances to be made for the principle of progressivity in tax rates. The major taxes raised by the Government are then allocated on certain principles to the two sectors, taking into account such factors as the absence of an income tax on agricultural incomes or the commodity bases of indirect taxes, etc. The relative tax burdens are then compared to the measures of relative taxable capacity previously calculated.

The calculation of net burden is complicated by the fact that both the agricultural and the non-agricultural sectors receive a number of subsidies, on such things as power, imported inputs and machinery. We must also add to it the fact that the allocation of social overhead capital is very much biased in favour of the non-agricultural sector, owing to the urban concentration of schools, hospitals and other amenities. As mentioned earlier, Gandhi, and Lipton and Shetty, come to opposing conclusions, while Shetty finds some evidence that the 'rural-urban' gap in tax burdens was moving against the non-farm sector, i.e. the non-farm sector was being less undertaxed towards the late 1960s.[18] To give an example, Shetty found that during 1951-56, while the relative taxable capacity of the non-farm sector was roughly five times as high as that of the farm sector, its relative tax burden was slightly less than four times as high. If, however, we had tried to take account of the principle of progressivity in the calculation of taxable capacity, we would have reached a higher figure. Hence, we would have obtained a higher measure of undertaxation of the non-farm sector. By 1966-68, while relative taxable capacity was twice as high for the non-farm sector, its relative tax burden was four times as high. Taking account of progressivity will in that period merely have equalized the two ratios.[19] None of this, however contradicts the fact that there is a considerable amount of tax potential, both in terms of income and wealth, in the rural sector that is exempted to no good purpose from tax liabilities. This view has been cogently argued by the Committee on the Taxation of Agricultural Wealth and Income.[20] Needless to say, there is also a high degree of evasion

[18]Shetty (1971).
[19]*Ibid.*
[20]India, Ministry of Finance, Ras (1972).

and non-payment of taxes in the urban sector as well.[21]

While it might remain a matter of controversy whether welfare is reduced to a greater or lesser extent in the rural or the urban sector through the operation of fiscal policy, it is clear that most rural taxes fall on consumption rather than production, while a number of productive inputs are subsidized below the market clearing price. While I agree that indirect taxation of a number of essential consumer goods must reduce the welfare of the rural population, it is rather difficult to believe that such taxes will discourage production via some general disincentive effects. The question then arises whether, taxation apart, there has been a disincentive effect on agricultural production through any worsening of that sector's terms of trade.

Any argument about intersectoral or intercountry terms of trade tends to be somewhat inconclusive, because it is not possible to settle unequivocally what constitute ideal terms of trade.[22] Moreover, the extent to which and the direction in which terms of trade are seen to change, often vary substantially according to the reference period chosen. Thus, Dantwala has argued that overall terms of trade have moved in favour of agriculture.[23] A careful study of Thamarajakshi for the period 1951-66 shows that there was a small movement in favour of agriculture.[24] Since then, agricultural prices have risen much more rapidly than non-agricultural prices, as we noted earlier.[25] It is, therefore, difficult to hold the view that the movement of relative prices has been such as to discourage the expansion of agricultural output.[26]

[21]See p. 86 above
[22]See Bhagwati and Chakravarty (1969) on terms of trade.
[23]Dantwala (1952).
[24]Thamarajakshi (1969).
[25]See p. 90 above.
[26]It has been argued, for example in Lewis (1968), that the real deterioration in agricultural terms of trade is to be measured in terms of the difference between the prices paid and received by agricultural producers, as opposed to the prices they would pay or receive if allowed to trade at world prices. This argument applies more strongly to those countries where a large proportion of agricultural output is exported or where agriculture is a large buyer of imported inputs. Both these assumptions would hold more strongly for pre-split Pakistan than for India. Moreover such an argument takes rather a micro-economic view of the problem. Given that tariffs and quotas are one means of restoring equilibrium in the

The 'Green Revolution'

I have put forward the view earlier that before the middle of the 1960s traditional agriculture was operating near to a technological frontier and any substantial increase in agricultural output required a technological breakthrough of some kind. This statement has to be interpreted cautiously. Contrary to what might be thought, the realization that yields in Indian agriculture could be increased substantially through better irrigation or choice of seeds or application of fertilizer is not new.[27] However, that realization had not sunk into the policy makers' minds sufficiently to influence the formulation of strategy. This distinction is somewhat similar to the Schumperterian distinction between invention and innovation.[28] Moreover, there is now quite a bit of evidence to show that yields per acre in small holdings under traditional practices were higher than in larger holdings. Therefore, it is possible that if land reform had been more effectively pursued, there might have been an increase in food production and also possibly in total agricultural production.[29] It does not follow, however, that there would have been an increase in the rate of growth of output without technical change.

The question that we have to consider is whether the particular package of new agricultural practices that embodies the so-called 'green revolution' constitutes such a technological breakthrough for Indian agriculture; whether the new agricultural practices have opened up a new technological frontier, thus easing the technological constraint operating upon the economy. In order to deal with this question, we have to consider the nature of that technology, its impact on such variables as output, employment and distribution and the conditions that would determine its continuous spread and adaptation to changing conditions. What has the 'green revolution' achieved and what are its prospects?[30]

---

economy, it is not obvious that alternative policies to those already in operation will always leave agriculturists better off.

[27]For an early discussion, see Mann, H. (1967).

[28]An 'invention' is the acquisition of pure technical knowledge of a new combination of factors of production; an 'innovation' occurs when that knowledge is embodied by entrepreneurs into the actual allocation of resources.

[29]This may have come about in two ways, the higher productivity per acre of small farms and a better system of incentives.

[30]There is a vast body of literature on the subject, too numerous to be

The distinguishing characteristic of the new technology lies in the substitution of traditional robust but low-yielding varieties of seed by the so-called high-yielding variety. These seeds have the physiological attribute of being able to turn large amounts of soil nutrients into grain rather than leaf growth. This enables the plant to produce higher yields, especially so if the supply of nutrients in the soil can be increased. This in turn creates the demand for chemical fertilizers to supplement the natural fertility of the soil. The need is initially largely for nitrogenous fertilizers but also after a time for potassic and phosphatic fertilizers. Because these contain nutrients in concentrated form they have to be applied with adequate supplies of water to enable the plant to absorb them without damage to itself. A lack of adequate water supply not only reduces the yield but may do so substantially.

This seed-fertilizer-water package in turn calls for better agricultural practices for the effective utilization of the technology. First, the plant requires the fertilizer-water input at particular stages of growth to give the best yields. Secondly, as fertilizers can be absorbed by weeds as well as by the plant, effective weeding is required to prevent waste of expensive fertilizer. Thirdly, while the HYV seeds give higher yields, they are more prone to damage from excessive watering. For example, shorter-stemmed dwarf varieties are more liable to be flooded. They thus require more effective water control and better drainage. The need is for controlled and adequate water supplies. Fourthly, being relatively new and non-acclimatized strains, they are more prone to local pests and diseases than established indigenous varieties and therefore require a supply of germicides and pesticides.[31]

Two further physiological characteristics of the new seeds are that they are quicker maturing than the traditional varieties and they are non-photosensitive.[32] On the one hand, these two charac-

---

quoted in a footnote. For a very useful bibliography, see Byres (1972). The most fruitful single source is the Review of Agriculture, published quarterly in March, June, September and December, in the *Economic and Political Weekly*. See also the notes to the rest of this chapter. For an introduction to the subject, the best references are Byres (1972), Frankel (1971), Griffin (1974) and Rao (1974).

[41]For a description of the new technology, see Ladejinsky (1973).

[32]That is to say, their period of maturity is independent of the length of exposure to the sunlight.

teristics give rise to a shorter harvesting period, thus making it possible for farmers to practise multiple cropping, enabling them to use more intensively a given amount of land. Fertilizers, by enabling more production per acre to be achieved, and the quicker maturing HYV seeds, by making it possible to use each acre, so to speak, oftener during the year, both act as land-saving innovations.[33] Hence their attraction to a land-hungry south Asia. On the other hand, as the crop may be ready for harvesting during the monsoon season at a time when the cloud-cover has not yet dispersed, a possibility of loss of output due to a lack of drying and storage facilities is also opened up.

Thus, the basic *technological* characteristic of the new technology is the application of a number of inputs which are complementary to each other. The application of these joint inputs yields much larger volumes of output of foodgrains as a result, largely by increasing yield per acre.[34] However, in order to assess the impact of the technology on Indian agriculture, we have to take account also of some of the economic characteristics of that technology. In an economy where labour is relatively plentiful, it has low opportunity cost. Most agricultural holdings in India use either family labour or fairly low-paid agricultural labour, neither of which, generally speaking, can command high levels of alternative earnings.[35] For traditional agriculture, the most expensive input, other than land, is bullock-power. The new inputs are mostly of manufactured origin, such as fertilizers, pesticides or pumps, and are more expensive. In non-rain-fed agriculture, there are also costs attached to irrigation, in the form either of the capital costs of sinking a well or installing a pump or running costs in the form of purchase of diesel fuel or payment of water rates.

The new practices, therefore, are much more expensive to the farmer. This has three implications. First, the extent to which the various inputs are applied in practice depends not on some technologically efficient dosage but on an economically optimum one. This depends in turn on the relative prices of inputs and outputs facing the producer. Minhas and Srinivasan have shown that

[33]Sen (1960), on land-saving technology.

[34]Part of the increase in output may be due to changes in crop-mix, etc.

[35]On labour use in traditional agriculture, see Sen (1962), Mazumdar (1963).

fertilizer application is subject to diminishing returns, the econo-mically optimum dose being smaller than the technical optimum.[36] A later study by Parikh and Srinivasan also shows that fertilizer application is subject to diminishing returns.[37] As technologi-cally some of the inputs are complementary, the extent to which the application of a particular input can be profitably pushed depends also on the availability of, and the ability to purchase, other inputs. For example, the degree of fertilizer application that is profitable will depend on the availability of water and on the ability of a farmer to purchase the use of *both* inputs.[38]

Secondly, the new technology is only worthwhile in terms of private benefits, e.g. if the farmer receives yields which are not only larger than traditional varieties but are substantially so, to make up for the additional variable costs of cultivation. This in turn requires, thirdly, a more intensive use of the fixed factor, e.g. land. The new technology opens up the possibility of multiple cropping; the economic imperative drives the farmer to it. This is compounded by the fact that while the new technology yields larger outputs, it is also more subject to risks. We have noted that the HYV seeds are prone to damage from flooding, water scarcity and pests. Moreover, because the farmer is a newcomer to these practices, he is also ignorant of how to respond if something goes wrong. Additionally, where he is involved in substantial cash out-lays in order to utilize the new technology, he bears a liquidity risk. This is reinforced by the fact that very often the farmer may have to resort to borrowing in order to meet the additional costs of cultivation. A crop failure saddles him with the burden of debt.

These economic aspects of the new technology are as important as its technological characteristics to our understanding of the impact of the 'green revolution' upon the agrarian economy, espe-cially in relation to the problems of mechanization and of unequal incidence of acceptance and use between large and small farmers. That impact can best be studied in terms of the effects of the new technology on output, employment and the regional and inter-personal distributions of gain arising from the adoption of that technology.

---

[36]Minhas and Srinivasan (1968).
[37]Parikh and Srinivasan (1974).
[38]Parikh (1969).

Starting with output, there are two questions to be answered. Broadly speaking, the introduction of the new technology into India can be dated from the middle 1960s. Therefore, we have to ask, was there a substantial increase in agricultural output after the mid 1960s? Is there any positive evidence to show that that increase is attributable to the adoption of a superior technology? Initially, very high claims were made for the output effects of this technology, based on figures of yield obtained under trial conditions on experimental plots, and there is no denying the fact that agricultural output in India has expanded very much more substantially in the 20 years after 1950 than in the previous decades.[39]

However, the observed figures for output in the post-'green revolution' period do not bear out a conclusion that agricultural output has expanded at a significantly faster rate after the middle 1960s. Griffin has shown that in most parts of the world there has been no significant difference in the rate of growth of agricultural output or of food production, before or after the onset of the 'green revolution'.[40] According to Srinivasan, there has been no significant change in the rate of growth of production of food crops other than wheat after the introduction of the new technology. For wheat such a change is noticeable and Srinivasan has thus christened the new technology the 'wheat revolution'.[41] Allowing for the fact that agricultural output fluctuates between peak and through years, Hanumantha Rao has shown that the net contribution of the 'green revolution' to the increase in agricultural output has not been insignificant but it has not been very large either. According to him, between 27 and 41 per cent of the additional output between 1964-65 and 1970-71 can be attributed to the 'green revolution'. That is to say more than half to three-quarters of the change can be attributed to normal trend factors.[42] Similar conclusions are reached by Desai, who also shows that returns obtained by farmers using the new technology were not significantly higher than those obtained by non-users.

The conclusion of these studies is not that agricultural output has not expanded substantially during the 1960s but that most of

---

[39]Sen (1967).
[40]Griffin (1974).
[41]Srinivasan (1972).
[42]Rao (1974); Desai (1969, 1972).

the increase can be explained by the trend rate of growth of agricultural output that has been in evidence since before the 'green revolution'. Now, it is possible to argue that since the man/land ratio has been steadily rising during this period, agricultural output will have expanded even more slowly without the 'green revolution'. This argument is hypothetical, in that no one has so far been able to show what effect a rising man/land ratio has had on agricultural output in this period. In any case, the protagonists of the 'green revolution' have always put their case in more positive terms. Our conclusion would be that while an extra five to eight million tons of foodgrains is certainly welcome, there is no evidence in the output figures of a major sustained technological breakthrough in agricultural production in India.[43]

Why has the apparently productive new technology had such limited and disappointing effects on output? Partly the answer must be that the initial hopes themselves were exaggerated, based as they were on extremely high yields obtained under ideal trial conditions. However, that is not the whole story. As has been pointed out earlier, the new HYV seeds are the cornerstone of the new technology. First, it has to be borne in mind that the HYV seeds have been most successfully evolved for wheat. As we have noted earlier, the major food crop in India is rice. In addition, millets contribute a large share to food output.[44] While new strains have been developed for rice, they have so far given less spectacular results. Part of the failure of rice has been attributed by some to wider variations in local conditions that influence the cultivation of rice.[45] The initially introduced imported varieties of both wheat and rice have sometimes turned out to be unsuitable for local conditions and prone to rust and blight.[46] Even for wheat, yields had begun to stagnate by the early 1970s.[47] It is true that for both wheat and rice, there are attempts to develop indigenous strains and some of these offer better prospects for yield. For example, the indigenous Jaya and Padma varieties

[43]This is the volume of output attributable to the adoption of the 'green revolution' calculated by Rao (1974).

[44]For the weights of the various crops in total agricultural output, see n. 27, Ch. 3.

[45]Hopper and Freeman (1969).

[46]Ladejinsky (1973).

[47]*Op. cit.*

of rice have done much better in field trials than the exotic Taichung or IRRI strains.[48]

Apart from wheat and rice, there have been some improved varieties of hybrid maize introduced into India. There has as yet been no breakthrough in jowar, bajra or pulses. The same holds true for commercial crops like sugar cane, cotton and jute. From the point of view of the composition of food crops, it can be seen that there has not been any spectacular rise in the output of the major crop, i.e. rice. In addition, most of the non-wheat food crops and the major non-food crops have not been touched by the new technology. As these together make up a substantial part of total agricultural output, the impact of the new technology has been limited to crops which make up only a small part of total production. Part of the impact of the 'green revolution' has not been on the total volume of food or agricultural production but on the crop-mix. The discovery of more productive varieties of food crops, however limited, has led to changes in cropping pattern away from non-food cash crops in some regions. To that extent, the increase in food production has been at the expense partly of non-food crops.[49] That is not to say that individual farmers have not benefited from such switches but the new technology has not eased the overall constraint imposed by low rates of growth on agricultural production.[50]

There are also other reasons that explain the limited impact of the 'green revolution'. The resulting increase in output depends obviously on the extent to which the new practices are used by farmers. It has to be remembered that the new inputs are complementary and that they have to be applied in the recommended dosages. A study by Desai in the mid 1960s showed that there was no signi-

---

[48]Hopper and Freeman (1969).

[49]Dharm Narain (1972).

[50]The wage-goods constraint in agriculture operates in two distinct ways. As most of the basic consumer goods are of agricultural origin, the ability to expand this part of the output determines the ability of the economy to meet additional consumption demand arising out of increases in population, income and employment or changes in the distribution of income. In addition, many of the exportable goods in India are also of agricultural origin. The rate at which the supply of these goods can be increased, and their export prices, also acts as a constraint on economic growth, through the operation of the foreign exchange constraint.

ficant correlation between the degree of use of different inputs.[51] This implies that one of the conditions under which the new inputs will give maximum yields is not fulfilled. Secondly, many studies show that where the new technology has been adopted, farmers still use less than the recommended dosage of fertilizer. Part of the reason is no doubt that fertilizer application is subject to diminishing returns and the amount used depends not only on technical factors but also on the relative prices of inputs and outputs. However, there might also be other reasons for restricted application, such as risk aversion.[52] It is certainly the case that there has been substantial excess demand for fertilizers for most of the period. Farmers were unable to get hold of adequate amounts of fertilizers, even if they had wished to use more.

Part of the limited impact of the 'green revolution' has, of course, been a direct consequence of Government policy, which restricted the geographical spread of the technology to selected areas with favourable initial conditions. The extent to which the new technology could increase output would have depended naturally on how fast it could spread out of these pockets. Here, limited availability of such inputs as fertilizers has been responsible for a slow expansion of the area under the new technology.[53] However, of critical importance has been the availability of water for cultivation.

The new technology requires both adequate and controlled use of water. As monsoon rains are seasonal and variable both in terms of timing and volume, the 'green revolution' has been largely confined to those areas of the country that have assured irrigation. The proportion of irrigated area to total cultivable area in India is of the order of 33 per cent and it has not increased very much since the inception of the 'green revolution'. During the 1960s, net irrigated area increased by only 16.7 per cent, while gross area increased by 24.5 per cent.[54] For net irrigated area, the increase was less than in the previous decade.[55] While part of this was offset by very substantial increases in well irrigation, especially in

[51]Desai (1969).
[52]On risk aversion, see Lipton (1968).
[53]Throughout this period, fertilizer was in short supply and much of it had to be imported.
[54]Rao (1974).
[55]*Op. cit.*

the private sector, this has not counteracted the fact that the technology could at best extend to cover one-third of the total area and could then expand only as fast as the spread of surface and well irrigation. Thus, the proportion of the total foodgrains area under HY varieties went up from 5 per cent to only 15 per cent between 1967-68 and 1971-72.[56] At the latter date, it was 39 per cent for wheat, 19 per cent for rice, 16 per cent for bajra and less than 10 per cent for jowar and maize.[57]

It has been pointed out by Raj and others that the dependence of the new technology on the availability of water underlines an inherent tendency towards limited and regionally unequal growth.[58] It might be argued that this is the inevitable consequence of having to rely on a water-intensive technique in a land that depends on the vagaries of the monsoon. It cannot, however, be denied that the problem has been much exacerbated by the policies of the Government. It has been late in promoting work and investment in the development of ground-water resources. Where private initiative has tried to bridge the gap, as in the case of the bamboo tubewells of Bihar, it is not too much to say that the official response has been unhelpful and even hostile.[59]

Apart from the volume of output, the question of variability in the levels of output is also of great importance in the Indian context. Can it be that while the 'green revolution' has had limited effect on the level of output, it has led to more stability in its level? As has been pointed out initially by Sen, increases in output in this period have been accompanied by increased instability.[60] Rao also reaches the same conclusion. The bulk of the increase in the coefficient of variation occurs moreover from the side of yield rather than from fluctuations in acreage.[61] It is true, however, that the HYV seeds have been used more widely in the *rabi* season, when their use is more profitable. This has tended to increase the *rabi* output and to lead to a diminution in the *kharif-rabi* seasonality pattern in the production of foodgrains.[62]

---

[56]*Op. cit.*
[57]*Op. cit.*
[58]Raj (1969); see also Dantwala (1972), p. 36 f.
[59]Appu (1974); Clay (1974).
[60]Sen (1967).
[61]Rao (1974).
[62]*Op. cit.*

While most authors stress the importance of supply factors in explaining the behaviour of output, some have pointed out the role played by demand. Thus, Dharm Narain has pointed out that sustained expansion of output from agriculture will require a sustained expansion in demand for agricultural products. He explains the relatively poor performance of rice in terms of the lower expenditure elasticity of demand for rice, as opposed to wheat. It is obviously also explained by the fact that incomes in wheat-producing areas have increased faster than in rice-producing areas, partly as a result of the 'green revolution'. Lefeber[63] and Datta Chaudhuri[64] have further developed the theoretical implications of these relationships. As Lefeber points out, given limited export possibility the demand for agricultural products depends primarily on the expansion of domestic incomes and the expenditure elasticity of demand for foodgrains, the rate of population growth being of less importance to the problem. Moreover, the bulk of the additional demand for foodgrains comes from the poorer sections of the population,[65] who are the major consumers of foodgrains. The expansion of demand depends, therefore, on how rapidly the incomes of the poorer sections of the population can grow. As is argued later, they have so far benefited little from either the 'green revolution' or from the overall economic growth in India.[66] Thus, the supply and demand factors have interacted to prevent the wider adaptation of the new technology and hence limited its effects on agricultural output.

Any discussion of the growth and variability of agricultural output under the new technology would be incomplete without some discussion of the effects of the weather on agricultural output. It can be argued that our conclusion that the increase in agricultural output has been limited and that the rate of growth of agricultural production had begun to falter by the early 1970s, is too much conditioned by the effects of the failure of the monsoon during 1972. It is difficult to know to what extent the decline in foodgrains output of about 11 million tonnes during 1972 was due to the weather, although the latter must have had a substantial effect.

[63]Lefeber (1973).
[64]Lefeber and Datta Chaudhuri (1971).
[65]For a theoretical discussion of the issue involved, see Lefeber (1973).
[66]See below, Chs. 7 and 8.

The obvious point of comparison is the period 1965-67, which witnessed the worst drought in 40 years.[67] During 1965 rainfall was below normal in 20 out of 28 states. In 12 of these, rainfall was deficient by more than 20 per cent and in 6 by more than 30 per cent. In 1966, rainfall was below normal in 23 states. The margin of deficiency was over 20 per cent in 13 states, over 40 per cent in 4 of them. Thus 1966 was a far worse year than 1965 and it came after an already harsh year of drought. These conditions led to a fall in agricultural output of around 18 to 20 per cent or about 20 million tonnes. In 1972 rainfall was below normal in 28 states, the degree of deficiency exceeding 20 per cent in 17 of them; in 5 states the deficiency exceeded 40 per cent. The result was a decline in food production of around 11 per cent or 15 million tonnes out of a larger volume of production. Thus, the economy seems to have withstood the effects of the year 1972 somewhat better, although it was a worse year, taken by itself, than 1966. But it did not follow upon a year half as bad as 1965.

Broadly speaking, the states where food production declined most, in both periods, were also those where rainfall was the most deficient. On the other hand, there was no systematic relationship between the degree of deficiency in rainfall and food production.[68] We can conclude from this that the available data do not enable us to say anything very conclusive about the question, whether the slackening of the growth in agricultural output is, or is not, a statistical illusion.

If the effect on food and agricultural production has been limited, what has been the effect of the new technology on employment? The question of employment is intimately associated with the question of the mechanization of Indian agriculture. The seed-fertilizer technology is basically a land-saving technology. Hence, its potential attractiveness to the land-hungry areas of south and southeast India. By increasing the yield per acre, the new technology makes it possible to increase food production out of a given amount of land. Its effect on labour demand is somewhat more problematic. Some better cultivation practices, such as

[67]Sen (1967).
[68]The rainfall data are published in the Central Statistical Office publication, *Statistical Abstract of the Indian Union* (annual); more recent data are from the *Times of India Directory* (annual).

more careful planting, better weeding, etc., tend to increase the demand for labour. On the other hand, substitution of pump-irrigation for surface irrigation to obtain better control may reduce the demand for labour.[69] Equally, a larger harvest increases the demand for harvest labour to collect that harvest. Moreover, where the new technology makes possible the introduction of multiple cropping, that in turn increases the demand for labour over the year as a whole.[70] Without the introduction of mechanization, there is *a priori* reason to believe that the new technology will tend to generate more employment.

However, the question cannot be discussed without a considera-tion of the mechanization of agriculture and its effect on employ-ment. Although there is no technical reason why the new techno-logy should imply the mechanization of agriculture, there are very strong economic reasons why the two should go together. As we have mentioned earlier, the new technology is much more expen-sive than the traditional one and it is also more variable in yield.[71] It is only worth a farmer's while to introduce that technology if he can derive a sufficiently high rate of profit from it. In addition, the technology both offers an opportunity for reducing risk and makes it profitable, e.g. by substituting tube-well irrigation for uncertain rainfall or surface irrigation.[72] Moreover, it equally makes it both possible and profitable to practise multiple cropping. Under certain conditions, the time interval between the harvesting of one crop and the planting of another, *if yields are to be maxi-mized*, is so short as to make it necessary to use tractors for pre-paration of the land for sowing. Therefore, there is a strong tend-ency for the new technology to be associated with mechanization, where a farmer has the resources to undertake the initial investment for deriving a higher rate of profit. This has been strengthened by the underpricing of tractors and harvesters through the overvalua-tion of the rupee and access to subsidized credit by large farmers.

[69]Raj (1972), for example, argues that the new technology may also be labour-saving.

[70]Thus reducing the seasonal instability in the demand for labour.

[71]On variability, see Rao (1974) and Sen (1967).

[72]Extension of tube-well irrigation may also cause second-generation problems. Too many tube-wells can cause the water table to drop too far, an interesting case of an external diseconomy. Hence, the need for detailed technical information on water-resource availability.

In addition, the very dynamic possibility of increasing yields may itself encourage mechanization. It is, no doubt, also helped by the fact that by and large machines are less troublesome to handle than labourers.

It is not possible in this case to say *a priori* whether mechanization would tend to reduce or increase employment. Such things as pump-sets or tractors displace labour directly; however, in so far as increase in irrigation by pumps or multiple cropping by tractors make it possible to increase output,[73] the net effect on employment may well go either way. It seems fairly clear that such things as combined harvesters or threshers will tend to displace labour rather more than tractors. The few studies that have been done on India do not give any very clear directions. In a study relating to the Punjab, Hanumantha Rao has found that while tractors directly displaced labour, they also encouraged labour use indirectly so that there was very little net effect on employment from tractorization.[74] In an earlier study, also based on the Punjab, Billings and Singh found that for farms of over 10 acres, use of irrigation equipment tended to increase the demand for labour while the use of tractors or wheat reapers tended to reduce it.[75] A study by the NCAER also found that while tractors by themselves did not displace labour, the combined operations of tractors and threshers had that effect.[76] In any case, the spread of tractors and reapers has not been very wide in India until now and it is not possible to say how important the present displacement of labour has been in terms of total rural manpower.[77] Ladejinsky's reports on various trips point to the conclusion that while such effects may have not been very widespread, they have had significant if localized effect on the demand for labour.[78]

[73]Very often, a particular crop cycle to be followed under multiple cropping leaves a very short interval for soil preparation. In such cases, use of tractors may be an essential condition for multiple cropping to be profitable.

[74]Rao (1974).

[75]Billings and Singh (1969).

[76]NCAER (1973).

[77]As the introduction of mechanization is largely confined to the 'green revolution' areas, and the latter themselves cover a small proportion of total cultivable area, the total volume of labour force influenced may not be very large at the moment.

[78]Ladejinsky (1969a) and (1969b).

It might be objected that we are ignoring the fact that the growth of employment in India has been constrained by the supply of wage-goods. It can be argued that in so far as more capital-intensive farming succeeds in breaking this bottleneck, there will be longer-run dynamic effects on employment. There are several reasons for doubting such a prognosis, while accepting the existence of a wage-goods constraint. As we have seen, the increase in the supply of foodgrains that can be attributed to the new technology has been limited. Out of that, it is doubtful whether a great deal can be attributed to mechanization, which is the phase of development at which labour is likely to become displaced. Moreover, given that the tendency of labour to be displaced on account of mechanization is stronger for large than for small farms, it can be argued that the concentration of production on large farms, which has been a consequence of the 'green revolution', leads to a trading-off of employment, not against an increased output of foodgrains but against a larger marketed surplus.[79]

However, as we have noted before, the new technology implies the use of joint inputs. In such cases, it is difficult to determine the shares of individual inputs in the resulting increase of output. In my view, none of the available studies deals with this problem successfully. The studies tend to show that while the application of new seeds and fertilizers tends to increase both output and yield, the evidence relating to the returns to mechanization is less favourable. Thus, in the study quoted above, Hanumantha Rao found that the effects of irrigation were significant in explaining double-cropping but those of tractors were not; in terms of output, HYV seeds and fertilizer application were most significant in explaining the increase in output, while tractors had a small but significant effect on output and were not significant in explaining yield.

A great deal of attention has been devoted in the literature on the 'green revolution' to the distributional aspects of agrarian change. Economists and social anthropologists have drawn attention both to the unequal regional incidence of technical change

[79]On the relationship of farm size to the marketed surplus, see p. 30 above and the reference cited there.

and its interpersonal incidence.[80] It has been repeatedly argued that the 'green revolution' has tended to increase the gap between the rich and poor in the rural sector, by channelling the benefits to the rich farmers at the expense of the small peasant and the landless labourer.

Before turning to a consideration of this question, we can note that the interests of the two latter groups are not identical. The small peasant largely provides his own labour in the form of family labour, although he may hire in labour at the margin.[81] The bulk of his livelihood is derived from his land, which he may or may not lease in from a rich farmer. He is, in a sense, in competition with the latter for scarce land and where he markets part of his produce he is also in competition in the market for foodgrains as a seller. His benefits depend on the productivity of his land, his access to land, the terms of such access and the price he gets for his surplus. The agricultural labourer, in his turn, is not in competition with the rich farmer but derives his livelihood from the employment the rich farmer provides and the wages he is paid. He is in competition with the machine. At the margin, the two shade into the sharecropper, whose benefits depend mainly on the terms of the crop share and his share of the costs of production.

An example will make clear the point that the small peasant and the landless labourer do not benefit in the same way from a process of technological change. Let us suppose that the rich farmer can monopolize the access to scarce inputs that are necessary for the increase in production. It is possible that without mechanization, he may increase his demand for labour, and where part of the payment is in kind, say a share of the harvest, the landless labourer can benefit from both higher employment and higher wages. However, if own cultivation of land becomes profitable, the rich farmer may take over land he was previously leasing out. The increase in marketed produce that results from an increase in production may drive down the market price and adversely affect the small farmer, who is a marginal supplier. Similarly, it is possi-

[80]For economists, see Frankel (1971), Ladejinsky (1969a) and (1969b) and Wharton (1969); for other social scientists, see Gough and Sharma (1973).

[81]On the other hand, the small peasant may also act as a wage labourer for a larger peasant for part of his time.

ble that if more resources are channelled to the small farmer, he may hire less non-family labour than the large farmer and may market less of his output for the landless to buy. On the other hand, as the small farmer is less likely to go in for mechanization, he is not likely to affect employment very adversely in the balance.

The available data point quite clearly to the fact that both the small peasants and the landless labourers have tended to be left behind by the new technology. They have certainly lost out in relative terms to the rich farmers, who have gathered to themselves the bulk of the additional benefits of the 'green revolution'. The data relating to the incidence of poverty in India, which is discussed in Chapters 7 and 8 below, indicate that the small peasants and the landless labourers have probably also lost out in absolute terms.[82]

The case for holding the view that the new technology has largely benefited the rich farmers has been documented most thoroughly by Frankel.[83] Concentrating on the five IADP districts, Ludhiana, West Godavary, Thanjavur, Palghat and Burdwan, Frankel found that in each district, while there was evidence that small farmers had made some limited gains, the gains made by large farmers, especially those owning land over say 10 to 20 acres or more, were very much larger.[84]

The direct evidence on landless labourers is more ambiguous. As we have indicated earlier, the studies on the employment effects of the new technology do not offer very clearcut evidence of what is likely to happen. The data on wages are also somewhat ambiguous. In his field trips in Bihar and the Punjab, Ladejinsky found that wage levels were still low. Whereas money wages had risen in recent years, especially during the harvest seasons, real wages showed little improvement.[85] Bardhan noted a decline in agricultural wages in the Punjab, whereas Gough found a small increase.[86] There is also some evidence that in some cases casual labourers have done better than those in permanent employment. The attempt by the larger farmers to switch over from payment of wages in kind to cash payments, to take

[82]See pp. 201-7.
[83]Frankel (1971).
[84]*Op. cit.*
[85]Ladejinsky (1969a) and (1969b).
[86]Bardhan (1970a); Gough (1971).

advantage of rising food prices, has also tended to keep real wages down.[87] The work done on poverty in India indicates strongly that the fate of the landless labourers, who figure prominently among the very poor, could not have improved very much. It is quite clear that their real wages have not increased in any way in step with the incomes of the rich farmers. Some authors have pointed to the growing militancy amongst the landless in rural India as a sign of growing poverty, whereas it is equally possible that it is a sign of growing political awareness.[88]

How can we explain the perverse distributional effects of the 'green revolution'? It needs to be said at the beginning that they are not accidental. They are a direct consequence of particular policies followed through in a particular institutional framework. One reason why large farmers might have fared better under the new technology would be if increasing returns to scale were a major feature of that technology. There is a fairly substantial volume of evidence to show that under traditional technology small farms showed higher rates of yield per acre than larger farms.[89] However, that evidence is of limited significance to us in evaluating the characteristics of the new technology. There is some evidence, adduced by Patnaik, that the old technological relationship had broken down and that the 'green revolution' technology is subject to increasing returns to scale.[90] However, Bardhan has shown that non-constant returns are mainly an attribute of wheat farming and that rice is most subject to constant returns. As most of the inputs are themselves divisible, it would be a result one would intuitively expect to derive.[91] While we cannot be firm about the conclusion it would seem unlikely that the large farmers have been able to benefit from the new technology simply because they are more efficient.

It is likely that the reason why large farmers have done better under the new technology lies not in their being large so much as in their being rich. This point can be elaborated in two slightly different ways, although both rely on market imperfections to

---

[87]Ladejinsky (1969a) and (1969b).

[88]For discussions of agrarian unrest, see Beteille (1974), Gough (1955) and Gough and Sharma (1973).

[89]See references cited in n. above.

[90]U. Patnaik (1971).

[91]Bardhan (1974).

make their point. It has been argued by Griffin that factor markets for both capital and labour are imperfect in poor countries, both factors being available to rich farmers at more favourable prices. As the relative price ratios facing the large and small farmers are different, it is possible to have a new technology which it would be profitable to adopt at one set of prices but not at the other. Griffin argues in effect that the 'green revolution' is such a technology.

The second argument would hold that the new technology opens up the same kind of choice to both small and large farmers but that the small farmer is prevented from opting for it. This is partly because he suffers from a budget constraint and partly because the large farmer monopolizes the use of scarce inputs necessary for increasing production. As we have pointed out earlier, the new technology is more expensive, albeit more productive.[92] A small farmer can only use it if he has adequate access to credit. The regulations governing the rural credit agencies, which were set up to channel funds towards agricultural development, virtually rule out giving credit to farmers with less than 7 to 10 acres of land.[93] The practice of calling for land as security, instead of offering loans on the basis of a lien on the crop, make credit inaccessible to all without a title to land that can be pledged. This means that a small farmer can only obtain credit from the private money-lender who charges much higher rates of interest, a point stressed by Griffin.[94]

There are also other factors which militate against the small farmer. He is more sensitive to risk, because he has a smaller margin of savings to fall back upon. While these are insurable risks from the point of view of society, Government policy has done little to devise methods to underwrite such risks. The cost of sinking wells makes them unprofitable for those with less than 5 acres. Yet Government policy does little to encourage cheaper wells.[95] Where HYV seeds and fertilizers are in short supply, rich farmers are often able to obtain the major share of these inputs. In fact, Government policy makes it easier for them to do so, by

[92]See pp. 122-3 above.
[93]Rao (1974).
[94]Griffin (1974).
[95]Appu (1974) and Clay (1974).

enabling them to have easier access to cheaper credit from the modern sector. Naturally, this process strengthens itself in course of time. Higher productivity enables higher savings to be made and ploughed back, which in turn enables reinvestment to take place.

The small farmer has also been adversely affected by the growing tendency among the large farmers to reclaim land previously leased out under tenancy agreements, which has been made profitable by higher returns from the new technology.[96] The small farmer has been increasingly pushed into the ranks of the landless labourers. Schulter and others have noted that the rates of adoption of new technology are positively related to the size of landholdings.[97] Moreover, it has been found that large farmers use more fertilizer per acre than smaller farmers. This reflects not so much the inherent progressiveness of the rich farmer as his ability, under the existing system, to make a pre-emptive bid for scarce resources.

Studies of the effects of the 'green revolution' on regional development are harder to come by. While it can be established that there has been unequal regional growth in recent years in India, with some indication of growing regional inequality, it is not easy to attribute this to the 'green revolution' one way or another. Because the 'green revolution' is confined to irrigated land and especially to wheat, it would seem intuitively plausible that the new technology would have promoted growth in well-irrigated wheat producing areas, such as the Punjab. No doubt this has happened and the prosperity of the Punjab is now a byword. However, other non-wheat producing states have also shown substantial output gains. Part of the answer lies in the fact that agricultural output, both food and non-food, is highly sensitive to changes in climatic conditions that have nothing to do with the 'green revolution'.

Within the limits of our knowledge, Mitra has shown that with the exception of relatively rich states like Punjab and Gujarat, most have fared badly in terms of rates of growth of *per capita* food output.[98] Comparing the behaviour of food production

---

[96]Dharm Narain and Joshi (1969).
[97]Schulter (1971).
[98]Mitra (1970).

during the two periods 1959-61 and 1969-71, Vyas found that in 9 out of 15 states food production had expanded at a rate lower than could be expected on the basis of their relative contributions to food output.[99] The group included Bihar, Kerala, Madhya Pradesh, Maharashtra and Orissa, all of them poor states.[100] Hanumantha Rao also finds evidence of uneven rates of growth of *per capita* output of foodgrains, again with a number of poorer states like Bihar, Madhya Pradesh and Maharashtra doing significantly worse than Punjab or Gujarat.[101] The only exception to this pattern appears to be Rajasthan, which showed significant increases in production up to 1970-71.[102] On the other hand, Ladejinsky points out that substantial gains in food production during 1970-71 came from non-'green revolution' areas.[103]

The participants in the debate on the distributional aspects of the 'green revolution' are not always clear on whether such effects are to be attributed to the success or the failure of the output effects of the new technology to materialize. It is sometimes alleged that very substantial increases have been made in production but that these have accrued to a small section of the rural population. As we have indicated, for the period we are talking about the gains in agricultural output that can be attributed to the 'green revolution' are fairly modest.[104] On the other hand, the argument that rich farmers have done better out of the very failure of the expected output to materialize assumes that the price elasticity of demand for foodgrains is less than unity over the relevant price range. This is at least a precise testable relationship.[105] In

[99]Vyas (1973); the comparison is between actual output and the notional output required to maintain the states' shares in 1959-61 output.

[100]*Op. cit.*

[101]Rao (1974).

[102]Vyas (1973); Rao (1974). On the face of it, it is difficult to explain the 1970-71 figures for Rajasthan. According to the official figures, the output of jowar, bajra and maize went up from 1,740 thousand tonnes to 4,176 thousand tonnes between 1969-70 and 1970-71. The average level of output of these crops for 1971-74 was approximately 2,370 thousand tonnes.

[103]Ladejinsky (1973).

[104]See p. 124 above.

[105]The problem is simplified by the fact that, in the short run, the farmer is faced with a choice between two alternative levels of output, whereas he is faced with a particular demand curve. The more profitable

any case, it is unlikely that under a competitive system farmers could drive up prices by restricting output except under some form of collusive behaviour.

Those who adhere to the first formulation of the problem imply that the 'green revolution' is a technocratic solution that is unacceptable for its social effects. In my view, this poses a false dichotomy. As Ladejinsky has said, '...neither farm prices and incentives nor structural changes can solve the problem of productivity and more equitable distribution of income where the suitable technological solution does not exist'.[106] This is because foodgrains form the basic consumer good for the poor. It is neither possible to alleviate poverty without more food production nor is it possible for poverty to exist in such an acute form in a country where a substantial breakthrough has been achieved in foodgrains production. It is the poor who eat the grains; the additional consumption of the rich consists of meat, dairy products and manufactured consumer goods.

A possible explanation of the impact of the 'green revolution' can run along the following lines. The failure to achieve a breakthrough in food production has meant that nothing very much has happened to ease the overall wage-goods constraint facing the economy. On the other hand, purely localized gains have been made by the rich farmers in particular areas. While this has led to the accumulation of wealth on a large scale by a small group of farmers, an acceptable offset to this growing inequality in the form of a higher availability of foodgrains has been totally lacking. At the same time, the economy has not gained the advantage of a more stable level of output. The critical role of water in the new technology, together with inadequate development of groundwater resources, has left the economy sensitive to the vagaries of nature, as was the case before. To add to that, the increased reliance on manufactured and imported inputs to obtain higher yields has made output sensitive also to the non-availability of such things as fertilizer or diesel oil. The agricultural economy has not prospered so much as become open to all the disturbances arising out of the world economy, from which its previous structural insularity had shielded itself. What we are observing in

---

output is determined by the price-elasticity of demand.

[106]Ladejinsky (1973).

India today appears to be the kind of process that Geertz has characterized as 'agricultural involution' in a different context.[107]

Much discussion has taken place on whether the 'green revolution' has ushered in an era of capitalist agriculture in India, spearheaded by a new class of capitalist farmer. It is not my purpose here to dwell upon the doctrinal aspects of the debate on alternative 'modes of production'.[108] It would be helpful, however, to explain briefly some of the major points at issue.

If we ask the question whether the introduction of a more capital-intensive technology has led to the large-scale substitution of capital equipment such as tractors or threshers for labour or animal power, the answer is not far to seek. Such mechanization of agriculture has taken place so far on a very limited scale, with the exception of Haryana and Punjab.[109] However, there is more to the question of capitalist farming than that.

The basic point at issue is whether a new class or category of farmer has developed in India, who can be characterized as being capitalist, as opposed to being a feudal proprietor of land or a mere peasant. There are two distinct aspects to this question, which do not always emerge clearly from the debate.

The first of these concerns the identification of a particular species, i.e. the capitalist farmer, according to a set of morphological characteristics that are agreed upon by the protagonists. The other is the quite distinct question, whether the species so identified is the dominant form of a particular genus or is dominant in a particular environment. There is as yet no complete agreement as to the morphological characteristics that are the distinctive features of the capitalist farmer and whether he requires to display all or only some of these to qualify as an original Linnaean category.[110] Rudra has argued that, given a fairly complete set of the required characteristics, there is as yet no such breed as the capitalist farmer in India. Utsa Patnaik has argued the oppo-

---

[107]Geertz (1970).

[108]For a discussion of some of these issues, see Alavi (1975).

[109]Rao (1975).

[110]The four major characteristics are. production for the market, use of wage labour, mechanization, and reinvestment of the surplus within the farm. A full bibliography is given in Alavi (1975). The more important contributions are Byres (1972), Chattopadhyay (1972), Patnaik (1971) and Rudra (1971).

site, that it is not necessary for a capitalist farmer to display all the relevant characteristics of the category during what is a period of transition. According to the weaker definition, she does find the beginnings of capitalist farming in India. While there cannot be much fruitful argument about which definition one prefers, it remains to be seen whether a species which displays at the moment only some characteristics out of a particular set, will in the end come to display them all.

The second question, which concerns the importance of the capitalist farmer in Indian agriculture today, can be dealt with more easily. The answer must be that as yet the capitalist farmer is very much of a minority in Indian agriculture, in quantitative terms. While much attention has been given to the use of wage-labour, or the introduction of tractors and threshers in large-scale farming, the proportion of total area or activities covered by that kind of development is still very small. Whether that mode of farming will come to dominate the Indian farming scene remains a highly interesting but a highly speculative question.

Land Reform

The ability of the rich farmer to appropriate a very large share of the limited gains of the 'green revolution' rests on the dominant position that he occupies both economically and socially in rural society. That position rests in turn on his control over the major source of wealth in that society, i.e. land. The question naturally arises whether it is possible to introduce a system that would distribute the benefits of economic progress more equitably, without a radical change in the system of land ownership and land use in rural society. The question of land reform is, therefore very close to the centre of development policy in India.

A great deal of attention is paid in the plan documents and other policy pronouncements to the need for and the importance of land reform.[111] In the immediate post-independence period, there were roughly speaking five categories of people whose livelihood was derived in some form or other from their relationship to land. These were the *zamindar* or absentee landlord, the large and small

---

[111]See, for example, India, Planning Commission (1952), Ch. XLI; (1956), Ch. IX; (1961), Ch. XIV.

peasant, who may be a tenant or sub-tenant, the share cropper, and the landless labourer. Unfortunately, from the point of view of analytical purity, these categories are not, and never have been, mutually exclusive. Thus, a *zamindar* may have cultivated some of his land, the large peasant might have had some *zamindari* land, the small peasant may have cultivated some land as a share cropper, and the landless labourer may partly have worked as a share cropper and partly as hired labour, casual or permanent.[112]

From our point of view, the essential categories existing at that time in the immediate post-independence period were the absentee landlord, the cultivator who made a living by the cultivation of land over which he exercised user rights in payment for rent, and the worker who sold his labour to compensate for his lack of land. The last category has always consisted of a very large proportion of the total agrarian population and has always numbered amongst its ranks some of the poorest of the poor. The original policy of land reform was based on the famous slogan 'land to the tiller' and consisted of the following elements: abolition of intermediary tenancy or *zamindari* rights, redistribution of land under a 'ceiling' legislation laying down the maximum amount of land to be held by cultivators, consolidation of small holdings to counter one of the effects of excessive fragmentation of land, security of tenure for the tenant and reasonable, non-penal rates of rent.[113] It is worth noting that even as originally conceived, the policy did not include an element that would have directly benefited the poorest groups of landless labourers. Their needs were supposed to be met through various special schemes for creating employment.

The abolition of *zamindaris* was brought about by the implementation of the Zamindari Abolition Acts in the early 1950s. This is the only part of the programme that has been fully implemented.

---

[112]Compare this to the more fundamental categories established by Thorner (1962), of 'malik', 'kishan' and 'mazdoor'. There are two facts about the rural social structure that are of great analytical significance. One is that the same term, e.g. 'jotedar', often signifies quite different categories in different parts of the country. The other is that it is extremely difficult to match up the functional and personal categories. The same individual may perform more than one role in the socio-economic nexus. For a discussion of these problems, see Beteille (1974).

[113]For a survey of Indian land reform policy and its origins, see Joshi (1971). A general survey is also given in Warriner (1969).

It should be pointed out that initially this was not a measure for the redistribution of wealth, because the former owners were compensated for the estimated value of their land. It did, however, make a large amount of land available for redistribution. If the 'ceiling' legislation had been properly enforced, there would have been a substantial redistribution of land from the *zamindars* to the middle and small peasants. The actual effect was merely to create a body of owner-cultivators with substantial land holdings, a new rural elite who were an improvement on the former in that they were more involved in the efficient utilization of their landholdings than were the absentee landlords but who did not augur well for the prospects of future rural equality. This result was brought about by the wide-scale and systematic evasion of the ceiling legislation, part of which was made possible by the very letters of the law. As 'ceilings' were left to be fixed by the states, very different maxima were enacted.[114] More seriously, the logical basis of the legislation was shot out from under by numerous exemptions that allowed the acquisition of excess land over ceilings for *khas* or own cultivation and through the fixing of ceilings in terms of individual holdings rather than families that formed the production unit. Januzzi has documented in great detail the course of ceiling legislation in one state, Bihar. After *zamindari* abolition, one landowner gained back 600 acres of land in a state where the official ceiling was between 20 and 60 acres.[115] Moreover, only a small part of the land made surplus by the ceiling was ever redistributed.[116] The right of owner-cultivators to reclaim land for own cultivation led to widespread eviction and the so-called voluntary surrender of land by small tenants.[117] This tendency has been reinforced by the higher profitability of large farms made possible by the 'green revolution'.

If the small peasant and the share cropper have not been able to get hold of very much land, they have also not been served any better by the legislation relating to security of tenure and the fixing of reasonable rents. The tendency for the small peasant to be evicted has already been remarked upon. In addition, the practice of granting oral leases or switching cultivators from one plot to

---

[114]Wunderlich (1970).
[115]Januzzi (1970).
[116]Wunderlich (1970).
[117]Khusro (1958); Dandekar and Khundanpur (1957)

another, devices to withhold from him permanent occupancy rights, are widespread.[118] The *locus classicus* of the non-implementation of tenancy legislation is the report prepared by Ladejinsky, who documented the lack of security of tenure and continued high levels of rental. The record on land consolidation is equally poor.[119] There are not many areas of economic policy in India where one can categorically point out the direction in which events have been moving. Unfortunately, land reform, a vital plank in rural development policy, is one of these. It is an unrelieved account of false promises, of continued oppression and misery.

The final points have to be noted before the discussion can be rounded off. One is whether there was, in the field of land redistribution, an implicit conflict between the efficient use of agricultural resources and equity; whether, in allowing a continued, if not a growing inequality in the ownership of land, the Government was not encouraging higher levels of productivity. It is not easy, for a country so vast and varied as India, to say what is the optimum size of landholdings. It varies according to the type of land and the type of crop we are talking about, as well as which factor of production we wish to economize upon the most. However, according to Khusro, the viable size in terms of productivity and income appears to be somewhere between 7 and 15 acres.[120] Roughly one-third of the total operational area in India was held in units of over 25 acres, forming less than 5 per cent of the number of operational holdings![121] Moreover, studies based on the farm management surveys also show that small farms were no less efficient than large ones, in terms of returns per unit of land.[122] While it is possible that the incidence of the 'green revolution' might have introduced an element of increasing returns to scale in agriculture, it is clear that the failure to implement land reform in the first 15 to 20 years of independence cannot be rationalized in terms of a desire for an efficient agriculture.[123]

Lastly, the question remains of the policy towards the landless

[118]Ladejinsky (1965); see also Ladejinsky (1972).

[119]India, Planning Commission (1969).

[120]Khusro (1973), Chs. 5 to 8.

[121]Khusro (1973), p. 77.

[122]See above n. 35; see also references cited in n. 33, Ch. 2.

[123]On more recent data on increasing returns to scale, see Bardhan (1974) and U. Patnaik (1971).

labourers. As has been pointed out, not even the 'land to the tiller' policy was directed at this bottom stratum of society. Raj Krishna, Dandekar and Rath, and Minhas have all argued that the poverty of the landless cannot be solved through the redistribution of land, because there simply is not enough land to go round.[124] Given the optimum size mentioned above, a minimum of 7 acres calculated by Khusro, this is certainly true. Such an overall figure is slightly misleading, because such a size might be too small for dry cultivation in arid areas and too large for, say, deltaic rice-growing in southern India. However, as a broad generalization it is true that not enough land can be made available through land redistribution, even of highly radical magnitudes. Various remedies have been suggested for improving the plight of the landless. Policies of land consolidation have been put forward for those with very small amounts of land, to enable them to form economic holdings. Others have recommended the use of public works, although some studies show up the limitation of public works as a policy towards the eradication of poverty.[125] The Government's own predilection has been towards various special schemes to create employment in selected areas. As they have almost always been ill-thought-out and inadequately financed, it is difficult to evaluate their potential, except by pointing out that they have so far had very little impact upon the problem. The problem of the poverty of the landless is unlikely to find a solution within the present framework of economic policies in India.

[124]Dandekar and Rath (1971); Minhas (1974); Raj Krishna (1959).
[125]On the limitations of public works in this context, see Rodgers (1973).

CHAPTER SIX

Problems of Industrial Development

The main features of industrial growth were summarized in an earlier chapter.[1] On the credit side we noted that, starting from a small base that was largely devoted to the production of finished manufactured goods, the economy built up a substantial and more diversified modern industrial sector. Especially in terms of absolute volumes of production of capital and intermediate goods, the growth was quite substantial. Industrial output expanded much faster than production in agriculture. Casual empiricism suggests, for there is not much up-to-date information about the growth of small-scale industry,[2] that this would be even more true if we took account of the growth of small-scale industries.

A result of this growth was the ability of the economy to satisfy a much larger proportion of its total requirements of various goods from domestic production.[3] On the other hand, there is evidence that the growth of industrial production suffered a setback during the 1965-67 recession from which it has not yet recovered. The slowing down in the growth of production has been more pronounced for capital goods and consumer non-durables, which include most commodities of mass consumption. This has in turn led to an imbalance in the industrial structure. In any case, in spite of rapid growth, there has been little perceptible change in the structure of the economy. The balance of pay-

---

[1]See pp. 65-70 above.

[2]Dhar and Lydall (1961) is now very much dated, although it is widely quoted as one of the few studies of this sector. Some information is given in Shirokov (1973).

See Table 18, p. 70.

ments situation still remains critical, with a tendency for the demand for imports to run ahead of the capacity to import, held only in check by the low level of industrial demand occasioned by low levels of utilization of capacity [4]

This pattern of uneven development has to be viewed against a certain perspective. In any case, what was being attempted in India was an extremely difficult task. Most of the industrialized countries have long histories of industrial progress; in India the process was being telescoped into a small number of years. Moreover, the fact that there are relatively few poor industrialized countries and that the rich countries have completely different endowments of capital infrastructure, enterprise and skills makes it difficult to establish norms against which Indian performance can be judged.[5] Seen against this background, one could be expected to view Indian industrial development in a somewhat charitable light.[6] It is, therefore, perhaps a little surprising to find that economists geared to the neo-classical tradition are as critical of Indian industrial performance as are those who adopt a Marxian mode of analysis of industrialization.[7] Such a celestial configuration might not be due entirely to the 'objective' nature of economic analysis. Indeed, in the Indian case, it arises out of the relationship of Indian industrial development to the overall strategy of development.[8] In any evaluation of industrialization in India, we have to keep firm hold of the strategic base on which the process rests or flounders.

At the risk of oversimplification, one could put the problem in this manner. An import-substituting industrialization policy

[4]On underutilization of capacity, see p. 152.

[5]Snould, say, a steel plant built to operate under conditions prevailing in an industrially developed country be expected to produce at full capacity in a poor country? If a fertilizer plant can be assembled in, say, 18 months in Europe, is two and a half years taken in India too long? These problems are very real, although they may not justify some of the delays of plan implementation in India.

[6]For a balanced but kind interpretation, see Robinson (1970).

[7]Compare Little, Scitovsky and Scott (1970) and Bhagwati and Desai (1970) to say, Bagchi (1970), Chattopadhyay (1973), and Prabhat Patnaik (1975). For underdeveloped countries in general, compare the interpretation of Warren (1970) to that of his critics, Emmanuel (1974) and MacMichael *et al.* (1974).

[8]See Ch. 9 below.

forms a major link in the chain of Indian development policy. An industrialization policy requires decisions to be made not only about flows of output to be manufactured at home but also about inflows of foreign capital and technology. Indian policy is protectionist towards the import of foreign goods, ambiguous towards the import of foreign capital and ill-informed about the import of foreign technology.[9] Neo-classical economists have based the bulk of their criticisms on the protectionist and exchange rate policies followed by the Indian Government and have criticized their effects on the pattern of industrial growth. Marxian critiques, on the other hand, have concentrated on the continued reliance of the economy on foreign capital and technology and have questioned the feasibility of building up an industrial structure consistent with the objectives of a 'socialist pattern of development'.

Each of these viewpoints rests on one basic assumption, which may not be strictly speaking implicit in much of the literature but which certainly is not stressed as much as it ought to be. Thus, the neo-classical critique rests on the assumption that there is a smooth and continuous transformation function for all tradeable goods, so that India could always obtain any required volume of imports by exporting such goods as it has a comparative advantage in producing. That is to say there are no structural constraints on the transformation of domestic into foreign resources. Moreover, the prevalence of tariffs is seen as the result of a policy of maintaining an artificially high rate of exchange for the rupee; this in turn assumes that the international demand for Indian exportables is price-elastic over the relevant range.[10] These are in final analysis largely questions of fact but there is certainly no comprehensive study that proves the point.[11] The Marxist ap-

[9]The protectionist basis of Indian trade policy is discussed in Bhagwati and Desai (1970) and Srinivasan (1974). Indian policy is ambiguous towards foreign capital in two senses. One is that while the plans regard 'self reliance' as an objective, the economy continues to be dependent on aid flows. The other is that while a number of regulations are laid down about the control of foreign investment, in practice these are not always adhered to. On criticisms of import of technology, see Lall (1974), NCAER (1971).

[10]On the price-elasticity of Indian exports, see n. 11.

[11]On the price-elasticity of Indian exports, see Cohen (1964). Nayyar (1974) and Srinivasan (1974) both discuss the effect of devaluation on Indian exports and come to rather different conclusions. As the degree of effective

proach assumes that there is a potential supply of domestic capital, skills and knowhow that will step in to fill any gap left by the withdrawal or shutting out of foreign capital and skill and that the former factors have a higher productivity at the margin in terms of the given objective function. This also is ultimately a question of fact and needless to say it is no more possible to establish this position empirically than it is to establish the corresponding neo-classical one. The position that I have adopted in relation to these two implicit assumptions will become clear later on in the discussion.[12]

Problems of Industrial Production

The most serious shortcoming of industrial production has been quite simply the inability to maintain a sustained rate of growth beyond the middle 1960s. This has shown itself both in low increases in levels of production in all but a small number of industries and in serious shortfalls in meeting plan tragets set for key industries. The latter problem is by no means a new one and has been a persistent feature of the development process in India.[13] However, while one could have put down the early failures to the teething problems of a modern industrial sector, that argument must necessarily begin to wear a little thin with time.

We have noted earlier the serious implications for the overall development of the economy of a stagnant rate of investment and the sluggish rate of growth of the capital goods industries since 1965.[14] For the bulk of the population, however, what matters most is the production of wage-goods within the industrial sector

---

devaluation in 1966 was rather small and the economy underwent fairly severe disturbances owing to exogenous factors such as the 1965-67 drought, it is difficult to reach very definite conclusions about the price-responsiveness of Indian exports during this period.

[12]See pp. 163f below.

[13]On shortfalls in targets, see Medhora (1968); numerous instances are also listed in the review documents for various plans and reports of the Lok Sabha Estimates Committee and the Committee on Public Undertakings. For review documents, see India, Planning Commission (1957), (1963) and (1971); for the Estimates Committee and the Committee on Public Undertakings, see the reports cited in n. 37 below.

[14]See pp. 49f, 67-9 above.

and of certain key inputs to agricultural production, especially fertilizers. As most manufactured wage-goods are processed commodities of agricultural origin, such as cotton textiles, sugar, vegetable oils, etc., their annual output shows considerable fluctuation, arising out of short-period fluctuations in agricultural production. Bearing this in mind, flour milling and sugar are the only consumer goods that have shown sustained growth over the period 1960-72. Output of vanaspati or hydrogenated oil showed little increase until 1969-70 but has since performed better, whereas production of mill-made cotton textiles, which forms the bulk of the output of manufactured cotton goods, has been considerably lower in the early 1970s than it was in 1960-61.[15] The figures for some of the basic industries are given in Table 35.

TABLE 35

INDEX OF PRODUCTION OF SELECTED CONSUMER GOODS INDUSTRIES (1960 = 100)

	1961	*1965*	*1969*	*1972**
Flour milling and grinding	100.7	127.6	185.9	284.0
Sugar refining	110.0	124 7	149.1	132.5
Vanaspati	100.4	127.1	142.7	178.8
Tea	111.6	114.1	108.1	140.4
Cigarettes	106.7	146.1	161.4	167.0
Cotton weaving	100.3	100.0	91.5	93.3

*1972 figures provisional.

SOURCE: Reserve Bank of India, *Report on Currency and Finance* (annual).

As it is a little problematical to decide, so to speak, *in vacuo*, what rate of growth of production of particular industries should be regarded as satisfactory, a clearer picture emerges from figures of the availability of certain manufactured goods of mass consumption. In interpreting these figures, the point has to be borne in mind that figures of availability per head of population offer a picture which is slightly biased. Where any particular good is scarce and it is consumed both by the poor and the relatively wealthy, it is a fairly safe bet that it is the consumption of the poor that will go by default. Anyway, of the commodities we

[15]India, Ministry of Finance, Survey (1973-74), p. 71.

have so far mentioned, only sugar shows any significant increase in *per capita* availability; vanaspati shows a small increase in absolute terms but a much larger one in proportion to the average level of consumption. Availability of edible oils and cotton cloth was lower in absolute terms in 1970-72 than it was in 1960-61. Add to this the fact that the basic wage-goods, cereals and pulses, were also both down during the same period.[16]

Two other characteristics of the behaviour of industrial production should also be noted. One is that employment in organized industry increased much less rapidly than output. Thus, between 1960 and 1965, industrial output increased roughly by 9 per cent per annum, whereas employment rose by about 6 per cent. Between 1965 and 1970, the increase in output over the whole period was of the order of 18.4 per cent, whereas employment increased by about 5.4 per cent.[17]

Secondly, the low level of industrial production went hand in hand with a low level of utilization of existing capacity in a number of key industries. While substantial underutilization of capacity is much better documented for the public sector industries, it is by no means confined to that sector.[18] There is very little reliable information about the degree of utilization of industrial capacity in India. A study carried out by USAID in India noted substantial degrees of excess capacity in industry. Similar conclusions are reached in a study by Satyanarayana for the years 1970 and 1971. Except for aluminium, copper, jeep vehicles and polyester fibres, almost all industries in the private sector showed under-capacity working. The level was as low as 14-15 per cent of capacity utilized for cement and coal mining machinery, while very few industries operated at much above 60 to 75 per cent of capacity.[19]

The phenomenon of unutilized capacity introduces us to a paradox in the Indian industrial sector. A large number of industries

[16]See p. 60 above.

[17]Mitra, A.K. (1974). The figures for the two sub-periods, before and after 1965, are not strictly comparable, because they use data from different sources. For each sub-period, there are differences in the behaviour of production between different industries. For an analysis of industrial production, see also Bose (1974).

[18]Little, Scitovsky and Scott (1970), pp. 93f, 208.

[19]Satyanarayana (1972).

give the shortage of inputs, including both raw materials and power, as the most frequent explanation of low levels of production. This indicates the existence of excess demand for a number of industrial products. There are no reliable statistical studies of the state of demand, but the impression is certainly borne out at the level of casual empiricism. While, on the face of it, a scarcity of inputs seems to be an adequate explanation of low levels of output for particular industries, it is obviously an unsatisfactory one for industries in general. This is because outputs of particular industries are the inputs of others. There are a number of non-tradeable inputs, such as hydro-electric power generation, where the shortages can be attributed in part to exogenous factors, such as persistence of severe drought in particular years. For most other inputs, imports can in principle be substituted for domestically produced inputs. To a certain extent, therefore, the shortfalls in industrial production can be attributed to the inability to finance an adequate level of maintenance imports or, in other words, to the balance of payments problem.[20] However, part of the latter problem is due to the inability to meet production targets in a number of key commodities, especially foodgrains, fertilizer and steel, thus completing a vicious circle.

The other major criticism of Indian industrialization that is most commonly voiced is that it is high-cost, with reference to the international prices of comparable commodities. It is argued that data relating to the proportion of total demand supplied through domestic production give too favourable a picture of import substitution, in so far as relatively cheaper imports are replaced with dearer domestic products. There are no direct cost comparisons of Indian and foreign manufactured goods, partly at least for the very good reason that there are major conceptual and practical problems in making such comparisons.[21] The studies that exist mostly

[20]One of the main reasons for underutilization of capacity is the lack of imports of intermediate goods. The significance of maintenance imports is pointed out in Reddaway (1962). In recent years demand, too, has become a problem.

[21]Such comparisons are most difficult for heterogeneous equipment, which may vary considerably in terms of specification and performance. More general problems are introduced by the existence of oligopolistic prices divorced from factor costs and by the fact that for more complicated

ignore some of these problems. Thus, the study by Baranson of a Cummins Diesel subsidiary in India mentions but takes little account of the fact that the Indian firm undertakes production under completely different circumstances.[22] A study of the automobile ancillary industry in India, which incidentally finds evidence of negative value added in the industry, also follows a similar methodology.[23]

The basic data on which the charge of high levels of cost rest come from studies of Indian tariff policy that have been undertaken recently. They show that much of Indian industry is subject to high degrees of effective protection and infer that the tariff structure has allowed a highly inefficient high-cost industrial structure to be built up in India.[24] Thus, in the study referred to, Bhagwati and Desai find levels of effective protection varying in the range of 80-100 per cent for the years 1961-62.[25] While not too much faith should be put on their precise figures, their basic finding that large parts of Indian industry have continued to remain profitable with very low levels of productivity is no doubt correct. It is less easy, however, to attribute this low level of productivity to specific causes.[26] No doubt it partly reflects the low level of factor productivity that defines, in a sense, the 'underdeveloped' nature of the economy. High costs have also been attributed to incorrect choice of technology that favours excessive use of scarce capital rather than relatively cheap labour. Management is prone to lay the blame on rising wages and labour troubles. There is no evidence that real wages have risen to any significant extent in India during this period, although it is true that frequent strikes and other labour problems are a significant cause of both low utilization of capacity and high industrial costs. On the other hand, there is evidence also of

---

capital goods there is often no unique international price, in spite of all the pious prescriptions of project evaluation manuals.

[22]Baranson (1967); Lal (1975).

[23]Krueger (1970).

[24]The most influential of these critiques has been Bhagwati and Desai (1970).

[25]*Op. cit.*, Ch. 17.

[26]It is arguable that one should lay less stress on the distorting effects of tariffs and more on the quantitative controls and the degree of excess demand that is generated by the existence of such controls.

inefficient management practices reflected in the choice of technology or product-mix, or faulty and inadequate maintenance of
plant leading to expensive shutdowns and production losses.[27]

Performance of Public Sector Industries

The development of a number of key industries within the public
sector is very central to Indian development strategy. These
industries cover mainly certain key inputs such as steel and fertilizers and various capital goods, such as heavy engineering and
electrical equipment, transport equipment and machine tools.
The rationale for such a policy was threefold. First, it was felt
that domestic capacity for the production of these goods was
vital to a rapid and sustained development of the economy.[28]
Moreover, these goods required the setting up of a large-scale,
highly capital-intensive and expensive investment in capacity with
long gestation and pay-off periods, and it was most unlikely that
these industries would be set up within the private sector. This
was certainly a view that was shared by the so-called industrial
bourgeoisie at the time of the inception of that policy.[29] The
decision to build up a public sector was not, however, to be in
the nature of a passive response to circumstances. It was felt
that public ownership would make it possible to shape industrial
policy more in accordance with social rather than private profitability.[30] Moreover, the Government was concerned with the
problem of concentration of power in industry as part of the
general problem of unequal distribution of wealth and saw the
development of the public sector as a countervailing power to
private monopoly.[31]

The performance of this public sector has come in for even
more criticism than private industry. Some are, indeed, likely to
attribute all of India's ills to her predilection towards a 'socialist
pattern' of industry. While enough has been said in the previous

[27]The experiences of the steel plants at Durgapur and Rourkela provide
some of the best examples.
[28]See Ch. 9 below.
[29]Weisskopf (1972), p. 7.
[30]Although the terminology of cost-benefit analysis had not yet come to
be applied to Indian planning at that time.
[31]The concept of countervailing power is developed in Galbraith (1957).

section to indicate that the picture of a highly efficient private sector raring to go if given its head is largely a myth, some attention must be given to the major criticisms of the performance of the public sector. While there is, indeed, much to be unsatisfied about in that performance, there is also a need to put part of the balance right.

During the plan period, there has been a substantial volume of investment in public sector industries. Thus, at the end of 1968-69, total investment in 85 public sector enterprises stood at Rs 3,902 crores at current prices.[32] During the first two plans, the share of the public sector in total investment had been of the order of 50 per cent; during the third and the fourth plan, this share was expected to rise to 60 per cent.[33] Given the fact that the share of the public sector in total capital stock in industry was estimated at around 33.7 per cent for all industry and 58.3 per cent for mining, manufacturing and transport, in 1965-66 the figures do not suggest that the public sector got an excessive share of total investment.[34] Of the Rs 3,902 crores, 33.4 per cent was in steel, 24.6 per cent in engineering, 10 to 11 per cent each in petroleum and chemicals and the rest in mining, transport and various other categories. Ten enterprises accounted for 72.6 per cent of all investment, the smallest of these being the Fertilizer Corporation of India with a share of 4.0 per cent of total investment. The point to note is that the lion's share in investment went to one industry, steel, and the performance of the public sector steel industry to a large extent influences the figures for the overall profitability and performance of the public sector.[35]

Criticisms of the performance of public sector enterprises can be grouped most conveniently into those relating to investment or creation of capacity and those relating to output or utilization of capacity.[36] On the investment side, the three major criticisms are that the actual costs of projects have by far exceeded the

[32]India, Bureau of Public Enterprises (1970).

[33]India, Ministry of Finance, Pocketbook (1970) pp. 259, 276. The plan documents probably underestimate the volume of private investment.

[34]Hazari and Ojha (1970).

[35]India, Bureau of Public Enterprises (1970).

[36]These are obviously not unrelated. The creation of capacity affects the flow of output and output performance influences the capacity to mobilize resources for further investment.

original estimates, that the projects have taken very much longer
to complete and bring into operation than originally planned and
that they have often embodied inappropriate technology or product-mix.[37] Cost-escalation has often been of the order of 10-15
to 80-90 per cent of the original estimate, and has been particularly noticeable for such projects as the Bokaro steel complex.[38]
Projects 18 months to 2 years behind schedule are by no means
untypical.[39] Inappropriate product-mix and plant-mix have been
criticized for the drugs project at Pimpri and for the machine tool
industry.[40] Each of these shortcomings has in turn affected both
levels of costs of production and the ability of the public sector
to generate a flow of reinvestible surplus. The latter factor has had
particularly damaging effects on the ability of the economy to
generate an adequate flow of investible resources.

Undoubtedly, faulty investment planning and project appraisal
have been responsible for some of these shortcomings. What is
less appreciated is the fact that these defects are partly due to the
problems of having to finance these projects through foreign aid.
There are two major causes of cost escalation. One is last-minute
changes in project design. Sometimes this has been due to a bela-
ted realization that the product-mix that was chosen originally
was inappropriate to Indian market conditions. This in turn has
required expensive modifications to plant.[41] Sometimes it has been
due, however, to the need to add vital parts to the plant which
had not been included in the original contract.[42] The other major
cause of cost escalation is simply a result of the lag in starting or
finishing a project, which lands the project with higher costs due
to inflation in supplier countries. While some of these problems
arise from the Indian side, so to speak, for many others it is the
aid-relationship which is to blame. Very often, aid contracts have

---

[37]On the performance of particular public sector plants, see Lok Sabha
Estimates Committee (1968) and Lok Sabha Committee on Public Undertakings (1965), (1965a), (1966), (1966a), (1966b), (1968), (1968a) (1968b), and
(1968-69).

[38]Desai (1972).

[39]Reserve Bank of India Bulletin (1968a).

[40]On the drugs industry, see Lok Sabha, CPU (1966), and (1968b);
on machine tool industry, see Mathur, Valavade and Kirloskar (1967).

[41]See the reference cited in n. 40 above, for the drugs industry.

[42]Lok Sabha, CPU (1965a).

taken much longer to complete than originally thought. A classic example of this is Bokaro, where the project was considerably delayed owing to the American decision not to finance the project after prolonged negotiations.[43]

Another major cause of cost escalation has been due to the escalation in prices charged for plant and equipment by suppliers in donor countries, under the now familiar practices of tied-aid.[44] Given the strategic decision to finance a capital goods sector through foreign aid, at least some of the shortcomings of the public sector investment plans have followed more or less directly from that decision.[45]

On the operational side, there are two criticisms of fundamental importance. One is that public sector industries have failed to make profits and have in fact accumulated substantial losses over the years. As a consequence, instead of being a source of reinvestible surplus, they have become a source of negative saving in the economy.[46] Secondly, public sector plants have suffered heavily from low levels of capacity utilization and have thus failed to utilize optimally scarce capital resources of the economy. In addition, there are a number of specific criticisms, such as overmanning of public sector plants, bad labour relations leading to frequent strikes and closures, and excessive levels of inventories.[47]

[43]Desai (1972); on the problems of negotiations and the delays involved, see also Kapoor (1970).

[44]On the costs of aid-tying, see the references cited in nn. 47 and 54 to Ch. 4; see also Datar (1972).

[45]Aid obviously confers some benefit, because it is unlikely that at that time India possessed either the capital goods capacity or the technology to undertake the building-up of an industrial sector without foreign aid. The point is quite simply that the net benefits of aid were considerably smaller than the apparent benefits.

[46]See pp. 159-60 below.

[47]Labour problems have been particularly acute in the Hindustan steel plant at Durgapur; on high levels of inventories and overmanning, see Lok Sabha Estimates Committee (1968). Under the present regulations, if a new factory is built on what is called a 'green fields' site, the enterprise has to take any displaced agricultural workers and peasants on to the labour force, irrespective of requirements or suitability. It was said by one of the managers of such a plant that it would often be cheaper to the company to pay such people gratuities equivalent to the wage, rather than having to employ them in the factory. A classic case of diminishing returns.

However, these are largely relevant because they in turn affect the rate of utilization of plant capacity and the profitability of the enterprises.

Given that the scale of investment in public sector plants is typically large and that the technology they embody is highly capital-intensive, it is clear that the rate of utilization of capacity is likely to have a significant effect on the net profitability of the enterprise. The two major criticisms are, therefore, not unrelated. It is also clear that they are both fully justified. The net profitability position of the ten major public sector enterprises by size of investment is shown in Table 36, for the period 1959-60 to 1968-69. It will be noticed that the statement that the public sector enterprises have failed to make a profit needs to be qualified in two ways. One is that a very substantial part of the total losses arises from the operation of a small number of enterprises, mainly steel and heavy machinery, especially the former. As steel embodies the bulk of the investment, this does not alter our major conclusion that large-scale investment in public sector industry has by and large failed to generate a flow of investible resources. However, it is worth noting that a number of public sector plants have been able to make a profit, suggesting that the management of public sector enterprises has not been uniformly bad.[48]

I have pointed out earlier that lack of profitability was partly the result of a low rate of utilization of capacity. In 1970, the rate of utilization of capacity in the three public sector steel plants that were then operational was as follows: Bhilai—65 per cent; Rourkela—48 per cent; Durgapur—30 per cent.[49] By comparison, the utilization rate in the two private sector plants were: TISCO—65 per cent and IISCO—58 per cent.[50] At a time when there was a grave shortage of fertilizers in India and imports of fertilizers were costing large sums in scarce foreign exchange, the rate of capacity-utilization in the fertilizer plants was of the order of 65 per cent.[51] In 1969-70, the rate of capacity utilization in some of

[48]India, Bureau of Public Enterprises (1970).

[49]The main problem in Rourkela was plant breakdown; in Durgapur, it was labour trouble.

[50]TISCO—Tata Iron and Steel Company; IISCO—Indian Iron and Steel Company, which has since been nationalized; for capacity utilization, see Satyanarayana (1972).

[51]Satyanarayana (1972).

TABLE 36
PROFITABILITY OF SELECTED PUBLIC SECTOR
ENTERPRISES—1959-60 to 1968-69
(Rs million)

	Investment	Net profit
Hindustan Steel	11,226	—1,409.5
Fertilizer Corporation of India	2,127	119.9
Neyveli Lignite Corporation	1,809	—163.8
Bokaro Steel*	1,800	——
Heavy Engineering Corporation	1,796	—333.2
Indian Oil Corporation	1,723	403.0
National Coal Development Corporation	1,703	4.7
Bharat Heavy Electricals	1,270	—74.1
Hindustan Aeronautics	957	72.8
Heavy Electricals (India)	698	—229.5
Indian Drugs and Pharmaceuticals	508	—119.9
Hindustan Machine Tools	353	107.9

*Not operative.
SOURCE: India, Ministry of Finance, Bureau of Public Enterprises, *Handbook of Information on Public Sector Enterprises* (annual).

the major public sector plants was as follows: Heavy Engineering Corporation—mechanical items 17 per cent, castings and forgings 61 per cent; Bharat Earthmovers—93 per cent; Instrumentation Ltd—6 per cent. In 1968-69, the various units of Heavy Electricals Ltd were operating between 33 and 94 per cent, three out of four operating below 60 per cent; Bharat Heavy Electricals were operating below 30 per cent and Hindustan Machine Tools below 50 per cent.[52]

A major reason given by the Government for choosing to invest in a small number of centralized large plants had been the lower long-run average costs that would result from such a choice. However, such low operating costs could only be realized if plants could be operated efficiently under Indian conditions at somewhere near full capacity. With the benefit of hindsight, we can see that that decision had gone badly awry. The economy has been saddled with heavy investment costs without the realization of the anticipated benefits of low average costs of production. The capital structure chosen has turned out to be 'too deep'.

[52]India, Bureau of Public Enterprises (1969, 1970).

There is no doubt that the management of the public sector industries leaves much to be desired. In my view, too much emphasis has been laid on the problems facing these industries on the supply side. The extent to which these problems are a direct consequence of some basic inconsistencies in the economic policies followed by the Government has been largely overlooked.

In order to develop this point of view, we need to disaggregate public sector industries into three groups. First, there are some industries which provide an output largely consumed in the private sector. These are e.g. railways, power, and also major irrigation. Secondly, there are capital goods which are produced in the public sector but the demand for which originates largely in the private sector, being geared largely to either the rate of growth of industrial output or the overall rate of investment in the economy. These are e.g. railway wagons, electrical machinery, coal mining machinery or machine tools, as well as such intermediate goods as steel. Thirdly, there are the so-called products of heavy industries, exemplified by the products of such enterprises as Bharat Heavy Electricals or the Heavy Engineering Corporation, the demand for whose products is largely a function of the level of development expenditure within the plans and the rate of investment in the public sector.

As far as the first group of industries is concerned, the Government has for a long time charged too low prices for these inputs. This systematic underpricing has acted as a direct subsidy to the private sector, at the expense of profits and savings in the public sector.[53] The fact that, as we noticed in Chapter 4, there has been a net transfer of savings from the private to the public sector has to be qualified by the worsening of the terms of trade between the public and the private sector. The argument that is sometimes advanced that state capitalism in India is a covert means of boosting the profitability of private sector industries is largely applicable to the products of these industries.[54]

The low profitability of the capital goods industries in the public sector is due in part to the high level of excess capacity generated

---

[53]Irrigation is an example. It is an activity carried out by the state governments and most of them make losses on this account. See India, Planning Commission (1969), p. 258.

[54]Bagchi (1970).

in these industries. As far as the second group of industries is concerned, the low level of demand is in part a reflection of the low rate of growth of industrial production and the low levels of industrial investment in the economy since the middle 1960s. The argument developed by Amiya Bagchi, that the inability of the Government to influence the allocation of resources in a mixed economy away from luxury consumption has acted as a constraint on the rate of investment, and hence the long-run growth of the economy, is most strongly applicable to this group of industries. As demand for the products of these industries originates in the private sector it follows that the Government can only influence such demand indirectly.[55] That argument, however, is not applicable to those public sector industries which are suppliers of investible inputs to the public sector itself.

It is this third group of industries which absorbs the major part of total investment in the public sector, assuming that the public sector is also a major purchaser of steel products.[56] The rate of profit in these industries is highly sensitive to the rate of utilization of capacity, given the high ratio of fixed to variable costs. As the public sector is the main purchaser of the output of these industries, to a certain extent it is possible for the Government to maintain an adequate level of demand for these products, without facing some of the problems raised by Bagchi. It is the Government's inability to maintain a high rate of public investment and its tendency to shift its pattern of expenditure away from development-oriented projects that has had adverse effects on the profitability of these enterprises. Economic policy, in this respect, has been destabilizing. Inability to raise enough investible resources has led the Government to retrench. Moreover, political expediency and the lack of any clear economic strategy since the middle 1960s has led the Government to cut down on development rather than non-development expenditure. This in turn has caused larger losses to be generated by the public sector industries, resulting in lower levels of resource mobilization in the public sector. The Government has been caught in a trap of its

[55]Bagchi (1970); Bose (1974).

[56]There are no detailed figures for the proportion of steel output that is absorbed by the public sector. India, Ministry of Steel (1963) suggests that this is a reasonable assumption.

own making and has compounded the inefficiencies that have been caused by poor economic management.[57]

Foreign Capital and Technology

India has received foreign resources in the form of official aid as well as private foreign capital. In addition, she has acquired foreign technology, either embodied in capital goods or through the acquisition of licences or foreign collaboration agreements.[58] Foreign technology can be seen in analytical terms as an input which enables the recipient country to improve the productivity of its own resources.[59] In Chapter 4, I have discussed at some length the impact of official aid on the economy. I shall, therefore, confine myself in this section largely to the role of private foreign capital. To refresh our memory, we might note again the main conclusions of our discussion on foreign aid. These were that the actual amount of net aid received has been very much smaller than the nominal amount of aid and that while aid has had some positive impact on the economy, especially by financing the import content of manufacturing investment, considerable costs have attached to most official aid.[60]

There exists a lively polemical literature on Indian industrialization as a case-study in 'neo-colonial' or 'dependent' forms of industrial development.[61] I intend to confine myself here to a summary of the more important, observable phenomena of private investment, although the way I present the facts will no doubt make clear my own approach to this debate.[62] While some eco-

[57]The draft on savings by the public sector, referred to on p. 80 above, has to be qualified by the fact that the terms of trade are sometimes biased against the public sector.

[58]An agreement for a licence to manufacture certain commodities may include an agreement to import some capital equipment.

[59]Through different and superior combinations of inputs through technologies not known or available to the domestic entrepreneurs. It has to be borne in mind that there are institutional constraints in the form of patents etc. which restrict the use of already known technologies. See Penrose (1973).

[60]See p. 95f above.

[61]One of the best is Kidron (1965), which is also well-documented and carries the story on to the mid-1960s; see also the references cited in n. 7 above.

[62]I think the analysis of the effects of foreign investment by the above authors is substantially correct. The only point of difference is that I am

nomists, such as Chandra or Chattopadhyay, have covered the effects of both aid and private investment on the economy, much of what they have to say is more applicable to the latter.[63] I shall, therefore, not be presenting a very distorted view of the problem, even if my conclusions might not be acceptable to the authors I quote.

Generally, the point made against private investment is that it has had a harmful effect on Indian development, in the sense that the costs of private investment to the economy have been relatively large in relation to the benefits. The costs are seen to have arisen in two rather distinct ways. First, it is felt that the net flow of foreign resources that the economy has received has been small or even negative. A special case of this argument is that foreign firms have charged too high prices for technology or have sold inappropriate technology. Secondly, it is felt that private investment has distorted the pattern of industrial development in India. This in turn is seen to have arisen in two ways. Foreign investment has gone into sectors where the private rates of return are high but which from the social point of view should have low priority.[64] This in turn arises out of an unequal distribution of income and wealth in India. As foreign capital is not a free good and is complementary to other scarce domestic factors such as skilled labour or management, a diversion to low priority sectors imposes a cost upon the economy.[65] In addition, it is felt that foreign ownership of industrial capital has reduced the degree of indigenous control over the future pattern of development of the economy. There are sufficient data available to us to elaborate some of these criticisms, though not to put them to very rigorous tests.

The first point to make is that to put the question of private investment in the context of the overall development of the economy is to give it excessive importance. To discuss the issues of

---

inclined to discuss the effects in terms of the process of industrialization in India, rather than of the economic growth of the country as a whole.

[63]Such as the argument that private foreign investment tends to create monopolies in the profitable sectors.

[64]Bagchi (1970).

[65]It is a common experience in poor countries, large and small, that the public sector has increasing difficulty in recruiting and keeping the more able skilled people.

'neo-colonialism' or 'dependency' in the same terms for India as for the Caribbean or the Fiji Islands does violence to both commonsense and economic analysis. As we have noted earlier, even official aid is a very small percentage of net national product.[66] In addition, while the average inflow of foreign aid was of the order of Rs 3,122.7 million over the period 1956-69, the rate of inflow of private capital was roughly of the order of Rs 330 million for the same period.[67] It is unlikely that flows of that magnitude could dominate the overall pattern of growth of the economy.

It makes a great deal more sense, however, to put the question in the context of Indian industrial development, stressing the fact that the importance of the industrial sector as a supplier of a number of strategic inputs, such as capital goods or fertilizers, is more than is indicated by its share in GNP. It is the strategic importance of the industrial sector that gives relevance to the issue of foreign capital in India, rather than the somewhat ingenuous argument that the quantitative importance of foreign capital should be measured by leaving out of consideration the main wage-goods producing sector of the economy.[68] As far as the industrial sector is concerned, the relative importance of foreign capital is very much larger, especially for the organized sector. Thus, the total paid-up share capital of rupee companies quoted on the main stock exchange in India on 31 March 1972 was Rs 15,055.3 million in book-value. For 31 March 1971, the comparable figure for 200 branches and 492 foreign controlled rupee companies was Rs 6,348.7 million; that is to say of the order of 42.2 per cent.[69] It is quite clear that as far as the industrial sector is concerned, foreign investment is quantitatively a very significant factor.[70]

[66]See p. 104 above.

[67]My estimation of foreign aid is lower than that of Chandra, who calculates it to be of the order of Rs 3,886.9 million. It is possible that the higher estimate is due to Chandra's taking the rupee value of aid, which overestimates the resource flow for the post-devaluation period; Chaudhuri (1974), Chandra (1973).

[68]This is the position adopted by Bettelheim (1968), p. 58.

[69]Two points should be noted. The market value of shares can be different from the book-value of share capital as quoted in accounts. Gross assets are a better measure of the amount of capital controlled by a company than share capital.

[70]Foreign investment refers to the flow of capital, while the share

The data show that private investment increased very rapidly during the period 1951-70. In describing the pattern of this growth, I shall confine myself to foreign direct investment, as being strategically the more important part of capital flow. It has to be borne in mind that foreign capital is also tied up in banking and other financial institutions, so that direct investment accounts only for a part of total private investment.[71] In comparing capital flows over a period of time or in comparing the behaviour of foreign to domestic capital, a number of problems have to be faced. Unfortunately, within the present boundaries of our knowledge, it is not possible to resolve these problems satisfactorily and none of the contributors to this debate has done so. Book-value of capital invested is not a satisfactory measure of total investment, which should include also profits reinvested within the corporate sector. In addition, firms may have access to credit, which increases their command over resources, without increasing the amount of capital they own. In India, substantial amounts of funds have been advanced to the corporate sector by banking and other financial institutions.[72] Moreover, changes in the price level also add a spurious growth element to figures of capital invested over a period of time.

Most of these criticisms would apply to both domestic and foreign capital. However, as there is no reason to believe that these factors would affect these two magnitudes in a uniform way or that they would bias the result in any particular direction, it is not easy to see how we should take account of them. Equally, on the side of profits earned, there is now a considerable volume of evidence that foreign firms find various ways of disguising real profits, through such practices as transfer pricing.[73] Equally, however, it is widely believed that domestic firms underestimate their profits, to reduce their tax liabilities. In what follows, we should do well to bear these limitations in mind.

---

capital measures the stock, Ideally, one should compare the former to the new domestic capital raised by the private sector.

[71]The Reserve Bank of India studies quoted in the text exclude banking and financial capital. Some of the studies also do not distinguish between majority and minority holdings, except Reserve Bank of India (1968) and (June 1974).

[72]Kidron (1965) and Ghandhi (1972).

[73]Lall (1973), Vaitsos (1974).

In 1955, foreign direct investment stood at Rs 3,865 million, of which Rs 2,431 million was invested in branches and Rs 1,434 million in FCRCs. In 1968, total investment was Rs 7,012 million, of which Rs 4,421 million was in FCRCs. The proportion invested in branches had fallen from 67 to 33 per cent roughly, and the total volume of investment in them had risen but little. Investment in FCRCs had, thus, risen by 71 per cent in 13 years.[74] The sectoral distribution of private investment is also different for branches and FCRCs. Thus in 1968, about 41 per cent of branch investment was in plantations and about 23 per cent each in petroleum and services. In contrast, 74 per cent of FCRC investment was in manufacturing, 34.7 per cent being in metals and chemicals and about 15 per cent in petroleum. Comparing 1955 with 1968, the share of investment in plantations for branches had gone up by about 7 per cent, while the petroleum share had fallen by about 11 per cent. For FCRCs, the share of manufacturing had gone up by a little less than 20 per cent, mainly at the expense of services, whose share had fallen by a corresponding amount.[75] For the period 1967-68 to 1970-71, FCRCs earned rates of profit on sales of around 12 per cent, as compared to 3 to 5 per cent for foreign branches and 7 per cent for Indian companies. Rates of profit on total capital employed raise the profitability of FCRCs and Indian companies by about 2 and 1 per cent respectively, while the profits of branches are raised significantly. However, the ranking between the three groups remains unaltered.[76]

A more detailed study by the Reserve Bank of India covers the performance of FCRCs, which are both the more important and the faster growing sector of foreign controlled enterprises.[77] The survey covers both direct investment and technical collaboration, being based on a sample of 630 FCRCs and 247 companies involved in pure technical collaboration. It also provides us with useful additional information by distinguishing between the per-

[74]Chandra (1973), p. 231; Weisskopf (1972) gives a higher estimate.

[75]Calculated from Chandra (1973), Table 4, p. 231.

[76]Reserve Bank of India *Bulletin* (May 1972), (October 1973); both rates of profit and capital formation fluctuate from year to year; in some ways the rate of profit on sales is a better measure than the rate of profit on capital, because the former is more reliable.

[77]Reserve Bank of India (June 1974); for the earlier period see Reserve Bank of India (1969).

formance of foreign subsidiaries and those companies where foreign investors had a minority holding.

In 1964-65, the ordinary share capital of the 630 FCRCs amounted to Rs 1,322 million, of which about 64 per cent was in subsidiaries. By 1969-70, the total investment so measured had risen to Rs 189.5 million, the share of subsidiaries being 62 per cent. It is, therefore, clear that the substantial part of foreign private capital comes under majority control, in spite of the Government's policy towards encouraging minority participation.[78] The bulk of the capital so invested came from the UK with the USA a long way behind, although the US share was rising. About 77 per cent of investment in 1964-65 was in manufacturing; in 1969-70, the proportion had risen to 82 per cent. In manufacturing, about a third of the investment was in chemical companies, 'the companies which attracted foreign capital most were those manufacturing paints and varnishes, soap, cosmetics and toilet and beauty preparations'.[79] In addition, about 11 per cent of total investment in that year was in petroleum. Together, about as much was invested in food, beverages and tobacco, stationery and office equipment and rubber goods as in transport equipment, machinery and metals and metal products.

This hardly gives the impression that foreign investment always went to priority sectors or went to fill foreign exchange gaps which would have caused key shortages. It is interesting to compare in this respect the sectoral contribution of foreign aid. Of the total amount of project aid received during 1956-70, 0.9 per cent went into consumer goods industries. Of the rest, 27.7 per cent went into steel capacity, 11.5 per cent into heavy machinery, over 20 per cent each into transport and power (including irrigation) and 4 per cent into fertilizers. Over the same period, 56 per cent of non-project aid was disbursed on industrial inputs and capital goods, 6.4 per cent on fertilizers and only 1.4 per cent on consumer goods machinery for producing consumer goods.[80] One hardly gets the

[78]Reserve Bank of India (June 1974), p. 1046; the share of the group where control by the foreign collaborator was between 50 to 73.9 per cent went up, while that for 100 per cent went down. As full control is hardly necessary for effective control, it is not likely that the degree of domestic control increased during this period.

[79]*Op. cit.*, p. 1047.

[80]Chaudhuri (1974).

picture of a profligate public sector winkling away resources from more productive use in the private sector.

Of the major sectors, the relative importance of foreign capital was the most pronounced in petroleum, for both subsidiaries and minority companies, although the share was naturally lower for the latter.[81] For subsidiaries, next in order of importance came the food industries, textiles and pharmaceuticals. For minority companies, the major sectors after petroleum were chemicals and metals and machinery.[82] The importance of foreign capital in these sectors has been noticed by Kidron, Lall and Tanzer amongst others;[83] Kidron has also drawn attention to the important fact that a number of foreign firms involved in investment in India were large multinational firms.[84]

In 1964-65, gross profits of both types of companies amounted to Rs 1,889 million, rising to Rs 3,491 million in 1969-70. In absolute terms, gross profits were largest in chemicals, especially in medicines and pharmaceuticals. They were followed in 1969-70 by food, beverages and tobacco, rubber and electrical goods and metal products.[85] The rate of profit on capital, in terms of gross profits as a percentage of total capital employed, was around 16 per cent for subsidiaries and only around 9 per cent for minority companies. There has been little change in these rates during the 1960s.[86] Profit rates were higher than the average for subsidiaries involved in plantations and manufacturing for the period 1964-70, being around 17 per cent. Among manufacturing industries, profits were highest for pharmaceuticals, textiles, rubber goods and the food industries.[87] As we have noticed earlier, these rates were also much higher than those earned by Indian companies. For minority companies, the most profitable sector is petroleum.[88]

There is no specific evidence to tell us whether the observed

[81]Of the subsidiaries, 98.2 per cent of foreign capital was in petroleum; for minority companies, the corresponding ration is 49.8 per cent. Reserve Bank of India (June 1974).

[82]*Op. cit.*, p. 1047.

[83]Kidron (1965), Lall (1974), Tanzer (1969).

[84]Kidron (1965), Ch. 6.

[85]Reserve Bank of India (June 1974), p. 1048.

[86]These are the average figures; as explained earlier, the annual rates sometimes fluctuate quite significantly.

[87]*Op. cit.*, p. 1049.

[88]*Op. cit.*, p. 1049.

high rates of profit were due to higher levels of productivity of foreign subsidiaries or to oligopolistic factors. A study quoted by the Reserve Bank survey indicates that the ratio of net value added per unit of labour and capital costs is not uniformly higher for foreign than for Indian firms. Moreover, Lall and Tanzer have argued fairly strongly that high rates of profit realized in the pharmaceuticals and the petroleum industries are not due to either genuine productivity advantages or a return on higher degrees of risk. Putting these bits together, one builds up a fairly strong presumption that foreign firms are able to exploit a semi-monopolistic position to earn higher rates of profit.

One of the criticisms that has been laid against foreign companies is that they repatriate a substantial amount of their profits abroad, thereby reducing the proportion of profits reinvested, as well as adding to an outflow of foreign exchange. In 1964-65, foreign subsidiaries earned total net profits of Rs 412 million, of which 61.4 per cent was distributed. The corresponding volume of net profits for 1969-70 was Rs 755 million and the rate of distribution was a little lower at 55.1 per cent.[89] The comparable rates of distribution of profits for minority companies were 61.5 per cent for 1964-65 and 44.3 per cent for 1969-70.[90] Thus, there is substance in the charge that much less than half of profits earned were ploughed back into investment for cost reduction or expansion. Given that throughout this period foreign capital was flowing into India, that old chestnut that political uncertainty or talk of socialism was keeping the rate of reinvestment low will hardly suffice. It is possible, however, that a fairly prolonged industrial recession and a lack of any cohesive government strategy towards development discouraged the ploughing back of profits by both domestic and foreign firms.

The figures for profits repatriated were Rs 203 million for 1964-65 and Rs 299 million for 1969-70.[91] That is to say, 43 to 47 per cent of distributed profits was repatriated. Although these are not high figures, one should bear in mind that throughout the period

[89]*Op. cit.*, p. 1051.

[90]*Op. cit.*, p. 1052.

[91]*Op. cit.*, p. 1054; for the purpose of comparison, we can note that the balance of payments deficits for 1964-65 and 1969-70 were of the order of Rs 8,000 and Rs 3,000 million respectively.

there were official restrictions on the repatriation of profits.[92] As we have seen before, gross inflow of private capital was around an annual average of Rs 330 million during 1955-70. Taking account of capital outflows, the net inflow is reduced to around Rs 80 million from 1964 to the end of the 1960s.[93] Deducting an average level of dividend remittance of Rs 240 million during 1964-70, we are left with a substantial net outflow of foreign exchange from India.

This is, of course, a familiar problem with foreign private investment, as well as with official aid, that has been remarked upon by MacDougall and others. Given that profit earned and remitted relates to the total stock of foreign capital, it requires an increasing gross inflow of new investment to maintain a net inflow of foreign exchange over a period of time. In this case, there is the problem of an increasing proportion of the total capital stock becoming foreign-owned, if the post-tax rate of profit is higher than the rate of growth of capital stock in the economy.[94] It is worth noting in passing that dividend remittances as a percentage of net worth for foreign companies were around 3.7 per cent for minority holdings and 6.2 per cent for subsidiaries.[95] For subsidiaries, the highest rates of dividend remitted as a percentage of net worth were in pharmaceuticals, petroleum, textiles and rubber goods.[96] For minority companies, the highest rates were in petroleum, food and textiles.[97]

If this is the position regarding repatriation of profits, it might be asked whether the activities of foreign companies provided a partial balance of payments offset through exporting parts of the output they produced. On *a priori* grounds, it might be thought that they would have shared in the growth of exports of manufact-

[92]Profits may, of course, be channelled out through unofficial channels.

[93]Chandra (1973); this excludes retained earnings, which must be added on if we want an estimate of total profits accruing under foreign ownership.

[94]For a lucid statement of this problem, see Macdougall (1958).

[95]Reserve Bank of India (June 1974), p. 1055.

[96]The rates for the subsidiaries were as follows: pharmaceuticals=9.2 per cent; petroleum=8.9 per cent; textiles=9.6 per cent; rubber goods=8.7 per cent.

[97]The rates for minority holdings companies were: petroleum=9.2 per cent; food products=4.7 per cent; textiles=4.0 per cent. Figures quoted in nn. 96 and 97 are from the Reserve Bank study quoted throughout.

ured engineering and other goods, especially if they were more efficient or produced better quality goods than domestic firms. On the other hand, as one of the major reasons for foreign investment is to get across a protection barrier into a large domestic market, the incentive to export must be low. On balance, it turns out that the foreign firms imported a much larger volume of goods as inputs than they exported as output. Over the period 1964-65 to 1969-70, the excess of imports over exports amounted to Rs 14,411 million or roughly US $1,921 million.[98] At the same time, total merchandise imports were running at a rate of over US $2,000 per year.[99] Overall, the data bear out the conclusion reached by Raj that foreign private investment imposes a higher balance of payments cost on the economy than foreign aid.[100]

Another way in which foreign companies have been involved in Indian economic development is through the transfer of technology. It is not possible to quantify these benefits. It is also not easy to generalize about the quality of the technology that is bought. It is difficult, therefore, to determine whether India has paid too high prices for imported technology except for specific cases. While it might be possible to argue that technology imported from developed countries may be technically superior, it is by no means clear that it is also more economic. The main reason for this is that imported technology mirrors a response to an entirely different condition of factor scarcity than obtains in most poor countries, and thus tends to be more labour-saving than capital-saving.[101] The following discussion, therefore, is more an attempt to highlight some of the basic features of the process of transfer rather than an evaluation of its costs and benefits to India.[102]

Between 1964 and 1970, the number of collaboration agreements involving technical knowhow was 1,098, of which 442 were pure collaboration agreements.[103] Of the latter, 62 per cent were

[98]Reserve Bank of India (June 1974), p. 1065.

[99]See Table 19, p. 72 above.

[100]Raj (1965).

[101]For a discussion of some of the problems, see *Journal of Development Studies* (October 1972).

[102]Much useful information is contained in NCAER (1971) and Reserve Bank of India (1968) and (June 1974).

[103]See the two Reserve Bank studies quoted in n. 102.

with the UK, the USA and West Germany. Almost all the agreements related to manufacturing industries, most of them being in machinery, electrical goods and metal industries. The number of companies involved was 620.[104] The bulk of the agreements were with medium-sized firms, involving sales of less than Rs 50 million per year, rather than with the largest companies.[105]

Technical knowhow is transferred either under licences for the use of patents, brand names, etc., or as technical services for help in construction of plant or production layouts, etc. In the first case, payments take the form of royalties; in the latter, of technical fees. A particular agreement may, of course, involve an element of both factors and be paid for under two heads. It is also worth noting that quite often, especially in transactions involving capital goods, technical knowhow is sold embodied in capital goods rather than in its pure form, so to speak. For a country like India, which has a considerable amount of unused industrial capacity in capital goods industries but might lack a particular knowhow, this acts as a constraint. It is also worth noting that the market for technology is highly imperfect. This may be due to various factors, such as legal restrictions in the form of patents or the oligopolistic structure of industry.[106]

During the years 1964-70, India paid Rs 285 million in royalty payments and Rs 284 million in technical fees. In addition, she paid Rs 173 million in payments to foreign technicians.[107] This makes a total foreign exchange payment of Rs 742 million over a period of six years. The bulk of the royalties and technical fees was paid by private sector firms, while the government sector was the chief source of technicians' fees. Industry-wise, the highest share of royalties went to transport equipment, electrical goods, rubber goods, pharmaceuticals and machinery, which together accounted for Rs 223 million. For technical fees, the major buyers were the following industries: basic industrial chemicals, metal industries, rubber goods and electricals. They together accounted for Rs 176 million. If we take dividend remittances,

---

[104]Reserve Bank of India (June 1974), p. 1044f.

[105]NCAER (1971); medium-sized firms are obviously also more numerous than large firms.

[106]On the role of patents, see Penrose (1973).

[107]Reserve Bank of India (June 1974), p. 1057f; these figures cover FCRCs also.

royalty and technical fees, the total foreign exchange payment for 1964-70 amounted to Rs 2,021 million, of which 54 per cent accrued to petroleum, chemicals and rubber goods and another 23 per cent to transport equipment, metals and electrical goods.[108] To this, we shall have to add another Rs 649 million for technical fees and interest on foreign loans obtained by private sector industries, for which we do not have an industrial breakdown.[109]

Most technical agreements were for durations of up to 10 years and most conferred exclusive rights to use on the purchaser. On the other hand, most agreements had some restrictive clauses attached to them. The restrictive clause that concerns us most is one which imposes some restriction on exports to third-country markets. This might vary from total prohibition for a period to one where the agreement of the seller of technology had to be obtained; mostly the restrictions were of the latter type. Out of 1,098 agreements, 956 had export restriction clauses attached, most of them relating to machinery and electrical goods. In spite of the professed policy of the Government to the contrary, the proportion of agreements carrying restrictive clauses had actually risen from 50 per cent during 1960-64 to about 60 per cent during 1964-70.[110]

It was said earlier that the policy of the Government towards private foreign capital has been ambiguous and that towards technology, ill-informed.[111] Is it possible to substantiate these charges? That would depend on one's interpretation of what constitutes proof beyond reasonable doubt; as in many other cases, the data are perhaps fragmentary and suggestive rather than comprehensive and conclusive. The policy of the Government towards foreign capital has certainly changed in the course of time but that is neither surprising nor is it necessarily a bad thing.[112] Its basic policy can be said to have been that private foreign capital had a role to play in promoting development but that that role should be a diminishing one, that it should be strictly controlled by government policy and that it should conform to plan priorities.

We have enough data to indicate that none of these assump-

---

[108]*Op. cit.*, p. 1060.
[109]Excluding technical assistance under foreign aid.
[110]*Op. cit.*, p. 1069.
[111]See p. 149 above.
[112]For an account of Government policy, see Weisskopf (1972) *passim.*

tions has been borne out in practice. The flow of foreign capital has not diminished, it still controls a very substantial part of the industrial sector and it has not gone primarily into those sectors which can be said to be priority sectors. As one should not have too many things both ways, I should point out that by the same token it would be somewhat disingenuous to suggest that foreign capital has lain siege to the commanding heights of the economy. Its main 'cost' to the economy, other than as a net outflow of foreign exchange, has been the diversion of scarce domestic resources into lines of production that satisfy the wants of a limited part of the relatively rich urban population.

It is hard to escape the conclusion that, faced with an acute balance of payments situation in the short run, the Government has found it difficult to turn away from a continued dependency on foreign capital. Moreover, much that is said about the profitability of foreign investment and its attitude towards profit repatriation and reinvestment turns out to be valid, especially if it is put against a growing volume of evidence about the impact of foreign capital on developing countries.[113] On the other hand, the impact of foreign capital is largely limited to the industrial sector. To attribute the continued grinding poverty of millions of Indians to 'neo-colonialism' engendered by foreign capital is to distort its importance out of scale.

A matter of greater concern from the point of view of long-run growth and structural change in the economy is the continued dependency of the economy on imported technology. This is a cause for concern because there is ample evidence that imported technology is not necessarily suited to either relative scarcities of resources in India or to the stage of development of Indian industry. For example, imported plant and equipment require infrastructural support or a network of sub-contracting or complementary industries which is simply non-existent in India and whose absence in turn reduces the efficiency of the expensive imported technology.[114] Moreover, payment for imported technology often implies a payment for 'good looks', so to speak, rather than functional efficiency of the imported equipment. A poor country can

[113]On the role of multinational companies in developing countries, see *inter alia* Dunning (1971).
[114]Baranson (1967).

ill afford such payments.[115]

On the other hand, as pointed out in the Reserve Bank survey, the amount of research and development activity in domestic firms is very small and is grossly inadequate in such critical areas as industrial plant design. This lack of indigenous knowhow also makes it quite impossible for the Government to negotiate effectively with foreign investors or foreign suppliers of technology. In my view, Warren is right to draw attention to the growing political power of the industrial bourgeoisie in poor countries; these countries today suffer at least as much from ignorance as from a weak bargaining position.[116] The cost to the economy of the latter shortcoming has certainly been very substantial in the past. However, the Government has hardly done much in the past to encourage what little domestic development there has been in these areas, witness its treatment of Dasturco over the Bokaro negotiations or its more recent treatment of the Fertilizer Corporation of India.[117] The Government's distrust of the indigenous bourgeoisie is certainly greater than its distrust of foreign capitalists.[118]

[115]There is no evidence that the Hindustan steel plant at Bhilai, which is supposed to be less modern, is operationally less efficient than the more sophisticated plants at Rourkela or Durgapur. In fact, the operational record of the former is better, quite possibly because less sophisticated equipment suits Indian conditions better.

[116]On the experience in the oil industry, see Tanzer (1969); Warren (1973) draws attention to the growing strength of indigenous entrepreneurs in poor countries.

[117]On Bokaro, see Desai (1972); in more recent times, the management of the Fertilizer Corporation, which had pioneered very useful work on the substitution of domestically produced catalysts for imports and in fertilizer plant assembly and design, has fallen foul of the Government.

[118]The NCAER (1971) study refers to the obvious 'zenophilia' of Indian industry. One might argue that foreign products or plants are preferred because they offer better quality. While this may be true in some cases, there is also evidence that sophisticated imported plants etc. suffer from as many operational disadvantages as do cheaper and less sophisticated substitutes.

PART 2

CHAPTER SEVEN

The Structure of Poverty in India

Until now, the progress of the Indian economy has been described mainly in terms of production. We have seen that the outline
of the story that emerges is a somewhat complicated one, whether
we look at the economy as a whole or at its particular sectors,
such as agriculture or industry. Some growth there has been,
often substantial in physical terms or in terms of past performance.
It has not been large, however, in terms of needs or targets.
Moreover, the growth that has been uneven in the best of times
appears to be slowing down and the rate of capital formation has
remained discouragingly low. Especially in agriculture, and in the
production of basic industrial goods, that is to say in terms of the
production of wage-goods, the economy has failed to keep pace
with the growing needs of the population. In spite of brave
words and heroic statistics, there has not so far been any miracu-
lous breakthrough. The economy has remained open to the
gamble of a capricious monsoon. To the average Indian, growth
has meant modest benefits, grudgingly yielded.

In this chapter and the next, I shall shift the emphasis to the
question of how these benefits, modest as they are, have been
distributed amongst groups and classes in Indian society. In particular, to what extent the extent of poverty has been ameliorated
or eliminated. Although the answer is depressingly easy to guess,
a systematic approach to the problem is essential if we are ever to
find a way towards a solution. It is right to call this approach a
shift in emphasis, the taking up of a particular viewpoint, so to
speak, rather than a new departure. For I hope to establish
that the problem of distribution, in the Indian context, can-

not be separated from that of production.[1] While there might be situations which can be illuminatingly described in terms of a conflict *between* growth and distribution, the Indian situation is not of that *genre*. In order to argue that point, we need first of all to establish as clearly as we can the nature of the problem of poverty in India and the characteristics of an identifiable group of people who are called 'the poor'.

Contrary to what might be supposed from the current concern of development economists with poverty in poor countries, there has been a clear recognition from the first five-year plan onwards of the need for special policies to benefit the poor.[2] Indeed, the rationale for such policies as land reform or the development of a public sector is to be found, in part, in that recognition. While the plans explicitly stated the problem, planners have been less explicit in formulating and executing policies which could be regarded as intended especially for the benefit of the poor. Indeed, attempts to identify in operational terms a group of people who are the poor and who it is intended that one should channel benefits to, are not more than a few years old. Even then, most of the work that has been done so far has been outside the formal planning process.[3] For our part, in going over that area we have to try to answer three distinct questions. Who are the poor and what socio-economic characteristics do they share? How many are there of the poor, give and take a million?[4] To what extent have they benefited from past economic policies and what alternative policies are suggested for their benefit? Before we try putting numbers to some of the answers, it will be best to get the nature of the problem clearly stated.

[1]See pp. 220-3 below.

[2]An early recognition of the problem of poverty as one distinct from that of growth is in Viner (1957). He has had surprisingly little credit for it in the literature. For a seminal article on the issue, see Seers (1972). In the Indian planning context, see Planning Commission (1973), p.8f.

[3]See the references quoted in n. 1, Chapter 8, only two of which, Planning Commission, PPD (1974) and Vaidyanathan, are by economists attached to the Commission. Vaidyanathan's paper was a private contribution to a seminar on income distribution; see Srinivasan and Bardhan (1974).

[4]As the discussion in Chapter 8 will make clear, there are substantial discrepancies in the various estimates of poverty in India.

There are two aspects of interpersonal or the so-called size-distribution of income that have to be distinguished. One comprises the degree of inequality in the distribution of income and embraces the whole of the spectrum. The degree of this inequality is commonly measured graphically by the Lorenz curve or by the Gini coefficient, which measures the deviance of the Lorenz curve from the line of equal distribution. The other focuses attention on one end of the distribution spectrum, those with the lowest incomes or the 'poor', choosing a more or less arbitrary cutoff level of income. In this case, one can study the magnitude of poverty either in terms of the absolute number of the poor or one can look more appropriately at the different degrees of poverty within the group so designated as the 'poor'.[5] Roughly speaking, the first approach lays more stress on poverty as a relative concept, whereas the latter interprets poverty in the first instance in terms of some absolute level of deprivation.[6] Much of the work on India has concentrated on the issue of poverty and most of our discussion will be concerned with that issue. Given the degree and magnitude of the problem, that appears to be the right kind of emphasis.

However, we cannot ignore the wider if less immediate issue of income inequality. When we come to talk about actual figures, therefore, we shall be concerned with three indexes, the Gini coefficient, the number of people below some notional poverty line, and Sen's poverty measure, P.[7] For each of these, we may sometimes want to describe the situation at a point in time or we may be concerned with changes in any or all of these indexes during a certain period. Here, I may enter a word of caution. In talking about the poor and the relatively better-off, we have to remember that we are talking about a country which overall is very poor. Talking about 'rich farmers' or the 'urban bourgeoisie' is likely to create images of affluence in people's minds that are belied by the reality of existence in India.

The simplest measure of inequality, or of poverty, and one that we are most familiar with, is current disposable income. The degree of inequality can then be expressed in terms of the

[5]On the concepts of income inequality, see Atkinson (1970) and Sen (1973); on the poverty measure, P, see Sen (1973a).
[6]On the concept of relative and absolute poverty, see Townsend (1970).
[7]See references cited in n. 5 above.

distribution among individuals of total disposable income, the top and bottom 5 per cent, say, having x and y per cent of income. For some purposes, we may want to know the distribution of income among households, rather than among individuals. These will not necessarily be the same, because the size of households may itself vary systematically in some fashion according to income levels. At this level of the discussion, we shall see that India suffers from a substantial degree of inequality in the distribution of income between both individuals and households. Data from other poor countries indicate that in this respect she is neither the best nor the worst, which is not very surprising.[8] As richer households in India tend to be also smaller, the inequality is greater for individuals than for households.[9]

As our concern is ultimately with standards of living, we should be more concerned with the distribution of real incomes, rather than money incomes. This means that we have to deflate our money-income values with some price index. This poses the first problem that we have to face. Since, as we shall see, the patterns of consumption are different for different income groups, we have to choose appropriate price indexes for each group. Since we cannot assume that relative prices remain constant over a period of time, the problem becomes even more important when we are trying to measure changes in the distribution of income. For a large country like India, we have two additional problems. One is that the rural population may be faced with a different set of prices than the urban, because they do not buy in the same markets. The other is that different prices may rule and may change differently in the various regions or states within India. All these make the choice of the appropriate price deflator as hazardous as it is important.[10] For India, the distribution of real income is not substantially different from the distribution of money income but the degree of inequality of income does vary from state to state for both money and real incomes.[11]

In some ways, consumption is a better measure of standards of living than income. Although consumption is highly unequally

[8]On India, see the references cited in n. 1, Chapter 8; on the other countries, see Chenery *et al.* (1974) and numerous references cited therein.

[9]Dandekar and Rath (1971), p. 11 f. and Vaidyanathan (1974), p. 223f,

[10]Bardhan (1974), Rudra (1974).

[11]See pp. 207-10 below and the references cited in the text.

distributed in India, the degree of inequality here is smaller than for incomes. There is, as yet, no satisfactory explanation of this discrepancy. It has been suggested that it is partly due to some of the poor having access to non-marketed foods, such as game or forest products, or to fertility differences between large and small holdings.[12] There is also some evidence that the discrepancy is due to the fact that richer households save a larger than average fraction of their incomes, while the poorer ones, as a group, are net dissavers. A relatively more equal distribution of consumption is reassuring in the sense that the poor manage to eke out their levels of present consumption. On the other hand, if the savings explanation holds, it merely goes to strengthen the forces that make for the persistence of inequality in income levels.[13]

So far the discussion has been mainly in terms of the distribution of purchasing power among individuals or households. Both in developed and developing countries, the distribution of purchasing power determines the pattern of final demand. However, in the former, except under conditions both of full employment and low rates of growth of productivity, an increase in aggregate demand creates its own supply and changes in patterns of demand can be accommodated by factor movements between different lines of production. For an underdeveloped country, neither of these two propositions might hold true. This has major implications for the delineation of the problem as much as for policy.

Poor countries suffer from supply constraints. On the one hand, low availabilities of non-labour resources act as a constraint on aggregate supply. In such situations, an increase in purchasing power may lead, not to an increase in supply but to the generation of excess demand. Moreover, structural imbalances within the economy make for factor-immobility and make it more difficult for supply to adjust to changes in the composition of demand. Naturally, these statements are more true in the short run. However, part of the problem of underdevelopment lies precisely in the strength of short-run structural constraints.[14]

---

[12]On the poor having access to non-marketed food or forest products, see Minhas (1970) and Vaidyanathan (1974), p. 221 f.; on relative fertility on smaller holdings, see C.H. Hanumantha Rao (1966), and Khusro (1964).

[13]On the savings issue, see Bhatty (1974).

[14]Lefeber (1973).

The overall supply constraint and the structural rigidities of the system both lead to a situation in which an initial distribution of purchasing power is not reflected in an equivalent distribution of goods and services between ultimate consumers, *where purchasing power itself is very unequally distributed*. However, the *modus operandi* of the two are rather different. An unequal distribution of purchasing power implies unequal bargaining strength. In such a situation, faced with an overall supply constraint, any excess of aggregate demand over supply creates excess demand and leads to incipient inflation. At that point, it is the demand of the poorer parts of the population that remains unsatisfied, although it is true that under such circumstances they would tend to accumulate involuntary savings.[15] On the other hand, structural rigidities affect the system in the following way. If, for example, supply constraints are more severe in those sectors that figure prominently as producers of wage-goods, and there is factor-rigidity between sectors, the expenditure of the poor, who are major consumers of wage-goods, may remain unsatisfied and exhaust itself in raising the relative prices of these goods over a period of time. For both these reasons, in an underdeveloped country a given distribution of purchasing power cannot immediately be taken to reflect an equivalent distribution of real consumption.[16]

That this line of argument is not idle speculation is indicated by the data related to patterns of consumption expenditure by different expenditure groups, collected by the National Sample Survey.[17] These are given in Table 37, separately for the rural and urban sectors. It can be seen that the patterns of consumption of the poor and the rich are indeed very different, as is everywhere the case. This difference is noticeable not only between the broad groups, food and non-food, but also for components within each group, e.g. for such things as foodgrains, milk products and sugar. As we start from the lower levels of expenditure and work our way up, consumption patterns change in somewhat similar manner for both rural and urban households,

[15]Their real savings will increase less than their money savings, owing to the rise in the price level.

[16]This argument applies with greater force to the effect of money income redistribution to changes in damand.

[17]See the 19th Round, National Sample Survey, 1964-65.

except that for each expenditure class rural households spend a much larger proportion of total expenditure on food. For mean expenditure levels of Rs 22.4 for rural and Rs 16.5 for urban sectors, almost 80 per cent of total expenditure is on food, the bulk of which is directed towards foodgrains.

A number of alternative estimates are available for the income or expenditure elasticities of demand for foodgrains in India. For example, Thamarajakshi estimates the income elasticity of demand to be 0.6 for the rural and 0.3 for the urban sector. In a more recent study, Desai has estimated the expenditure elasticity for foodgrains for the bottom five deciles in the rural sector, according to expenditure groupings, to be between 0.6 and 0.5; while the corresponding ratio for the urban sector is around 0.5. The average overall ratio comes out as 0.4 approximately, the ratio falling off fairly sharply as higher decile groups are reached.[18]

The conclusion is inescapable that an increase in real consumption or income of the poor requires increases in the supply of a narrow range of goods, and especially of food products such as cereals and pulses, *all of which require land as an input*. Thus, any redistribution of purchasing power in terms of money can only increase real consumption in so far as the total supply of these products can be increased, because any decline in incomes of the relatively better-off will not release sufficient amounts of these products to meet the demands of the poor.

For this reason, it is often illuminating to look at some non-monetary index of growth, such as the *per capita* availability of certain basic commodities that are consumed mainly by the poor, or rather are major items in the consumption of the poor. Where the *per capita* availability of basic consumer goods is low or is not increasing significantly, it would be extremely implausible for the real consumption of the poor to be substantially increased. In chapter 3, I show that *per capita* availability of certain basic foodstuffs has been both low and stagnant for our period.[19] While it is clear how stagnation can be measured, how does one determine what level of *per capita* availability of, say rice or wheat, is too low and what is adequate? This question links up with a closely related one.

[18]Thamarajakshi (1969); Desai (1972).
[19]See below, p. 60; See also Table 38, p. 187.

TABLE 37
PATTERN OF CONSUMPTION—1964-65
(Percentage of consumption expenditure per person/month)

Expenditure class (Rs)	Percentage of population in class	Food of which	Food grains	Non-food	Total
RURAL INDIA					
0-8	3.18	83.68	63.52	16.32	100.0
8-11	5.99	84.14	62.20	15.86	100.0
11-21	42.13	82.24	58.28	17.76	100.0
21-28	22.02	77.57	49.93	22.44	100.0
28-75	25.01	65.52	36.44	34.48	100 0
75 and above	1.67	40.64	17.76	59.36	100.0
All classes	100.0	71.77	44.87	28.23	100.0
URBAN INDIA					
0-8	0.70	81.46	49.43	18.54	100.0
8-11	3.12	75.61	45.31	24.39	100 0
11-21	29.23	77.87	43.67	22.13	100.0
21-28	21.21	72.92	36.49	27.29	100.0
28-75	39 12	63.14	23.09	36.86	100 0
75 and above	6.12	39.22	6.97	60.78	100.0
All classes	100.0	64.02	24.13	39.98	100.0

The figures for expenditure classes Rs 11-21, 21-28, and 28-75 are average values for the following classes respectively:

11-21—11-13, 13-15, 15-18, 18-21
21-28—21-24, 24-28
28-75—28-34, 34-43, 43-55, 55-75.

SOURCE: *The National Sample Survey*, 19th Round, July 1964-June 1965.

Given that income is unequally distributed, at what point do we draw the line and call the people below the line the 'poor'? A number of attempts have been made recently to provide such a bench-mark. They all share the common attribute of basing such a distinction on some nutrition-based norm. We start from estimates of the amounts of calories, protein, minerals or vitamins, especially the first two, that are required for the sustenance of a healthy human being. Naturally an adult would require more than a child, and a man of sedentary habits will require less than a man doing arduous work. We can then work out the physical amounts of foodstuffs that are normally consumed that will give the necessary nutritional equivalent. In turn, valuing that particular basket of goods at current or base-year prices, we can derive the minimum level of income that will be required for subsistence. If we had to identify a hard core of poverty, we would find it amongst those people whose *per capita* incomes were less than the nutrition-based minimum. From that, given the average size, age and sex composition of households, we can calculate an equivalent household or family income level. It is worth noting that in doing this, we exclude not only any 'luxuries' but also necessary items of private and social consumption such as housing, health and education.[20] On such bases, somewhere between 40 and 60 per cent of the Indian population has in the recent past been designated as poor.[21]

The nutritional approach to the problem provides a little more than an index of poverty. It enables us to gain some very necessary insight into the structure of poverty and, by implication, the policy requirements of any poverty-eradication programme. It must be said at the outset, however, that much of the bio-medical issues are still matters of controversy. In addition, much of the data relating to India are derived from sample surveys conducted in selected areas and it is not clear to what extent their findings can be generalized. Whatever the limitations, some statements about the nutritional aspects of poverty can be made with a reasonable degree of confidence.

Let us suppose that we are considering a modest objective of development, which is to ensure that all members of the population have enough to eat consistent with absence of malnutrition and a moderate level of activity. For a long time, the view was held that the major nutritional deficiency consisted of a protein deficiency, rather than a simple calorie deficiency. This has an important policy implication, because by and large proteins are

[20]There is no objection in principle to including these items in a poverty budget, although there are quite difficult problems of valuation of these items. The point remains that most studies of poverty levels do not include these items; see the references cited in n. 1, Chapter 8; on nutrition see Berg (1973), Joy (1971) and Sukhatme (1971) on problems and issues; for data on nutrition, see Gopalan *et al.* (1971), (1971a) and Gopalan and Vijaya Raghavan (1971); see also Panikar (1972). Most studies of the poverty level in India use one or other of the basic sources of data cited above; see also India, Planning Commission, *Task Force* (n.d.).

[21]See p. 199f below.

more expensive forms of food to produce than most cereal or root crops. However, recent research, admirably summarized by Sukhatme, shows that most of the malnourished suffer mainly from calorie rather than protein deficiency. People who do not suffer from calorie deficiency also do not suffer from protein deficiency. On the other hand, people who suffer from protein deficiency suffer simultaneously from calorie deficiency, that is to say they simply do not have enough to eat.

This is mostly because of two reasons. Most cereals, but not the staple root crops, contain enough protein to supply normal bodily need, if enough is eaten to meet the calorie requirement. In addition, as living tissues fulfil energy requirements, prior to any growth a calorie-deficient organism simply burns up the more expensive growth-producing protein to supply energy needs. This is not to say that protein is not important as a constituent of human diets. It is simply that there is not much point in providing human beings with protein foods, if they do not have enough to eat in the first place.

The priority in nutritional policy is what commonsense dictates, that is to feed the hungry.[22] Apart from calories and protein, the body also needs certain minimum amounts of minerals and vitamins, absence of which causes various diseases of malnutrition.[23] While cereals provide some of these, they do not provide either all or enough of them so that the fulfilment of a calorie target for the poor will still leave them with some degree of malnutrition, if the other elements of a 'balanced diet' are absent.

Figures for *per capita* availability of cereals and proteins for India, as Table 38 shows, indicate that the country produces roughly enough major foodstuffs to meet, or almost meet, the minimum nutritional demand of the population. On the other hand, there are two kinds of evidence that point introvertibly to the existence of large-scale malnutrition. The first, which I shall discuss later in greater detail, is that various studies done for India, both on a regional and a national basis, indicate that a very

[22]Sukhatme (1971) and Sukhatme (1972); on root crops, see Panikar (1972).

[23]On the effects of malnutrition in India, see Gopalan and Vijaya Raghavan (1971).

large proportion of the population have incomes that are insufficient to buy a nutritionally minimum diet. Secondly, all too overt proof of malnutrition is present in large numbers of children and adults who suffer from one or other of the diseases and deformities associated with such a state. The problem of ensuring the minimum of subsistence for human existence is not merely one of ensuring an adequacy of supply.

TABLE 38
PER CAPITA AVAILABILITY OF FOODGRAINS
PER DAY—SELECTED YEARS

	Cereals (grammes)	Pulses (grammes)
1951	334.1	60 8
1956	360.5	70.4
1965	418.6	61.6
1966	360.0	48.2
1972	420 2	47.1
1974	408.5	39.9

SOURCE: India, Ministry of Finance, *Economic Survey* (annual).

This is not an entirely surprising conclusion to arrive at in a mixed economy. Whatever the requirements of the population, their capacity to satisfy them depends on their effective demand. This depends in turn on their incomes, which derive from either wage-employment or ownership or user rights over productive assets, especially land. The poor are malnourished because they are poor. Just as it is true that mere creation of money incomes will not increase the real consumption of the poor if wage-goods remain in short supply, so it is also the case that availability of wage-goods does not ensure that they can be consumed by those that need them most. Wage-goods, by definition, require wages to command their purchase.

While maldistribution of purchasing power or its inadequacy is the major explanation of the persistence of poverty below levels of subsistence, there are other reasons why particular sections of the population suffer from undernourishment. For example, the protein requirements of young children and of expectant and nursing mothers are very much higher than those of the rest of the population. It is precisely these groups that suffer particularly severely from protein and calorie deficiencies within families, for various socio-economic reasons. The result is deteriorating standards of health and welfare for both present and future generations.[24] This shows that quite apart from the major instrument of creating adequate purchasing power, one would need complementary policies specifically directed towards particularly needy or vulnerable parts of the population.

It can be objected that we have so far concentrated on aspects of private consumption of the poorer parts of the population. The standards of living of the population depend also on the distribution and availability of goods and services that are components of social consumption. That is to say those goods and services such as education or health services that are made available for collective consumption, either free or upon payment, by the population. While this objection may be valid in principle, it is quite clear that taking account of these factors will heighten the degree of deprivation suffered by the poor in India.

Little is known about the distribution of educational and medical facilities among people of different income levels. Casual empiricism strongly suggests that the poor are by and large not the chief beneficiaries of these services. We have already drawn attention to the low levels of literacy in India, most of the illiterates being obviously poor. While we do not know much about the educational facilities available to the rich and the poor, we do have information about the amounts of resources devoted to primary, secondary and higher education respectively, as well as educational expenditure and wastage rates in rural and urban areas. The poor figure prominently among those that will benefit most from primary education and most of them live in rural society. The Government has always spent much larger sums on higher education than on primary education. For example, during 1969-72, expenditure on primary, secondary and university education was Rs 88,5, 50.1 and 93.1 respectively; *a fortiori*, higher education gets much more in *per capita* terms.[25] Moreover, educational spending gets much lower priority for the rural sector, where most of the poor live, and wastage rates are much higher there

---

[24]On the effects on children's health, see Cantor (1973) and Gopalan and Vijaya Raghavan (1971).

[25]Planning Commission (1974), p. 203.

than amongst the urban middle-class population.[26] Even within the rural sector, the poorer elements such as the scheduled castes suffer more educational neglect than their more prosperous neighbours.[27]

Medical facilities pose a greater problem, because less is known about this area and conventional health statistics are often not very accurate estimators of real benefits.[28] But low as the overall levels of medical facilities are, a disproportionate amount of these are concentrated in the larger metropolitan areas. For most of the poor, especially the rural poor, access can be had mostly to indigenous medicine, because it is much cheaper. As in some other fields, while the Government offers much encouragement, it offers very little hard cash to develop these areas of health care.[29] As the poor must have their reward in heaven, little obstacle is put in their way.

Poverty in India, whether we measure it in terms of income or nutritional levels, is concentrated among certain occupational classes in both the rural and the urban sectors. In 1960-61, roughly 63 per cent of the rural and 54 per cent of the urban population could be classified as poor, according to the estimates of Dandekar and Rath.[30] This reflects the fact that the degree of income inequality is lower in rural than in urban India, although the average urban income is 38 per cent higher than the average rural income. At 1960-61 population levels, this gives a total of roughly 224 million in the rural and 48 million in the urban sector. Most of the rural poor are to be found among two groups, peasant cultivators with very small holdings and landless labourers. In the urban sector, most of them are the unemployed or underemployed people in what has come to be termed the 'informal sector'.[31]

There are a number of socio-economic studies of Indian cities.[32]

---

[26] Agro-economic Research Centre (1971).

[27] *Ibid.*

[28] On health policy, see Banerji (1973).

[29] For a very useful introduction to the health situation in India, see Myrdal (1968), Vol. III, Chapter 30; on health policy see a very stimulating article by Banerji (1973)

[30] Dandekar and Rath (1971).

[31] ILO (1972).

[32] Gadgil (1945-52), Lubell (1974), Rao and Desai (1965), Sen (1960) and Sovani (1951).

Although they are not confined to a study of poverty in these areas, they do provide some useful information about the conditions of living in cities. The causes of poverty in cities are mostly open unemployment, underemployment in various low productivity occupations such as porterage, street peddling, insecure employment, and low real wages in some industries. In some cities, such as Calcutta, migrant workers figure prominently amongst the poor. Moreover, as none of the urban poor are producers of food and have to buy a part of their total requirements in the open market, they are extremely susceptible to rising food prices.[33] In addition, the urban poor suffer from extremely bad conditions of housing, water supply and sanitation. While availability of an assured water supply, which could be regarded as a major factor in improving standards of health in cities, is a matter for public expenditure, in housing the problem is not only of making available more houses but of ensuring that the people who need it most have the wherewithal to pay the required rents. In this area, public policy is little short of perverse. While eyesore slums, which incidentally are close to the places of work of the poor, are knocked down, the poor are abolished to shanty-towns in the outskirts, where lack of transport facilities is added to their troubles.[34] At the same time, subsidized low-cost housing is provided for higher paid workers and subsidized credit is made available to middle-class salary earners to strengthen the property-owning democracy.

A great deal more is known about the rural poor in India and it is possible to be more specific about the nature and causes of the poverty.[35] Unfortunately, most of the data relating to aspects of the economic structure of the rural society, such as the pattern

---

[33]Part of the diet of the urban poor is subsidized in the sense that they can buy part of their consumption requirements in fair price shops, at prices below the 'free' market price. As access to these shops is not restricted by the income levels of the purchasers, this acts as a fairly indiscriminate subsidy to all, including the more affluent middle classes.

[34]A not untypical example is that of workers in a factory in Calcutta, some of whom leave home around 6 a.m. to be able to clock-in at 8.30 a.m., finally returning home around 7 p.m. During the monsoons, they may have to walk about two miles either way through a flooded street.

[35]Ministry of Labour and Employment, Labour Bureau (1950), Department of Labour and Employment, Labour Bureau (1968); for a criticism of the Second Agricultural Labour Survey, see Thorner and Thorner (1962).

of distribution of landholdings, are not up-to-date. They relate
mostly to the early 1960s. As a substantial part of the debate on
agrarian change in India relates to issues of structural change, the
lack of more recent data is a serious limitation to analysis.[36]

If, following Dandekar and Rath,[37] we take a monthly income
level of Rs 13-15 *per capita* as a poverty line, approximately 35
per cent of rural households and 38 per cent of the rural population falls into this class. Together, they account for only 19 per
cent of total rural consumption, an indication of their level of
poverty.[38] The average size of a rural family is 5.25 and the
poorer families tend to be larger than average. Thus, the two
lowest quintiles have family sizes of 5.77 and 5.97 respectively.[39]
On the other hand, larger family sizes are associated with the
larger holdings.[40] It is possible to say, somewhat tautologically,
that one reason for higher *per capita* incomes is that the income
has to be shared between fewer persons. On the other hand,
poorer families that are dependent on scraping together a living
from various sources tend to be larger because they have to rely
on casual, uncertain, low-productivity activities to keep the family
pot boiling.

In 1958-59, out of a sample of 7,416 households, 1,477 had
a monthly consumption of less than Rs 11 per capita.[41] Out of the
latter, 41 per cent were farmers and a similar percentage consisted
of farm workers or agricultural labourers. Land being the chief
source of income in rural India, it is obvious that lack of access
to land is a major course of poverty. In Chapter 2, I have shown
that both ownership and operated holdings of land are extremely
unequally distributed in rural India. Thus 42 per cent of rural
households had holdings of less than 1 acre in 1960-61, covering
1.3 per cent of area operated and 2.1 per cent of irrigated area.[42]
The fact that smaller holdings are relatively better irrigated

[36]Recently, an agricultural census has been completed, which will give
vluable evidence. However, the report of the census is yet to be released
for publication; Ministry of Agriculture (1974).
[37]Dandekar and Rath (1971), p. 5f.
[38]Vaidyanathan (1974), p. 220.
[39]Dandekar and Rath (1971), p. 12.
[40]Vaidanyathan (1974), p. 222.
[41]*Ibid.*, p. 231.
[42]*Ibid.*, p. 223.

contributes a small degree of amelioration to the poor. As irrigated land tends to be more productive, the income disparities,
although very great, tend to be smaller than would be indicated
by the data on land use.[43] But while it is true that the poor lack
land, it is not true to the same extent that land ownership necessarily precludes proverty. Thus, in 1956-57, 1.3 per cent of
rural households possessed more than 50 acres. Of these, only one-
third had income levels of more than Rs 21 per month per
person.[44] In 1958-59, 7 per cent of all households with *per capita*
income levels of less than Rs 11 per month had land of more than
10 acres. Moreover, rich households, i.e. those with income levels
of more than Rs 28 *per capita*, tend to come fairly evenly from
households owning little or much land. As Vaidyanathan says,
'The rich households do not consist exclusively of big land holders
nor are all big land holders "rich".'[45] This underlines the point
I have made earlier that redistribution of land cannot be the whole
answer to the question of rural poverty, albeit it must provide a
major component of any such answer.[46]

By all accounts, the major group of the rural poor consists of
landless agricultural labourers or those who own or have access
to so little land that they are forced into wage labour to earn a
subsistence. Interestingly enough, according to the 1961 census,
about 44 per cent of agricultural labourers came from the untouchable castes or tribal people. Only about 40 per cent of agricultural labourers in 1958 59 were listed as being gainfully employed,
the rest being either unemployed or persons 'not in the labour
force'. Of those who were gainfully employed, some 24 per cent
had work of less than 4 hours per day. In 1956-57, the average
number of days worked by men was 196.8 and by women 137.1.[47]
This gives an average of about 16.3 days per month, for men.
The so-called minimum statutory wage fixed by the Minimum
Wages Act 1948 was mostly in the region of Rs 2 to 3 per day.
It is widely known that very often actual rates are lower than
this and women's wages are lower by far than men's. Even taking

[43]On the size-productivity debate, see Hanumantha Rao (1966) and the
references cited in n.1, Chapter 5.
[44]Vaidyanathan (1974), p. 223.
[45]Vaidynathen (1974), p. 223.
[46]See p. 146 above.
[47]Department of Labour, Labour Bureau (1968), p. 40.

account of the fact that some households will have more than one wage earner, it is not difficult to see that these households figure prominently amongst the Indian poor.[48]

The prevalence of poverty amongst agricultural labouring households is underlined by the prevalence of rural indebtedness. In 1956-57, 63.9 per cent of all labour households were indebted, the burden of debt, significantly, being higher among attached households. The average debt per indebted household was Rs 138. A higher percentage of untouchable households were indebted. In 1960-61, the average outstanding debt per indebted household was recorded as being Rs 469. We should not take this to mean that average indebtedness had risen, because the two figures are derived from two different sources and disagree on other points as well.[49] Most of these debts were incurred from village moneylenders who, it is well known, charge much higher rates of interest than commercial sources. The reasons for the predominance of the village moneylenders are many, not least of which is that most loans, about 46 per cent in 1956-57, are incurred for consumption purposes. Although it is often not possible to prevent the diversion of the so-called productive loans to sustain the consumption of the poor, commercial channels are not willing to advance money overtly for consumption purposes. The poor, therefore, have no option but to borrow at high interest rates if, for some reason, their incomes fall below subsistence. In practice, in rural societies, there are close structural links between the lending of money, the purchase and sale of land and patterns of labour use. The main purpose of rural moneylending is not only to earn interest, which is often unpaid, but to obtain liens on land and labour services performed by the poor, e.g. through sharecropping for the moneylender/landowner. Interestingly enough, the percentage of indebtedness, measured by the percentage of households in debt, is lowest amongst the landless, who presumably need such loans most. It is much higher among those who own small amounts of land. There have been some studies of rural indebtedness, purporting to prove that the rural moneylender performs a useful service at 'normal' rates of profit.

[48]Department of Labour, Labour Bureau (1968), pp. 56-7.
[49]The first figure is derived from the National Sample Survey, the second from the Second Agricultural Labour Enquiry; on a critical review of concepts and procedures used, see Thorner and Thorner (1962).

There is no doubt that he does perform a service, within the existing structure of rural society. However, whether he earns a 'normal' rate of return or not cannot be proved by misspecifying the problem and concentrating solely on the cash-loan nexus in the total relationship. It is as if, in evaluating medieval feudal society, we were to concentrate on the level of quit rents and ignore the persistence of *corvées*.[50][51]

The fact that the relationship of the rural poor to the money-lender overlaps the relationship between owners and users of land serves to illustrate an important aspect of the problem of rural poverty that is of considerable significance. Poverty is the outcome of a complex set of relationships within rural society that controls the distribution and use of resources in that society and spills over from the narrowly economic to the wider social life of the countryside. We have already noticed the unequal distribution of land ownership and use and its implications.[52] While the study by Vaidyanathan indicates that ownership of land is not a sufficient condition for being or becoming better-off, lack of access to a minimum amount of land is certainly a major cause of poverty.[53] Indeed, work by some social anthropologists has shown that only in exceptional cases can a group break out of a poverty trap, without access to land. These are cases where, through some exogenous factor, new sources of income or new opportunities are opened up to certain sections of the community.[54] In the absence of such exogenous changes, the same lack of land that defines in a sense the problem of poverty, equally leads to a perpetuation of that state.

Where technological change, again largely exogenous to the system, opens up the possibility of profitable use of non-land resources such as credit, the same inequality of access to such inputs also perpetuates the existing state of poverty.[55] Here, a further point is worth noticing in passing. Because land is the

---

[50]On the incidence of indebtedness by size of holdings, see Department of Labour, Labour Bureau (1968), pp. 188-96, esp. p. 193.

[51]On the relationship between rents and labour services under feudalism, see Ganshof and Verhulst (1971).

[52]See pp. 27-9 above.

[53]Vaidyanathan (1974), p. 221f.

[54]Two such case studies are Bailey (1957) and Epstein (1962).

[55]See p. 137 above.

scarce resource *par excellence*, hardly any attention has been given by economists to the fact that control over the use of labour power is itself a matter of some importance in rural society and can serve as an objective of economic behaviour. There are several reasons why this should be so, even in a labour-surplus economy. To an individual, leisure may have some utility in itself and a moneylender may use his power over the debtor to substitute the latter's labour for his own through some system of sharecropping [56] This is reinforced by the fact that certain forms of cultivation may be physically more onerous than others and a landowner may be more eager to buy labour power in such cases.[57] Furthermore, there are strictly speaking non-economic or ritual uses of labour in society, which would also add 'value' to command over the labour of others.[58]

Lastly, the fact that the poor may have to bear the disutility of additional labour as well as the rigours of poverty is really a special case of the more common phenomenon, that people who are poor in terms of income also tend to be deprived of other privileges in village society. Thus there is a large volume of evidence, mostly derived from work done by social anthropologists, that the ranks of the poor are manned substantially by people of low caste or 'ultra-caste' tribal groups, who are discriminated against in numerous ways in rural society.[59] These may take various forms, from the exclusion of the poor low-caste groups from access to the best wells in the villages to the dominance of higher-caste groups in village *panchyats*, where the superior bargaining power is used, for example, to monopolize access to scarce credit or fertilizers.[60]

---

[56]On the relationship between leisure preference and supply of labour input, see Sen (1966); on practical implications of valuing disutility of work, see Lal (1972).

[57]See Beteille (1974), for an interesting discussion of this problem.

[58]Such non-economic uses will be marriages, religious ceremonies etc.

[59]For studies of such discriminations, the reader can pick up any number of village studies conducted by social anthropologists but see especially Beteille (1965) and Gough (1955); because low caste-status almost always goes with low levels of income, it is difficult to be sure whether the observed discriminations in society are discriminations against caste or more generally against the poor.

[60]See pp. 137-8 above.

CHAPTER EIGHT

The State of the Poor, 1950-1970

In the previous chapter, I have looked at certain attributes of the problem of poverty in India, in terms of alternative ways of measuring the state of poverty and certain socio-economic characteristics attached to that state. In the present chapter, I shall briefly summarize the quantitative aspects of the question and try to give some indication of how poor the poor are, how numerous they are and whether they are getting less poor or less numerous with the years.[1] However, there are certain qualifications that have to be borne in mind, before the data can actually be presented.

The first point to bear in mind is that none of the available data are very up-to-date. Most of the studies take the year 1960-61 as a bench-mark year for purposes of comparison. The most recent data to which comparisons can be made relate to the late 1960s, e.g. 1968-69. This is an important point, for there is evidence in the form of an acceleration in the rate of inflation, a faltering in the growth of agricultural production and continuing industrial stagnation that matters have grown worse for the poor and the lower-paid since the late 1960s. Whatever our conclusions are regarding the state of the poor in India, they are likely to be an understatement of the problem, on the basis of the available evidence.

[1]There is now a growing specialist literature on 'poverty' for a general review of the problem of persistence of poverty in poor countries, see Chenery *et al.* (1974); on India, see Bardhan (1970), Bardhan (1973) Bhatty (1974), Dandekar and Rath (1971), Ojha (1970), Minhas (1970) Vaidyanathan (1974) and other references quoted in the text; on policy see Lefeber (1973), Minhas (1974), Srinivasan (1974a), Leys (1974), Vaidyanathan (1974a), Planning Commission (1974), UNO (1975).

Secondly, no two studies give quite the same answer to all the problems. Not only do they yield different numbers for, say, the proportion of people below the 'poverty line'; they also differ with respect to such issues as the ranking of different states in terms of the extent of poverty and whether the poor are growing or diminishing in numbers.[2] However, our conclusion would be that although the different studies yield different answers in relation to the magnitude of change, their conclusions together point quite unequivocally towards the same direction of change.

The reasons for the discrepancies between the different studies can be grouped into three: different estimates of income, consumption and minimum nutrition levels: the issue of the correct price deflator to be used in a particular case; *a priori* choice of some key conversion factors to overcome the lack of availability of appropriate disaggregated empirical data. Let us look at each of these in turn:

1. Most of the studies calculate the size distribution of income and/or consumption from data derived from the National Sample Survey. However, the estimates of aggregate consumption derived from the NSS data for particular years, e.g. 1967-68, are 10 per cent below the consumption estimates derived from the national income statistics.[3] This indicates that one or the other must be an under- or over-estimate of actual consumption. However, Srinivasan and others have argued that the discrepancies are greater for point estimates than over a period of time but that each is subject to error.[4] Moreover, different studies, e.g. the NSS and NCAER surveys, conducted for roughly the same period, give slightly different figures for the size distribution of consumption expenditure.[5]

2. The concept of a required minimum level of nutrition and its purchasing power equivalent forms the basis of all the studies that have attempted to estimate the numbers of people living below some notional poverty line. There are a number of these

---

[2]See below, *passim*; compare e.g. Bardhan (1970) to Minhas (1970) or the ranking of states in Bhatty (1974) to those in Dandekar and Rath (1971) or Vaidyanathan (1974).

[3]Dandekar and Rath (1971), p. 27.

[4]Srinivasan *et al.* (1974).

[5]For a review of the various studies on poverty, see Bardhan (1973).

studies, which give somewhat different estimates of nutritional requirements for the whole of India.[6] Moreover, there is some evidence that a regional low-cost diet might, for fairly obvious reasons, differ significantly from the national one, in composition.[7]

3. As most income or consumption expenditure data are available initially at current prices, one needs to deflate them to obtain real values for purposes of intertemporal or spatial comparisons. Different expenditure groups have different consumption patterns; they often buy these goods either at ex-farm or retail prices; some indeed obtain them in kind. Prices of identical goods vary from region to region. For these reasons, there are problems involved in the choice of a correct price deflator for purposes of comparison, either on an all-India basis or between states. Some researchers reach different conclusions because they use different price deflators.[8]

4. Because of shortcomings in the availability of data, one often has to resort to the use of some conversion factors to build up a complete picture from fragmented data. Thus, Dandekar and Rath *assume* that the top 30 per cent of the population would have fared no worse in terms of consumption between 1960-61 and 1967-68 than the lower income groups.[9] Similarly, in order to derive an estimate of total expenditure from expenditure on food items, Bardhan uses a conversion factor appropriate to the bottom 50 per cent, no more and no less, of the population.[10] While we may argue which number is the more plausible it is clear that there cannot be a 'correct' estimare that can be derived from such assumptions about what are ultimately questions of fact.

Bearing these points in mind, I shall look first at estimates of inequality of incomes and consumption, turning later to estimates of people below a 'poverty line'. Lastly, we shall look at some data relating to the overall availability of certain basic commo-

[6]See Akroyd (1951), Planning Commission, PPD (1974), Gopalan *et al.* (1971) and Sukhatme (1971) for different estimates of nutritional 'norms'.

[7]Panikar (1972); See also UNO (1975).

[8]On the use of alternative price deflators, see Bardhan (1970) and Minhas (1970).

[9]Dandekar and Rath (1971), p. 27 f.

[10]Bardhan (1970); for a critique of Bardhan, see Rudra (1974).

dities to see if they are consistent with our general findings.

TABLE 39
DIFFERENT ESTIMATES OF INCOME INEQUALITY, INDIA

Source	Ojha-Bhatt	Ranadive	Ahmed-Bhattacharya	NCAER
Period Covered	(Ave. 1961-62 to 1963-64)	(1961-62)	(1963-64)	(1964-65)
Share of top 10%	35	45.47	31.5	33.35
Share of bottom 20%	7	7.80	7.6	7.50
Lorenz ratio	0.377	0.351	0.372	0.39

The Ranadive estimate is the lower (i.e. gives a more equal distribution) of the two estimates. The higher esitmate gives a Lorenz ratio of 0.367.

SOURCE: Bardhan, 1973a. The studies quoted are: Ahmed, M. and Bhattacharya, N., 'Size Distribution of Per Capita Personal Income in India', *EPW*, July 1972; NCAER, *All India Consumer Expenditure Surveys*; Ojha, P.D. and Bhatt, V.V., 'Some Aspects of Income Distribution in India', *Bulletin of the Oxford Institute of Economics and Statistics*, August 1964; Ranadive, K., 'The "Equality" of Incomes in India', ibid., May 1965.

Table 39 summarizes the results of a number of studies relating to the early 1960s. They lead, broadly speaking, to a similar conclusion that the degree of inequality in the distribution of disposable incomes was quite severe in India. The distribution of consumption for the same period shows a smaller, although still a substantial, degree of inequality. Thus, the NCAER survey shows the bottom 20 per cent as receiving 8.66 and the top 20 per cent 42.39 per cent of total consumption. According to the NSS estimates, the corresponding figures are 8.47 and 37.87 per cent, although there is some indication that the NSS underestimates the percentage of income accruing to the higher income-groups.[11] The corresponding Lorenz ratios in the two cases are 0.32 and 0.29 respectively. The theoretical reasons for expecting a lower degree of inequality for consumption than for income distribution have been discussed earlier in Chapter 7.[12]

There are no more up-to-date studies for income distribution

[11]Bardhan (1970).
[12]See p. 181 above.

for the whole of India. However, a number of people have estimated the pattern of distribution of consumption expenditure for the late 1960s. Thus, according to Vaidyanathan, the Lorenz ratio for distribution of consumption in rural areas for 1967-68 was 0.29, whereas a similar study by Bhatty gives an estimated value of 0.27, indicating a lower degree of inequality. The work by Vaidyanathan indicates a decline in the degree of inequality in the distribution of consumption expenditure between 1957-58 and 1963-64, with a subsequent worsening during the later 1960s.[13]

Much debate and controversy has taken place around a number of studies that look not so much at the whole spectrum of income distribution in India but at the problem of poverty. More specifically, the question that has attracted most attention is whether the proportion of the population living below the 'poverty level' has increased or diminished in recent years. Starting with the work of Minhas and Bardhan in 1970, there have been studies by Dandekar and Rath, Ojha, Vaidyanathan and Bhatty.[14] I shall summarize very briefly the main points of these studies below.

Roughly the same procedures are used in the various studies. Most of them use NSS data to obtain a percentile breakdown of consumption expenditure; Bhatty uses data collected from a sample survey carried out by the NCAER. An independent estimate of minimum level of consumption is derived from more or less explicit nutritional data; some studies use an estimate formulated by an expert committee of the Planning Commission in 1962; Bardhan uses the levels recommended by the 1957 Pay Commission, based on the work of Akroyd; Ojha, as well as Dandekar and Rath, uses an estimated minimum calorie intake level of 2,250 per day. By estimating the cost of the minimum diet and comparing it with the sample survey data, one can obtain the number of people whose incomes are below the level required to purchase the minimum level of subsistence. These are 'the poor'. Where changes in the magnitude of poverty have to be estimated between two different dates, account has to be taken of changes in the price level. Some studies, like Minhas's, use

[13]Vaidyanathan (1974), p. 236.
[14]See references quoted in n. 1 above.

the national income deflator, whereas Bardhan and Vaidyanathan use the agricultural labour consumer price index, on the ground that it is more representative of the price level facing the poorer parts of the population. While some studies are confined to the rural poor, who in any case form the bulk of the poor, others look at both urban and rural poor. Most of the studies look at both all-India and state level data, which some are confined to the all-India data.

In one of the earliest studies, Minhas uses a *per capita* annual income level of Rs 240 at 1960-61 prices as that necessary for bare subsistence, which is recommended by the previously mentioned expert committee of the Planning Commission. For rural population, he takes a slightly lower figure of Rs 200, on the ground that the urban cost of living tends to be somewhat higher. Using the latter figure, he finds that between 1960-61 and 1967-68 the number of poor people decreased from 164 million to 154 million; expressed as a proportion of rural population, this gives a decline from 46.0 to 37.1 per cent. If we took the higher level, i.e. Rs 240, as the poverty level, the number of the poor would remain more or less unchanged at 210 million, while the proportion would drop from 59.4 to 50.6. He finds, as one would expect to, that the numbers of the poor tend to rise in bad harvest years. Two points are worth noting. The first is that, whether we take Rs 200 or Rs 240 as a minimum, it is the rock-bottom so to speak and allows for no margin of expenditure on health, education or contingencies of any sort. The second is that whether the numbers are seen to be rising or falling, 154 million people living in very deep poverty is a staggering magnitude to contemplate.[15]

The study by Bardhan reaches results which are in direct contrast to those of Minhas. While he uses the same NSS data for distribution of consumer expenditure, Bardhan uses a different minimum level of income of Rs 15.0 per month at 1960-61 prices.[16] Starting from that level, he argues quite rightly that the national income deflator is not an appropriate price index to use, because it does not accurately reflect the set of prices facing the poor consumer. If we take that index to reflect the behaviour of the average price level, there is a great deal of evidence to show that

[15]Minhas (1974).

[16]Bardhan's estimate has been criticized by Rudra as being too low. Rudra cites Patwardhan's estimate of Rs 15.63 and Sukhatme's of Rs 22.73. See Rudra (1974).

prices of commodities have risen faster for the poor than for the better-off parts of the population.[17] He, therefore, uses an alternative deflator which is the agricultural labour consumer price index referred to above. While he is right on the point of principle, it can be argued that the set of prices facing, say, the small cultivator who buys in only part of his consumption but who may still figure among the poor as defined in this context, might have behaved differently from the prices facing the agricultural labourer. *A fortiori*, this may be true of the urban poor who are, however, not covered in Bardhan's study. In any case, after allowing for the rise in prices, he calculates that an expenditure level of Rs 28.4 would have been required in 1968-69 to purchase the same minimum diet. Using the latter figure he finds that, in sharp contrast to Minhas, the proportion of people living below the poverty line in the rural sector had *risen* from 38 per cent in 1960-61 to 54 per cent in 1968-69. In other words, more than half the rural population was living in 1968-69 below a notional level of subsistence.

The next study we should look at is the one by Dandekar and Rath, which has probably attracted the most attention.[18] While their use of statistical procedures is somewhat eccentric, in that they make a number of fairly arbitrary adjustments to the basic NSS data, it is unlikely that their basic conclusions are very much off the point.[19] The importance of their study is that it covers both the urban and rural sector, whereas most of the other works are confined to the measurement of rural poverty. They assume a daily intake of 2,250 calories per adult male as the required minimum intake for subsistence. This is the figure estimated by Sukhatme for Indian conditions and it is somewhat lower than the intake recommended by the Nutrition Advisory Committee of the Indian Council of Medical Research.[20] In 1960-61, it would have required an income of Rs 170.8 *per capita* for an individual to be able to afford such a diet. For a number of reasons, the urban consumer would typically need to spend a higher amount to purchase the

---

[17]See above, pp. 00; see *inter alia* Bardhan (1973), Rajaraman (1974) and Vaidyanathan (1974).

[18]Dandekar and Rath (1971).

[19]For criticisms of Dandekar and Rath's statistical methods, see Bardhan (1973) and Srinivasan *et al.* (1974).

[20]Sukhatme (1971); Gopalan *et al.* (1971a).

same amount of nutrition, i.e. Rs 271.7.[21] Thus, according to Dandekar and Rath, the urban consumer would have needed to spend roughly 59 per cent more to attain the same level of nutrition, whereas the average urban income was only 37 per cent higher.[22]

To return to the main point, in 1960-61 roughly 40 per cent of the rural population and a little under 50 per cent of the urban population would have been living below the level of poverty. In 1967-68, allowing for changes in the price level, roughly 40 per cent of the rural population and a little over 50 per cent of the urban population would still have been living below the poverty line.[23] As far as the rural population is concerned, therefore, the Dandekar and Rath results lie in between the Minhas and Bardhan estimates, in that they find no significant change in the proportion of the people living below the poverty line in the late 1960s. The additional point made by them is that urban poverty had deepened in the intervening period, although urban average incomes still exceeded the average rural income, albeit by a smaller margin than before.[24] Whereas all but the bottom 5 per cent of the rural population had shown some improvement in rural incomes, no less than the bottom 40 per cent of the urban population had suffered a decline in their real standard of living.

Ojha's study looks at both rural and urban poverty for 1960-61 and at rural poverty only for 1967-68. For 1960-61, he compares actual food consumption in grammes per head of rural and urban population derived from the NSS surveys with a nutritional minimum level of consumption of 518 grammes per head daily for rural and 432 grammes for urban population. Ignoring shortfalls of less than 10 per cent, he finds that nutritional deficiency persisted in the rural area for expenditure levels up to Rs 15-18 per capita per month. For the urban population, the corresponding level at which consumption ceased to be deficient was Rs 11-13 per month. On this basis, Ojha estimates that in 1960-61 roughly 51.8 per cent of the rural population, or 184.2 million people, lived in poverty, while for the urban area the proportion was only 7.6 per cent, a total of 6 million people.

[21]Dandekar and Rath (1971), p. 7.
[22]*Ibid.*, p. 7 f and p. 31.
[23]*Ibid.*, pp. 25 f and 29 f.
[24]*Ibid.*, p. 31.

Given the fact that urban households tend to spend a smaller percentage of their incomes on food and that urban food prices tend to be higher, it is at first sight surprising that the urban consumers should be able to reach a level of self-sufficiency at a lower absolute level of spending. This is a result, of course, of estimating a nutritional norm for urban population, that is 86 grammes or 16.4 per cent lower. If we took the same calorie level of nutrition for both sectors, the urban dweller would need an expenditure level of Rs 21-24 to avoid nutritional deficiency and the proportion of urban people living in poverty would increase to about 45 per cent. Moreover, for each particular expenditure level, the urban sector would show a higher level of nutritional deficiency.

The discrepancy in the results obtained by Ojha on the one hand and Dandekar and Rath on the other, follows largely from the different assumptions made in the two studies about what is the minimum level of nutrition. Ojha's calculations for 1967-68 cover only the rural population. He finds that 70 per cent of rural households were living in poverty in the later year, giving a total number of 289 million. Moreover, at each expenditure level, the degree of nutritional deficiency was higher.[25]

The two remaining studies are by Vaidyanathan and Bhatty.[26] Taking an income level of Rs 132 per year to denote poverty, which is roughly half the national average for 1960-61 and is considerably lower than the range of Rs 170-240 used by others, Vaidyanathan finds that 15.7 per cent of the rural population were then living in poverty.[27] This would give a total number of about 56 million, which can be taken as some sort of a minimum estimate of poverty. He also points out that the NSS survey data and the national income statistics give quite different answers to the question of the degree of poverty, which has also been noted by others mentioned before. The NSS data give a higher estimate of the proportion of the rural population living in poverty for both 1960-61 and 1967-68 than the national income data and they indicate an increase in the incidence of poverty over a period of time, whereas the latter data indicate a more or less stagnant level of

[25]Ojha (1970).
[26]Bhatty (1974), Vaidyanathan (1974).
[27]Vaidyanathan (1974).

poverty. The study by Bhatty refers to the extent of rural poverty
in 1968-69. His results are summarized in Table 40 below. It will
be seen that his estimates of the proportion of the population below
the poverty line are lower than those of Bardhan, Dandekar and
Rath, Minhas and Ojha, while for the lowest poverty level, i.e.
Rs 180, his results correspond roughly to Vaidyanathan's.[28]

TABLE 40

PROPORTION OF RURAL PEOPLE BELOW THE
'POVERTY LINE'—1968-69

	Poverty Line		*(Rs per capita)*	
	180	*240*	*300*	*360*
All Households %	24.19	42.43	56.41	67.15
Cultivators %	22.66	39.31	52.48	62.36
Agricultural Labourers %	31.64	56.21	71.36	82.84
Non-Agricultural Workers %	21.95	39.55	55.87	69.70

SOURCE: Bhatty (1974), Tables 11-14, pp. 318-19.

Of all these studies, Bhatty alone has attempted to make calculations for India of Sen's poverty measure P; if for no other reason
than that the other poverty studies were conducted before Sen's
work on measurement of inequality.[29] According to Sen, the
poverty measure P, which measures the area between the actual distribution line and the poverty line, differs from the Gini coefficient,
'in being concerned only with the people who lie below the poverty
line...and...in calculating the income differences from the
poverty line and not from the average income of the distribution
itself'.[30] As the estimates are available for only one year it is, of
course, not possible to use the results to show whether poverty
has been increasing or not. The results do indicate, however, that
for all poverty levels above Rs 180 *per capita*, the incidence of
poverty was most severe among agricultural labourers and least

---

[28] The references are to the various studies quoted in n. 1 above.

[29] Sen's work arises partly out of his dissatisfaction with the use of the
numbers of people below the poverty line as a measure of poverty. As
Sen points out, this takes no account of either the degree of poverty or the
degree of relative poverty amongst the poor; see Sen (1973a).

[30] Sen (1973a), p. 80.

among non-agricultural rural workers.[31]

So far, we have confined our attention to the problem at the level of the whole economy. The question arises whether our results would have to be modified in any way if we took account of differences at the state level. Do the data available for particular states bear out the broad conclusions that can be reached from the all-India studies? Is the incidence of poverty more severe or has it grown more severe in some states than in others? Does the work on poverty substantiate the regional image of India depicted earlier of a country divided into rich states and poor? There are very few studies that have concentrated on these questions although Bardhan, Bhatty, Dandekar and Rath, and Vaidyanathan provide us with some information for different states as well. The two studies that I shall consider are Panikar's work on Kerala and Rajaraman's study of the incidence of poverty in the Punjab.[32]

Panikar is largely concerned with the question of choice of a nutritional minimum or, more strictly, a low-cost diet for poor households. He does not say anything explicitly about numbers of the poor in Kerala, to which his study relates. He criticizes both the nutritional measures used by Dandekar and Rath and by the Nutrition Advisory Committee. His basic conclusions are that by ignoring regional factors, they both reach wrong conclusions about the cost of a nutritionally adequate diet in Kerala. Moreover, that by using aggregated, all-India estimates, Dandekar and Rath have overestimated the numbers of the poor in Kerala. Whether we agree with his particular estimates or not, he does raise an important point of principle, that a nutritional minimum diet for the whole of India is not likely to be a very useful basis for the formulation of economic policy relating to the eradication of poverty or malnutrition.

Indira Rajaraman's study is confined to the incidence of poverty in the Punjab between 1960-61 and 1970-71.[33] In the former year, the bottom 10 per cent of the rural population accounted for 4.3 per cent of total consumption; the next highest decile for

---

[31]Bhatty (1974), pp. 316-17.

[32]Panikar (1972), Rajaraman (1974). Rajaraman's article is based on her unpublished PhD dissertation, bearing the same title, submitted to Cornell University in 1973.

[33]Rajaraman (1974).

another 6 per cent, making a cumulative share of 10.4 per cent. In 1970-71 the bottom 20 per cent represented only 8.9 per cent of total consumption, the decline being largely in the second lowest decile. The figures show a small increase in the share of the top 10 per cent of the population, their share having gone up from 23.2 to 24.7 per cent. Taking a figure of Rs 16.36 for 1960-61 and a corresponding level of expenditure of Rs 33.86 in 1970-71 as the poverty line, Rajaraman found that the percentage of the population below the poverty line had increased from 18.4 to 23.3 per cent in the ten years. The largest increase in poverty was among the agricultural labourers. In 1960-61 and 1970-71 agricultural labourers formed 17.5 and 23.2 per cent of all rural occupational groups, whereas in 1960-61 they comprised only 22.6 per cent of the households living in poverty, and in the later year that share had become no less than 40.5 per cent. In contrast, the incidence of poverty among cultivators showed a small decline.[34] Rajaraman's findings are consistent with those of Bardhan, for example, who found no signs of rising prosperity among agricultural labourers in the Punjab following the 'green revolution'.[35] It is a matter of some significance that even in the Punjab, which is regarded both as a prosperous and a rapidly growing area, a little over one-fifth of the population would still be below the poverty line.[36]

This brings us to the question, whether there are major differences in the incidence of poverty amongst the different states. As mentioned before a number of studies have touched on this question. However, their coverage is too dissimilar for us to be able to compare their results in any satisfactory manner. Thus Dandekar and Rath calculate the proportions of the population living below the poverty line in different states but only for 1961-62.[37] Vaidyanathan also gives estimates of rural population living below a poverty line but his poverty line, as we have mentioned

[34]Rajaraman finds that while the increased incidence of poverty amongst agricultural labouring households is statistically significant, the findings relating to cultivating households were not; see Rajaraman (1974).

[35]Bardhan (1970a).

[36]We must bear in mind that in terms of population, Punjab is relatively a small state.

[37]Dandekar and Rath (1971).

before, is drawn at a much lower level of expenditure.[38] He also gives the Gini coefficients for different states for a number of years, including 1960-61 and 1967-68. Bardhan gives the proportions of people living below the poverty line but not any overall measure of inequality for both 1960-61 and 1967-68.[39] Lastly, Bhatty gives the P measure, as well as the Gini coefficients for different states for 1968-69.[40] Given the fragmented nature of the evidence, one can but summarize their main findings.

Dandekar and Rath list 9 out of 16 states where the proportion of rural population living below the poverty line was higher than the all-India average; for the urban population, the number rose to 12. The major reason for this different incidence of poverty was the difference in regional prices, which necessitated a much higher level of expenditure in some states to buy the nutritional minimum diet than in others. For the rural sector, Kerala headed their list with a staggering 90.75 per cent of poor people. As we have mentioned earlier, this point has been questioned by Panikar.[41] Next in the order came Andhra Pradesh, Maharashtra and Tamil Nadu.[42] For the urban sector, Kerala again headed the list, with roughly 89 per cent poor, followed by Tamil Nadu, Maharashtra and Andhra Pradesh.[43] Interestingly enough, whereas Punjab had one of the lowest proportions of the rural poor, together with Rajasthan, for the urban sector the proportion for Punjab was as high as 52 per cent. The two best-off states from the urban point of view turned out to be Rajasthan and Assam.[44]

For 1960-61, Vaidyanathan found that the following states had a higher proportion of the population below the poverty line than the national average: Andhra Pradesh, Kerala, Madhya Pradesh, Tamil Nadu, Orissa and Uttar Pradesh. The 'poorest'

[38]Vaidyanathan (1974).

[39]Bardhan (1970).

[40]Bhatty (1974).

[41]Panikar (1972).

[42]Others in the group are Mysore, Bihar, Orissa, West Bengal, Assam and the Union Territories; Dandekar and Rath (1971), p. 9.

[43]Others in the urban group are Madhya Pradesh, Punjab (including Haryana), Mysore, Gujarat, Orissa, West Bengal and the Union Territories; Dandekar and Rath (1971), p. 11.

[44]Dandekar and Rath (1971), p. 11.

state was Orissa, with 32.6 per cent of the population below the poverty line, Kerala coming second with 23.2 per cent. Bihar, Maharashtra and Mysore came close to the line of demarcation, having percentages of population below the poverty line quite close to the average. Assam and Punjab turned out to be the two least 'poor' states, with proportions of poor people of around 1.2 per cent.[45] Vaidyanathan also calculated the Lorenz ratios for the distribution of consumption for rural India in the different states for a number of years. For 1960-61, Punjab had the highest degree of inequality of consumption, followed by Bihar and then Andhra Pradesh, Kerala and Orissa. For 1967-68, the highest degree of inequality was registered by Rajasthan, followed by Kerala and Madhya Pradesh. In the intervening period the value of the ratio had declined for Andhra Pradesh, Assam, Bihar, Orissa, Punjab and Uttar Pradesh, although it still remained high for Bihar, Orissa and the Punjab. It had increased most substantially in Gujarat and Rajasthan.[46]

If we select two alternative poverty levels out of the five utilized by Bhatty, Rs 180 and Rs 300 *per capita*, the following four states come out as being the poorest in the sense that they show the highest proportion of the population below the poverty line for both the norms: Gujarat, Tamil Nadu, Rajasthan and Madhya Pradesh. If we take the higher figure, Orissa comes out as the fifth poorest state, changing places with Uttar Pradesh. On either count, Punjab comes out as the most prosperous, with Andhra Pradesh, Assam and West Bengal fairly high up in the ranks of the rich states. Somewhat paradoxically, Bihar also comes out in this group, while Kerala sits fairly squarely in the middle, with a rank of 6 in both ranking orders. The proportion of the population that falls below the poverty line naturally varies according to how high that line is drawn. Thus, with a poverty line of Rs 180, Gujarat will have 49.1 per cent below the line, the percentage rising to 75.8 for the poverty level of Rs 300. At the other extreme, Punjab, which shows only 3.9 per cent below the line at Rs 180, will show 21.0 per cent below the poverty line at Rs 300.[47]

---

[45]We should note that the 'poverty line' used by Vaidyanathan is lower than those used in the other studies; see p. 204 above.

[46]Vaidyanathan (1974), p. 235 f.

[47]Bhatty's figures quoted here refer to all households; he also gives

This leaves us with Bardhan's study, to which we have referred earlier when looking at the data at the national level.[48] For 1960-61, Bardhan found that eight states had a higher than national average for people below the poverty line. The highest percentages were registered by Orissa, Tamil Nadu and Andhra Pradesh, all between 47 and 56 per cent, the lowest being registered in Assam and Punjab. For 1967-68, nine states showed poverty levels higher than the national average, Andhra Pradesh dropping out of the list and Mysore and West Bengal moving in. The higher overall incidence of poverty that Bardhan found is reflected in the states' figures. Thus, the highest levels were registered by West Bengal, Bihar, Kerala and Orissa, in that order; the range extended from 74 per cent for West Bengal to 64 per cent for Orissa. According to Bardhan, in no less than nine states, including the Punjab, the proportion of the rural population living below the poverty line had substantially increased.[49]

Enough has been said, perhaps, to indicate that the findings are too dissimilar for us to draw very clearcut conclusions about the extent of poverty at the state level. Some states figure consistently as among the poorest in all the studies. However, no two studies include and exclude precisely the same states. The ranking order of states within the broad groups, 'rich' and 'poor', varies from study to study and from period to period. No two authors agree on the extent of poverty in the various states or on the extent to which the problem has worsened or improved within a certain period. A state which scores high on an inequality index sometimes scores low in terms of numbers of poor below the poverty level. While it is possible that many of these differences may eventually be reconciled, much work needs to be done before anything very precise or certain can be said about the regional pattern of poverty in India.

An interesting nutrition study carried out in Tamil Nadu indicates that differences in the incidence of poverty, or rather nutritional levels, do not stop at the state level. Within a particular state there might be significant variations among districts.

---

separate estimates for agricultural labouring, cultivating and non-cultivating households; see Bhatty (1974), p. 316 f.

[48]Bardhan (1970).

[49]Bardhan (1973), p. 249.

Thus, out of the 14 districts in Tamil Nadu, more than 90 per cent of protein requirements are fulfilled in only two districts: Thanjavur and Tiruchirapalli. Over 90 per cent of protein requirements were fulfilled in seven of the districts. In three districts, the calorie deficiency was higher than 25 per cent.[50] Much micro-level work remains to be done before all the major facets of poverty can be unearthed in India.

We have argued previously that the bulk of the consumption of the poor, especially the rural poor, is concentrated on a narrow range of goods, especially foodgrains. The bulk of their total expenditure is absorbed by these commodities and the income elasticity of demand for these goods in high. It follows that some insight can be gained into the state of the poor by looking at the data relating to the total availability of these goods within the country. This is so, even if we allow for the fact that the available goods are not uniformly distributed among the population. Nor do some of the population have adequate purchasing power to buy a minimum sufficiency of these goods. Indeed, in so far as the distribution of these goods is uneven, increasing availability becomes, *a fortiori*, more important as providing a necessary though not a sufficient condition for any substantial amelioration in the conditions of the poor. The data given in Tables 35 and 38 tell their own story, without further embellishment. For most of the major commodities that are consumed by the poor, the economy has at best marked time. For some important commodities such as pulses, which provide a cheap source of protein, or for the so-called inferior grains, the position has actually deteriorated.[51] Take this together with the point that the industrial production of such basic manufactured goods as textiles has been stagnant and it is not surprising that very little change has been wrought in the conditions of the poor in India.[52] No amount of talk about redistribution will overcome the constraint of a stagnant level of production of wage-goods in the economy.[53]

[50]Cantor (1973).
[51]See Table 38, p. 187 above; for Table 35, See p. 15.
[52]On the behaviour of industrial production, see Chapter 6, pp. 150-2.
[53]Obviously the stagnant level of production of wage-goods is not a development that is independent of the existing social structure. It is, of

Faced with this fragmentary and contradictory evidence about the incidence of poverty in India in recent years, one can react in one of two ways. One is to say that we do not know enough to say for certain whether the problem of poverty has grown more or less acute; whether it is the numbers of the poor that have increased or the proportion itself risen. These are all pertinent questions to raise. However, the numbers that we are talking about are hundreds of millions and the level of subsistence in question is a bare minimum. Where all the data that we have, however unsatisfactory, point steadily in the direction of increasing poverty and there is no evidence to point in the opposite direction, it will be neither too rash nor too soon to draw the conclusion that economic development and economic planning have largely by-passed the people who were supposed to be their chief beneficiaries.[54]

course, possible that the factors which prevent any substantial degree of redistribution also act as a constraint on the production of wage-goods through their influence on the allocation of resources.

[54]This paragraph owes much to a very sensible and balanced assessment of some of these issues in Robert Cassen's forthcoming book on the population problems of India.

PART 3

CHAPTER NINE

The Role of the State: Formulation of Economic Strategy

In the previous chapters, I have discussed the nature of economic progress in India. It is a commonplace that the Government has played an active role in that process. Here I shall describe the basic planning strategy followed by the Government during 1950-74. As India is not a fully planned economy but a mixed economy, it will be necessary to discuss what instruments of control were used by the Government to try to ensure that the economy followed the path devised by the planners. That aspect of the question is deferred until the next chapter.

Before I come to a discussion of the role of the State, I should recur to a point made earlier in the book that the State or the Government cannot be assumed to play a neutral role in the economic process. It represents, rather, some interest groups as opposed to others, whether these groups are designated 'majority-minority', 'right-left' or 'rich-poor' or whatever suits our purpose. An evaluation of the role of the State in the formulation of economic policy can hardly be attempted without some clear understanding of who the Government saw as the ultimate beneficiaries of that strategy.

Unfortunately, in the Indian context, it is somewhat difficult to determine in simple terms which interest groups the Government is supposed to represent. To say that it represents those in power is a tautology. To say that it serves primarily the doctrinal dictates of state socialism is to perpetrate a gross travesty of the facts. While much is said about socialism in India, it would be difficult to recognize it as a socialist state in terms of any objective criteria.

In some ways, it can be said to represent the interests of the rural rich, the so-called ·kulaks' or large farmers. That would explain the emphasis on high procurement prices and low rates of procurement that co-exist; or the failure to redistribute land or levy taxes on large agricultural incomes. In other ways, however, the State can be said to represent the interests of the urban bourgeoisie as a class. While the Government might depend on the 'kulaks' for the votes, it depends on large industrialists for party funds. In some ways, the Government's policy towards the industrial bourgeoisie is antagonistic. That this is so can be argued in the context of the Government's policy towards foreign technology or towards monopoly. On the other hand, high rates of protection and import restrictions help the industrial sector, as does the systematic underpricing of some industrial inputs produced by the public sector. More significantly, while high food prices may help the rich farmer, they can hardly be in the interests of the industrial bourgeoisie.

I do not raise these questions to show that a political analysis of the role of the State is impossible. I wish merely to state that the problem is sufficiently complex to be treated in a peripheral fashion in a fairly broad discussion of Indian economic development. For the rest of this chapter, therefore, I shall not pay much attention to political motives guiding the formulation and implementation of economic strategy. It will be worth bearing this *caveat* in mind when we come up against certain seeming inconsistencies in the economic policies that the Government has followed. For such inconsistencies might spring in part from the need to resolve conflicting interests of different classes in society.

There has been a number of excellent technical studies of the various planning models that have been constructed to help or explain the process of economic development in India. Some of these have formed bases for particular plans, while others have been devised as critiques of the official models.[1] I shall confine myself here to a non-technical discussion of the economic rationale behind the planning strategy, laying particular emphasis on

[1]The best known example of a model behind a plan is Mahalanobis (1963) which contains the plan-frame for the second five-year plan; on criticisms, see especially Bhagwati and Chakravarty (1969), Rudra (1974) and Tendulkar (1974); there is a comprehensive bibliography covering the literature in Bhagwati and Chakravarty (1969).

the interrelationship between the various objectives of the Government and its policies. Here, one must enter a certain note of caution. Indian plans, taken as statements of intent of the planners, are very comprehensive documents. If one reads any particular plan document carefully enough, one will find almost all desirable objectives set down and almost all accorded priority. Indian plans recognize neither conflict nor constraints. They are couched in terms of targets and the desirability of attaining those targets. Needless to say, they are also innocent of concepts of trade-offs between different objectives.[2] Therefore, which objectives are to be taken seriously, so to speak, is to a certain extent a matter of judgement.

I think it will be fair to say that the Government put forward three major objectives fairly consistently in the plans, although the various plan documents differ in the order or the manner in which the objectives are presented. These three are self-sustained economic growth, a reduction in inequality and 'a socialist pattern of society'.[3] Growth is expressed both in terms of output and employment, although it is quite clear in the context that the planners put the emphasis on the first. The realization that growth has to be self-sustained leads to the emphasis on investment as a strategic variable, as well as to the objective of a diminishing reliance on foreign aid.[4] The desire to reduce inequality, which is sometimes explicitly associated with the need to abolish poverty, leads in turn to a concern with a reduction in concentration of economic power and land reform.[5] Industrialization and the promotion of agricultural growth are very much in the nature of proximate objectives and means to a higher end.

The decision to pursue a socialist pattern of development was an explicit political decision, adopted at the Avadi Congress in

[2]Hanson (1966), p. 92. Readers who have a liking for intellectual history may find this quotation from Kosambi interesting. 'The logic advanced by the brahmins took good care to avoid all reality. The end result is seen in the philosophy. . .(which) threw out the proposition that "A thing is either A or not-A". . .This ability to swallow logical contradictions wholesale also left its stamp upon the Indian national character. . .' Kosambi (1970), p. 174.

[3]India, Planning Commission (1956) Ch. II (1961) Ch. I.

[4]India, Planning Commission (1956) Ch. I (1961) Ch. I.

[5]India, Planning Commission (1951) Chs. I and II.

1954.[6] A decision not to follow a socialist pattern would have been equally a political decision. Either decision would have prescribed the institutional context in which development would occur. As the term 'socialist pattern' has sometimes been misinterpreted, it is worth making its implications clear. Whatever might have been its original conception, it is not easy to find an operational definition of the term, except such vague notions that it had to be a kind of socialism that was congenial to the native genius of the people.[7]

Its significance has to be inferred from the activities of the Government. As the Government has always interfered in the running of the economy in various ways, from taxation to rationing and famine relief, it had to mean something more than Government regulation of economic activity. It did not imply the setting up of a welfare state with substantial diversion of resources towards such sectors as health or education or subsidized consumption for the poor. Indeed, given the magnitude of the problem of poverty in India and the scale of the country, that would hardly have been feasible. Neither did it imply any significant interference with the existing structure of property or other institutional arrangements. There was hardly any nationalization and no confiscation of any kinds of assets. What it meant in effect was that the Government was to take an active part in certain kinds of economic activity; it meant the setting up of public sector industries. As I have indicated earlier, there were in any case sound economic and non-ideological reasons behind such a decision which were not disputed by the private sector. However, the fact that the planning strategy had to be implemented within the institutional context of a mixed economy, with the Government as one of the protagonists, is of some significance.[8]

The objective of economic policy that is most fully articulated and the one which the Government has regarded as the most important is economic growth. India was, and is, a poor country with a low level of income per head. It is quite clear that the average level of real income could not be increased substantially

---

[6] On the Avadi Congress, see Hanson (1966), p. 123.
[7] See the quotation from Nehru in Hanson (1966), p. 123.
[8] That the Government is an interest group and is not neutral is an imortant point to bear in mind; on this, see Alavi (1973).

merely through redistribution, even if that were feasible. What was required was a substantial increase in the total amount of goods and services produced by the economy. This in turn raises the question why the level of output was low in the first instance. In the planners' view, the chief limiting factor was the low level of the capital stock of the economy and the chief imperative was to increase the capital stock through a high rate of investment.[9]

The identification of the scarcity of capital led during the second plan to the formulation of what has come to be known as the Mahalanobis strategy.[10] The capacity to produce output at any point in time is embodied in a given volume of capital goods of particular composition. To increase output capacity one needs then to increase the stock of capital goods within the economy.[11] The process of capital formation is thus seen as a process of production of capital goods. If the economy is 'closed', or is virtually 'closed' owing to a limited capacity to import, the major part of these capital goods will have to be produced at home.[12] Here, it is vitally important to distinguish between two kinds of capital goods: those that produce consumer goods and those that produce other capital goods. If the immediate objective is to increase the output of capital goods over a period of time, the former constitutes a leakage from the capital accumulation process. The rate of growth of output capacity can be increased by minimizing that leakage and increasing the share of resources devoted to the production of those capital goods which in turn will produce other capital goods. The basic strategy then becomes a maximization of the share of investment going to the production of 'machine producing machines'. For brevity, we can call the

[9]India, Planning Commission (1956), Ch. V, provides an example of this form of reasoning.

[10]Mahalanobis (1963); see also Fel'dman (1964). The Fel'dman model is summarized in Domar (1957); see also Raj and Sen (1961).

[11]The fact that the same capital equipment can produce more output through changes in productivity is not stressed by Mahalanobis. For a critique of the model, see Bhagwati and Chakravarty (1969) and references cited therein.

[12]This underlies the so-called 'export pessimism'. To my way of thinking, it is reasonable to assume in the Indian context that the bulk of the capital goods required will have to be domestically produced. This still leaves open the vital questions of the phasing of that investment and its methods of finance.

industries which produce these goods 'heavy industries'.

As has been pointed out before, in the present state of technology, 'heavy industries' require typically large-scale investment,
being subject to increasing returns to scale. The requirement of
large initial capital outlay meant that it was unlikely under Indian
conditions that domestic private industry would be able to undertake this type of investment. However, a bigger deterrent would have
been that the markets for the products of these industries did not
exist at the time of the second plan but would have needed to be
developed in the future. It was therefore likely to involve considerable risk, which would tend to keep private capital away
from such investment. Thus it became necessary to locate this
investment in the public sector, which in turn fitted in nicely with
the objective of a 'socialist society'. However, a problem remained that India at that time did not have the technology to produce
these capital goods. This meant importing the technology, and
as the technology is generally embodied in the machines themselves and is not commonly sold except as plant and equipment,
it meant in turn importing the capital goods from abroad.[13] It
was never seriously discussed what priority should be given to the
building-up of domestic technology so as to minimize this dependence, although there was a vague feeling that eventually the
economy would learn 'by doing'.

On the face of it, it does not seem to be an unrealistic strategy
for a large, semi-industrialized country like India to have followed.
In any case, that it was feasible under certain historical and institutional conditions had been demonstrated by the USSR. However, it has certain peculiarities that have to be brought out into
the open. First, such a strategy basically implies trading-off a relatively lower level of present consumption for future consumption.
Unless the Government has complete freedom of policy over
patterns of distribution, it also implies some choice about whose
consumption should be forgone for whose benefit. Neither of these
issues was faced in the formulation of the strategy. The first of
them concerns the problem of mobilization of an adequate
volume of savings to finance a given planned volume of invest-

---

[13]The fact that imports of capital goods are not synonymous with
import of capital, i.e. the import surplus, is often ignored in the development literature.

ment. The criticism that the strategy assumed that a given investment plan would finance itself by generating its own savings has been made by Bhagwati and Chakravarty and others. We shall shortly return to its wider implications. For the moment, let us underline the implication of the distributional issue.

Given the recognition that there is a large number of poor people in the economy and that the bulk of their incomes is spent on consumption, a redistribution of income really means increasing the *consumption* of the poor. If one believes that the possibilities of redistributing existing incomes, or consumption, is small—in Nehru's telling phrase, 'in a poor country there is only poverty to redistribute', the additional consumption can only come out of incremental incomes or output. However, while one leg of economic policy was pulling in that direction, the basic strategy implied keeping the increment of output going towards additional consumption as low as possible. This obvious contradiction largely escaped the planners' notice.

Let us now return to the question of the aggregate volume of savings required to finance investment. As Bhagwati and others have pointed out, there was a fallacy involved in the assumption that because capital goods were not themselves available for consumption purposes, a given level of output of these goods would automatically generate their own savings.[14] Unless the *ex-ante* rate of savings was equal to the planned rate of investment, the outcome might simply generate excess demand and put pressure on the price level and the balance of payments. Whether the economy could maintain the planned volume or rate of growth of investment in such circumstances, would depend partly on the Government's concern for price and balance of payments stability on the one hand and on the other the ability of the public sector to maintain its share of investible resources against pressure from the private sector.

Our previous discussion of certain aspects of the performance of the public sector has to be seen against this light. A substantial programme of investment in heavy industries required a large volume of public sector savings to finance it on the supply side and a high rate of public investment on the demand side to obtain the benefit of high rates of utilization of capacity. The lack of a clear

[14]Patel (1969); Bhagwati (1962).

and consistent strategy on resource mobilization led to the generation of excess demand and inflationary pressures on the economy. The failure to control non-essential expenditures in the private sector and especially its own non-developmental expenditure led to a cutback on public sector investment.[15] This in turn undermined the only basis on which heavy capital expenditure in public sector industries could have been made to justify itself and saddled the economy with underused and expensive capital goods capacity. The stagnation of these industries led in turn to continuous technological dependence on foreign knowhow and the inadequacy of domestic resources led in its own turn to a continuing dependence on foreign capital.

There is another intellectual sleight of hand involved in the planning strategy. Given the objective of maximizing the rate of growth, the Mahalanobis strategy lays down an allocation rule that is of general applicability, *whatever is the scarce input that is required to attain a given rate of investment*. Because the problem was discussed in the Indian context in terms of the scarcity of foreign exchange, the solution was formulated in such a way as to imply that one could derive both a particular composition of investment as well as a particular allocation of foreign exchange; for example, as if devoting a high proportion of investment to heavy machinery implied allocating a high share of foreign exchange directly to the imports of that machinery. As Bhagwati and Patel have pointed out, the last conclusion again involves a fallacy. At given sets of international prices facing the economy, the economy might well have gained by obtaining a given amount of heavy machinery at a smaller resource cost through trade.[16] That would depend on comparative costs, interpreted in some dynamic framework.[17] The fact that the planning approach sidestepped the problem had an interesting implication. As capital goods imports were accorded high priority, the question of the development of an indigenous technology receded further into the background. In addition, the failure to distinguish between the savings constraint and the foreign exchange constraint, as Tendulkar has shown, led to an underestimation of the overall resource

---

[15]See pp. 87, 108-9 above.
[16]See the references cited in n. 14 above.
[17]Chenery (1961).

requirements of a given investment plan.[18]

All the discussion so far has been in terms of generation of output. That is how the planners saw the problem of growth primarily. The issue of employment was treated separately as an objective. Although full employment was regarded as a desirable objective, its achievement was seen to depend on the fulfilment of achieving a capital stock objective and that in the long run.[19] There was no serious concern in the formulation of the strategy for the compatibility of the employment targets with the various output and investment targets. As we have seen, in fact, the employment targets in the plans were never even remotely fulfilled.[20]

The treatment of employment as a side issue, so to speak, had particular implications for the question of removal of inequality and poverty. In Chapters 7 and 8, I have discussed at length the questions of who are the poor and what a policy of eradication of poverty entails. We saw there that a major cause of rural poverty was lack of access to land ownership and land use, whereas urban poverty was largely a result of a lack of employment and low wages. A necessary condition for both was an expansion in the production of wage-goods, especially food products on which the bulk of the income of the poor is spent. To take the urban poor first, in a mixed economy incomes are earned through employment, the real wage rates determining the adequacy of that level of income. In such an economy, there are no other ways of increasing the incomes of the urban poor, except through the provision of employment at adequate levels of productivity.[21] An adequate rate of creation of employment is, therefore, central to the issue of reducing inequality or poverty, as far as the urban poor are concerned. The objective of urban poverty cannot be discussed separately from the employment question.[22]

---

[18]Tendulkar (1971).

[19]India, Planning Commission (1956), Ch. V.

[20]See pp. 46-9 above.

[21]People employed in the service sectors in the urban economy do not always earn wages but are self-employed. Their productivity depends not so much on the stock of capital equipment as on the level and composition of demand. See, for example, Reddaway (1962), ILO (1972).

[22]The fact that there is widespread 'underemployment' in India has been freely recognized in the plans.

The position regarding the rural poor is somewhat different. As we saw earlier, this group consists of small peasants and landless agricultural labourers, the two categories shading into one another at the margin. The planners laid stress on the redistribution of land as the major instrument for reduction of rural poverty. In formulating this policy, there was never any discussion in the plans of how much land would have to be redistributed, what the required levels of ceilings on maximum holdings would be and whether the proposed ceiling levels for the states were consistent with the plan objectives.[23] There was no discussion along the lines initiated long after by Minhas, whether alternative policies of land consolidation and public works would provide a better and more workable solution. In any case, land redistribution was never intended to help the plight of the landless, who are amongst the poorest of the poor. For them, the plans merely proposed an expansion of *khadi* and handicraft production to provide employment and various totally inadequate make-work schemes which would hardly have made a dent in the problem and which in no sense were part of any core plan.[24] The first part of the scheme also ignored the question of where the demand for handicraft products would come from, seeing that the bulk of the additional incomes were going to be directed not towards *khadi* but basic foodgrains.

The attitude towards the problem of poverty highlights the approach of the planners to the central problems of the economy. At a general level, there is obviously a serious concern for the poor and their poverty. On the other hand, there is little attempt either to identify the poorer parts of the population or to estimate the magnitude of poverty and hence the likely dimensions of any programme that would make a significant impact. Until the draft fifth plan, there was also no discussion of the implications for the overall growth of the economy of any diversion of resources

[23]The inadequacy of land redistribution as a solution to the problem of rural poverty has been pointed out by Raj Krishna (1959), Minhas (1974) and Dandekar and Rath (1971). See also the discussion in p 142f above.

[24]See, for example, India, Planning Commission (1956), Ch. V; on the inadequacy of the various rural works schemes, see Lok Sabha Estimates Committee (1964) and Minhas (1974); on the limited impact of land reform on the landless labourers, see India, Planning Commission (1952), p. 193.

towards the poor.[25] While the first five-year plan clearly posed the problem that a rise in incomes of the poor required as a condition an increase in the supply of wage-goods and foodgrains output, in later plans the relationship between these two factors became far less clearly defined.[26] While there was a general awareness of the complementary nature of agricultural and industrial growth, there was very little recognition that if planning was to benefit the poor, it had to produce a great deal more of the basic wage-goods that the poor consumed and generate purchasing power amongst the poor.

The question naturally arises how was the Government's attitude to the concentration of economic power in the industrial sector related to the objective of reducing inequality and poverty. An anti-monopoly policy was obviously more relevant to the reduction of the overall degree of inequality in incomes and wealth in the economy than to raising the absolute levels of incomes of the very poor. Even then, the policy was of limited relevance. What was proposed was a levelling down from above, partly through the fiscal system and partly through direct controls on expansion of large enterprises. However, as the efficiency of the fiscal system was very limited and the Government had no effective means of controlling monopolistic practices in the non-corporate sector such as the wholesale trade in foodgrains, little effective change could have been wrought by the strategy that was followed. Amaresh Bagchi has shown how the fiscal system has for the most part been regressive rather than progressive; Hazari has shown for the early years how concentration of economic power increased even in the corporate sector.[27] It would appear that quite apart from failure in implementation, Government strategy towards the control of monopoly was largely borrowed from the European social democratic tradition, without much regard for its appropriateness to Indian situations.[28]

[25]India, Planning Commission (1973); see also Tendulkar (1974).

[26]India, Planning Commission (1952), Ch. I.

[27]Amaresh Bagchi (1974); see also Gupta (1975) for a review of studies on tax incidence; on the concentration of economic power in India, see Hazari (1966).

[28]In a developed country, an anti-monopoly policy can be directed solely at the organized sector. In a poor country, monopolistic practices may exist outside the organized corporate sector, e.g. in the wholesale

We can now turn to a brief consideration of the Government's strategy on agricultural development. It was seen in our discussion of the problems of agricultural change in India that it is not easy to come to a definite conclusion on the question of the alleged neglect of the agricultural sector in the allocation of resources.[29] It is quite clear, however, that while the planners were aware of the interrelationship between agricultural and industrial development, they seriously underestimated the critical importance of agricultural development to some of the basic objectives of the plans. For example, there is no clear appreciation of the importance of the wage-goods constraint on both the employment and the elimination of poverty objectives. Bhagwati and Chakravarty have pointed out that the importance of the wage-goods constraint was first raised by Vakil and Bramhanand and Vakil in 1956.[30]

Although the Government noted that industrial inputs were necessary for increasing agricultural production, they gave very little importance to investment in industrial capacity for producing these inputs. We have seen that the share of project aid going to fertilizer production was as low as 4.1 per cent during 1956-70.;[31] this in spite of the fact that the importance of investment in fertilizer capacity was first pointed out in 1959.[32] It is, perhaps, the low priority given to the expansion of capacity in those lines of production that were immediately relevant to the needs of the agricultural sector such as fertilizers, small pumps, better agricultural implements, etc., rather than a low overall allocation of funds to agriculture, that most strongly underlines the low priority given to agricultural development by the planners.

The combination of a solemn appreciation of the problems of agricultural development and a sustained inability to provide an adequate supply of inputs to bring about that development is a characteristic of Indian economic policy. It springs, in turn, from the planners' view of the nature of the constraints on agricultural development. As Raj has pointed out, there is an underlying con-

---

trade in foodgrains. For a long time Indian policy ignored these areas of monopoly, which even now are untouched. Except, that is, for the abortive attempt to regulate the grain trade.

[29]See pp. 113-15 above

[30]Bramhanand and Vakil (1956).

[31]See p. 168 above.

[32]Sen (1960), App. A.

tinuity in that view. From time to time, the Government has identified a particular shortcoming as the critical one and has concentrated its attention on that particular aspect of the problem. What has changed in course of time has been the identity of the critical factor.[33]

During the first plan, the view was taken that 'underemployed' labour provided a hidden reserve of resources for expansion of output. While inputs such as seeds and fertilizers and facilities such as improved marketing channels were necessary, the main problem was to bring about a better organization of that idle manpower through the dissemination of information and incentives to a potentially receptive peasant community. Hence, the major effort was concentrated on a widely dispersed network of community development and extension services. The effect of that policy was minimal, although its failure was partially hidden by the effects of a run of good monsoons which increased food output.[34] The failure of that policy was due in substantial part to the inability to relate the community development and extension services to specific problem-solving advice and inputs.[35]

The seemingly correct lesson was then learned and the policy switched to the provision of certain identifiable inputs to select areas such as fertilizers, irrigation and credit to select areas in the country, so as not to dilute the impact of that strategy. As the need was to increase the level of agricultural output, it was thought that this could best be achieved by concentrating these inputs on areas which were already better endowed with such facilities as irrigation. As to the obvious regional and interfarm imbalances that this would create, reliance was placed on strong spread effects emanating from the larger farmers and more fertile areas to the less fortunate ones.

Essentially the policy that was embodied in the IAAP and the IADP programmes was carried forward into the HYV stage, when the technological breakthrough was thought to have been established by the discovery of new high-yielding varieties of seeds. As Weisskopf has pointed out, the policy was directed from the

---

[33]Raj (1969).

[34]During the first five-year plan food production increased by 15 per cent mainly as a result of favourable weather conditions.

[35]On the limitations of this policy, see Brown (1971).

beginning towards helping the richer farmers and the richer areas.[36] As to the spread effects, there was very little empirical evidence to encourage belief in their existence and the Government did little to bring them about. Moreover, even in the restricted area of its operations, the economy has been faced with frequent shortages of fertilizers, seeds, etc., in spite of the fact that the rates of application, especially of fertilizers, have been below the recommended dosage. Here, again, the Government has lacked the will to will the means that its chosen strategy required.

Basically, the same strategy has continued in operation since the beginning of the 1960s, in the face of continued evidence of failure to achieve a breakthrough for any crop other than wheat. Even the evidence on that is none too firm.[37] The official view is that agricultural stagnation is the result of periodical failure of the monsoons. We have already seen what evidence there is for the view that the poor harvests of recent years are to be explained largely in these terms.[38] What, say the planners, can one expect to do in the face of exogenous shocks such as the failure of the monsoons? In my view, the best answer to that has been provided by Postan in a different context. Writing about the Middle Ages, he says, 'Yet the unprecedented heavy toll that these harvest failures took, like the toll which similar calamities have taken in certain countries in modern times, could not have been due to natural causes alone but to the calamity-sensitive constitution of society, and above all to the precarious balance between men's needs and the productivity of their holdings characteristic of an overpopulated country and an overextended agriculture'.[39]

It is interesting that there is no evidence that the planners at any stage considered any alternative strategies. There is a great deal of evidence that the productivity of small holdings in traditional Indian agriculture is higher per acre than that of large holdings. There is also evidence that one of the key constraints on the growth of agriculture has been the inadequacy of water supply and irrigation. It has also been known since the inception of the IADP/HYV strategies that they are expensive in terms of resour-

---

[36]Weisskopf (1972).
[37]See p. 124 above.
[38]See pp. 129-0 above.
[39]Postan (1971), p. 565.

ces, although they yield higher outputs than traditional strategies, and that the ability of the economy to provide enough inputs to cover a substantial part of either the area or the farming population was going to be severely limited for years. Yet there is no evidence that the Government ever considered whether an alternative strategy based on a wider dispersion of a cheaper if less productive technology would have been more optimal than the strategy that was chosen. It is quite possible that the answer would have been the same. The loss of agricultural output it would have entailed might have turned out to have been unacceptable. The interesting point, however, is that a strategy that is supposed to have as its major objective the elimination of poverty should have largely ignored even the existence of such a choice.

The comment by Postan brings us to the last element of planning strategy that I wish to consider, which relates to the growth of population in India. In a sense, it can be argued that the relatively poor performance of the Indian economy is due not so much to any inefficiency in the field of production but simply to the fact that so much of any increase in total output is used up to provide for a growing population. Thus, the Mahalanobis committee estimated that roughly 51 per cent of the total increase in net national product between 1950-51 and 1960-61 was required to maintain the same *per capita* level of output, on account of the growth in population.[40] However, as the growth of population is a fact of life, one has to assess the performance of the economy in relation to the needs of that population.

A peculiarity of the population problem in India is its asymmetrical impact for different planning horizons. That is to say over a period of, say, 25 years, the rate of growth of population has to be taken more or less as a datum. The size of the child-bearing population for that period is given and the only way to affect the position is to influence the number of births per head of that population. Over a longer period, both variables become policy variables and thus a much larger impact is possible upon the rate of growth of population. In the very long run, too, one could argue that the population question in India is the key question, in the sense that no improvement in the standards of

[40]India, Planning Commission, Mahalanobis Committee Pt. I (1964), Table 2.1, p.59.

living of the population is possible in the long run if population continues to grow at anything approaching the current rates. So that, while not much that is tangible can be expected from any population control policy in the medium run, the long-run battle might be lost unless a great deal is done in the short term. Faced with this paradox, what has been the strategy of the Government on population control?

As with many other problems that we have looked into, it must be said at the outset that the data do not permit an evaluation of the strategy of population control followed by the Government that would provide a conclusive answer as to its appropriateness. There are a number of reasons for this. First, although we know that decisions relating to family size in *any* population are influenced by a large number of socio-economic factors, we know too little to be definite about the precise relationships between these factors and desired family size. Equally, not enough is known about the effectiveness of alternative policies in influencing these relationships towards smaller family size. Thirdly, in the narrow sphere of technology a number of alternative methods are available; there is some evidence that they are not equally effective over periods of time and over different geographical areas. Much of our ignorance springs from basic uncertainties that still remain in our knowledge of reproductive biology and social psychology. One should not, therefore, be too eager to blame the Government for some of the shortcomings of its family planning programme. In addition, the empirical data relating to some of these problems in India cover only small geographical areas and periods of time and it is not clear to what extent their conclusions can be generalized for the whole of India.[41]

Although they were aware of a growing population, until the middle 1950s Indian planners generally underestimated the urgency of the problem. No doubt this view was held partly because the rate of growth of population was itself underestimated until the 1961 census. Since that time, Indian plans have given increasing emphasis to population control, although substantial resources have been devoted to it only since the middle 1960s.[42]

---

[41]Thus, Wyon and Gordon (1971) and Mamdani (1972) both cover a small area in the Punjab.

[42]On cost-benefit studies, see Cassen (1968), Enke (1966) and Simmons

The strategy on population control, the family planning programme as it is called, has been fairly narrowly conceived. The emphasis has been directed towards policies to bring down the birth rate. There are a number of known techniques of birth control that vary in cost and effectiveness. They are mainly condoms, IUDs, vasectomies or sterilization, and the contraceptive pill. While the Government has encouraged all these, reliance has been placed mainly on one or two of them to achieve a 'breakthrough', to use a favourite planning term. While in the middle 1960s IUDs were seen as the main answer to the problem, the emphasis has now shifted towards sterilization.

How effective have these strategies been? According to Simmons, the official birth control programme has had some but only a limited effectiveness.[43] A similar conclusion is reached in a study relating to some Punjab villages by Wyon and Gordon.[44] Simmons estimated that the post-programme birth rate has been 10 per cent lower than it would have been in the absence of such a programme.[45] Of the various methods tried, sterilization has had the widest impact and been the most effective.[46]

Why has the impact been so limited? There appears to be a number of reasons for this. First, there is the problem of the effective implementation of such a programme over a country as large as India. For a long time, the scale of expenditure on the programme was not very large. Thereafter, there have been administrative problems both of expanding the area covered and of effectively manning the programme with suitably skilled workers. The impact of the programme and its effective implementation has varied considerably from state to state, thus reducing the overall effect below what could have been possible with more uniform and better implementation. According to Simmons,

---

(1971). For a review of Indian policy towards family planning, see Banerji (1972); see also India, Planning Commission, PEO (1970).

[43]Simmons (1971), Chs. 3 and 4.

[44]Wyon and Gordon (1971).

[45]Simmons (1971), Chs. 3 and 4.

[46]According to Simmons (1971), sterilization was four times as effective as other methods. This is estimated by comparing the actual births in a sample population with the expected number of births calculated from age-specific fertility rates, birth-intervals between conceptions etc; see Simmons (1971), Ch. 3.

levels of acceptance of contraceptive devices were three times as
high for Punjab and Maharashtra as for Bihar and Uttar
Pradesh.[47] Secondly, the impact of any given technique has been
seen to diminish with its continuous use. This has been true of
both IUDs and sterilization. A third reason, which partly explains
the second, is that a number of traditional methods of birth control are already practised by a part of the population.[48] The birth
control programme has quite often simply had the effect of making
some of the people who were already undertaking some methods
of control switch to the modern methods. The catchment area of
the programmes has not extended to include those who were not
already practising birth control and this too has reduced the
effectiveness of the chosen strategy.[49] As far as one can determine,
professed unwillingness to adopt these practices has not been a
serious problem in India.[50]

A number of studies have drawn attention to what may be a
more fundamental shortcoming of the Indian strategy. If these
criticisms are valid, the family planning programme will offer
another example of the proclivity of Indian planners to adopt a
particular technical solution to a problem without either fully
appreciating the nature of the problem itself or considering possible
alternative solutions.[51]

The basic issue raised by these studies is whether the birth rate
is not determined by certain socio-economic variables relating to
a particular structure of society, so that any sustained attack on
the birth rate requires policies that would affect the operations of
those variables, rather than the provision merely of various contraceptive techniques. In the Indian context, it has been argued
that a particular birth rate is related to a desired family, which in
turn is critically influenced by the prevailing infant mortality
rate.[52] Families aim for a particular number of live births in rela-

[47]Simmons (1971), p. 145f.

[48]Mandelbaum (1974).

[49]Wyon and Gordon (1971).

[50]The actual and effective degree of acceptance, as shown by continuous
adherence to particular practices, may of course differ from people's initial
response to the idea of birth control.

[51]See Simmons (1971), Wyon and Gordon (1971) and Cassen (1974) on
the influence of family size; Mandelbaum (1974) discusses the role of social
factors.

[52]See above p. 43, on the infant mortality rate.

tion to the prevailing rate of infant mortality, so as to have a reasonable chance of achieving the desired family size. The analytical significance of the continuing high level of infant mortality that we have noticed earlier will now be appreciated.[53] In such a situation, although the infant mortality rate is falling slowly, there may be a recognition lag that will tend to keep the birth rate high. It might then require quite a dramatic fall in the infant mortality rate for the birth rate to show a decline. A policy that is directed towards reducing the infant mortality rate may, therefore, be a more effective means of bringing down the birth rate than some more narrowly conceived birth control policies. As the infant mortality rate is, in turn, influenced by a variety of factors, such as malnutrition of expectant mothers and infants, contaminated water supplies carrying waterborne diseases, insanitary living conditions, etc., a population control policy may have to be conceived broadly covering wide areas of nutrition and health policy.[54]

[53]On the relationship between some of these factors, see Banerji (1973), and Nair (1974).

[54]Mamdani (1972). In a critique of the Khanna study, Mamdani has argued that large families are required as a source of labour for individual households, where they make a positive contribution to household output and incomes. It would be wrong in such circumstances to expect the birth rate to fall unless conditions of labour use were changed in rural society. It is a stimulating thesis but based on somewhat limited evidence. The policy implications of his findings are the same as for the previous ones, indicating that a successful family planning strategy may have to cover a much wider area of operation than has been realized by the planners. The section dealing with the family planning programme, like the rest of the book, was written before the impact of the 1975 'emergency'.

CHAPTER TEN

The Role of the State: Instruments of Control

The object of the present chapter is not to provide a detailed account of the policy instruments used by the Indian Government to direct and control the economy. The instruments used are often extremely complex and detailed and they have undergone changes from time to time. The formal nature of an instrument and the way in which it is actually deployed may also be different. Moreover, quite an elaborate institutional structure has also been built up for the administration of some of these rules. It is obviously not possible within a short space to give an account of such a complex system. What I propose here is to give a short description of the nature of the policy instruments used by the Government and their main areas of operation, and without attempting any detailed evaluation indicate the extent to which they can be said to have been successful in achieving their major aims. In doing so, I shall exclude those instruments which are largely used to cope with emergencies, such as famines or wars.[1]

To start at the most general level, we can note that whatever the merits and demerits of the economic strategy that has been pursued by the Government, its implementation has been very poor. While the former will continue to be a matter of controversy, few will be found to defend the Government's record of implementation of its chosen policy.[2] The failure of implementation can be obser-

---

[1] That is, policies concerned with famine or flood reliefs, emergency rationing, gold control orders, etc.

[2] The criticisms are too numerous to note. They are contained in the mid-term reviews of various plans, reports of the Estimates Committee and the Public Undertakings Committee, quoted in Ch. 6 above, and in the

ved at both an aggregative and at the specific sectoral or project level. The most critical failures at the aggregative level are, perhaps, the failure to achieve the planned rates of investment and of domestic resource mobilization, with its consequent continued dependence on foreign aid.[3]

With the exception of the first five-year plan, all the others have suffered from this shortcoming.[4] At the sectoral level, we have noted the failure of agricultural output to expand at the planned rate since the 1950s.[5] Medhora has usefully summarized for us the failure of particular targets of industrial output to be reached during the planned periods, as well as the delays in completing various industrial projects on target.[6] Critical shortfalls in the production of steel, fertilizers and other inputs continue to be a feature of economic life in India. The failure of public sector industries to reach their investment and output targets has been amply documented in the various reports of the Lok Sabha Committee of Estimates, the Committee on Public Undertakings and the reports of the Programme Evaluation Organization of the Planning Commission.[7] The failure of implementation at both the macro- and the micro-levels is obviously not unrelated. While a particular development plan is something more than a sum of the individual projects, in that it embodies a particular strategy in the choice and phasing of the projects, it only materializes through the successful implementation of the projects. In this connection, it would be true to say that while the non-achievement of some targets may merely reflect the unreality of those targets and hence faulty plan formulation, widespread shortfalls across the board cannot be explained away in such terms alone.

It has to be borne in mind that the Indian economy is not a centrally planned economy but a mixed economy, with the Government having direct control over that small part of it that consti-

---

literature relating to the 'green revolution' discussed in Ch. 5. See also Gadgil (1972).

[3]See pp. 79-80 above.

[4]The first five-year plan used very small amounts of deficitfi nancing or running down of external assets.

[5]See p. 223 above.

[6]Medhora (1968).

[7]See n. 37, Ch. 6.

tutes the public sector.[8] Its capacity to control the economy depends, therefore, on its ability to influence the behaviour of a large number of individual decision-making units through a system of incentives and disincentives. Moreover, while it can devise alternative systems of incentives and disincentives, it cannot determine the degree to which allocative decisions within the private sector would respond to any such system. In this context, it is important to distinguish between those policies that influence the total level of demand for resources and those that affect the allocation of resources without directly affecting the level of demand. In turn, the second type of policy can be divided into those that operate through the price system and those that bypass that system, such as various forms of quotas and directives.[9] While some of the criticisms that have been made of Government economic policy tend to give the picture of a distinctly *dirigiste* regime, in fact the Government has used both types of allocative policy, with greater emphasis on the latter.

In the short run, the Indian economy suffers from two distinct types of pressure on the level of demand. First, the output of the agricultural sector is subject to wide and random fluctuations owing to variations in rainfall. A severe and prolonged drought such as was observed during 1965-67 obviously affects the level of demand as well as output. Less severe failures in rainfall, however, reduce the supply of the major wage-goods without necessarily reducing the purchasing power of the population in terms of money.[10] Such situations obviously give rise to excess demand within the economy. Secondly, in a capital-scarce economy, and we have seen that the planners view the economy very much in such a light, supplies of various kinds of output are restricted by sectoral ceilings imposed by the limited output capacity of such sectors. Indeed, if we adopt the view that it is the lack of investment that keeps agricultural output from increasing, the wage-goods bottleneck in agriculture will simply be an important special case of such

[8]See p. 12 above.

[9]On price and non-price controls, see Little, Scitovsky and Scott (1970). Of course, the two different types of policy may affect each other. For example, quotas affect prices, if they do not eliminate excess demand.

[10]That is to say the purchasing power of the non-agricultural population may not be reduced. The agricultural producer may suffer from a reduction in real income and have to resort to dissaving or borrowing.

a sectoral constraint.[11] In an economy subject to the operation of sectoral full employment of capacity ceilings, there is no automatic mechanism that would keep demand in balance with capacity. Under normal circumstances, an economy of that nature can cope with such short-run imbalances by drawing in net imports from abroad, allowing its balance of payments to worsen, and calling in the international economy to redress the balance of demand in the domestic economy. If the balance of payments problem is as acute as it has been for India such an accommodation of excess demand is virtually ruled out. The economy thus has to operate directly on the level of demand to maintain stability.

It is obvious that in so far as the Government has a budgetary policy, its fiscal measures must have some effect on the level of demand. It would be fair to say, however, that the Government has made no systematic attempt to adopt a short-run stabilization policy to control the level of effective demand in the economy. So far as it has had a strategy, it is perhaps to control the level of deficit financing within certain limits. As we have seen earlier, its definition of deficit financing makes it underestimate the inflationary effects of the budgetary policy. Moreover, even within the limits of its own definition it has failed to keep the level of deficit financing within acceptable limits, especially during the second five-year plan and in the 1970s.[12] We must not underestimate the problems of running an effective demand management policy in an underdeveloped economy, where knowledge of the basic expenditure-income relationships is extremely meagre.[13] The fact remains that it has done little even to collect any information that would help it to perform that task more adequately.[14] Instead, it has relied on direct controls to keep balance between output and demand. In the agricultural sector, this has taken the form of buffer stocks and price policies; in the non-agricultural sector, of quotas and licensing policies. The efficiency of such policies is sensitive to the degree of excess demand that they have to accommodate

[11]The concept of sectoral ceilings is put forward, e.g. in Raj (1948).

[12]See p. 81f above.

[13]Compare the current experience of many a developed country, where the data-base of economic policy is very much firmer.

[14]For example, while a lot of work has been done on long-term planning, the Planning Commission has developed no short-term forecasting models.

and they tend to break down if the excess demand assumes too large a proportion. The Indian experience has, in this respect, not been an exception.

Before we go on to discuss the methods that have actually been employed by the Government to regulate the agricultural and industrial sectors, we have to face up to a very pertinent question as to the use of the term 'excess demand' in the Indian context. On the one hand, a low level of savings, an adverse balance of payments and inflation are traditionally recognized signs of excess demand. On the other, I have several times pointed to a lasting industrial recession and substantial volumes of excess capacity in particular public sector industries.[15] Whether one recognizes the presence of excess demand in the economy in this admittedly confused body of evidence depends on whether one accepts the proposition that there are severe structural maladjustments within the economy.

In my view, the recognition that the Indian economy suffers from severe structural imbalances and discontinuities between sectors is central to an understanding of recent economic development in India. In such an economy there are certain factors and inputs, such as land or heavy machinery, which are specific to particular sectors. On the other hand, there are other inputs, such as steel or cement, which are non-specific and can be used, say, to produce investment goods, basic consumer goods or luxury consumer goods. Moreover, there are some consumer goods, such as foodgrains or edible oils, that are consumed by both rich and poor. If aggregate supply is less than aggregate demand, and the deficiency cannot be met by a further worsening of the balance of payments, part of the demand generated has to remain unfulfilled in real terms. It is the demand of the poorer consumers, and hence the derived demand for inputs for the production of those goods, that suffers; so does the investment plan of the public sector, although I have argued that the latter is partly due to the higher priority given to non-developmental expenditure by the Government.[16] Moreover, shortages of specific inputs such as land and the diversion of non-specific inputs such as steel, from one sector to others, perpetuate the shortages that gave rise to the imbalance in the first

[15]See e.g. pp. 159-60.
[16]See pp. 86-8 above.

instance. Admittedly, I have not rigorously established the presence of structural factors in the Indian economy. However, such a view is perfectly consistent with the observed realities of the economy.

To return to the pattern of controls used by the Government, a major concern of policy has been that of maintaining some sort of a balance between the supply of foodgrains and the demand for food. This policy has to be viewed against the background of virtually no improvement in *per capita* availability of foodgrains in the last twenty-odd years.[17] As the average level of consumption in a 'normal' year has been fairly close to the nutritional minimum, any shortfall in the harvest causes shortages of serious consequence. This has been exacerbated by the fact that the distribution of foodgrains amongst rich and poor consumers is unequal, indicating that the poor have less than the nutritional minimum. The Government's view has also been that shortages are made more acute by speculative withholding of foodgrains by grain dealers.[18] In addition, the food problem has a regional dimension in India, in that some states are surplus producers of foodgrains while others have a chronic deficit.[19] Over the years, the Government has tried to deal with these problems, partly through the import of foodgrains, partly through the building up and running down of buffer stocks and partly through trying to control the price and distribution of foodgrains.

The policy of the Government towards maintaining an overall balance between supply and demand for foodgrains has been based on imports of foodgrains. If the Government's objective were to use imports to build up buffer stocks of foodgrains, in order to even out consumption between good and bad years, the policy of food imports has not conformed to it. In the pre-1965 period, when imports were available under PL 480, imports were used to increase the consumption of certain groups of consumers. The inability to build up buffer stocks in earlier years has meant increasing reliance on imported grains to make up for bad harvests, even when grain has had to be purchased at rising, free-

[17]Table 38, p. 187 above.
[18]For a criticism of food policy, see Chandra (1973). Chandra criticizes the NSS estimates as being too high.
[19]The 'surplus' states are *inter alia* Punjab, Madhya Pradesh, Rajasthan, Uttar Pradesh and Andhra Pradesh.

market prices. The net effect of foodgrains imports, especially in
the earlier years, has been not so much to even out fluctuations in
imports as to depress the relative price of wheat.[20] As Raj Krishna
has shown, the Government's buffer-stock policy has also been
inefficient, in the sense that its major objectives could have been
achieved through smaller volumes of buffer stocks.[21]

Part of the reason for such inefficiency in the operation of buffer
stocks is the inability of the Government effectively to control the
distribution of foodgrains among different groups of consumers.[22]
As Chandra has shown, the total availability of foodgrains during
this period was just about sufficient to ensure a nutritionally adequate level of consumption for the population, *on the assumption
that there was no inequality in levels of consumption* [23] However, the
institutional constraints within which the Government chooses to
formulate its policy rule out such an assumption.

The avowed policy of the Government has been to effect the
distribution of foodgrains through a system of partial rationing.
This takes the form of the sale of foodgrains through fair price
shops, at a price lower than the ruling market price, of a given
amount of grains per head. Ideally, such a policy should be directed towards providing food for those who are the most needy and
a necessary condition of such a policy is that the Government gets
hold of a sufficient amount of the marketed surplus from the surplus farmers and surplus areas. On the first of these, an adequate
comment is that such fair price shops exist mainly in urban areas,
whereas the bulk of the poor live in rural areas. Nevertheless, it
is true that some of the urban poor are very poor and are denied
any access to non-marketed foodgrains, which at least part of the
rural poor might have.[24]

However, as the fair price shop 'ration' is not related to the
income of the consumer, the effect of such a distribution policy
has been to offer an indiscriminate subsidy to all income groups in
urban areas and none to even the poorest groups in rural areas.
In addition, even that limited policy has been ineffective through

---

[20]Rath and Patwardhan (1967); Raj (1966); Mann, J. (1967).
[21]Raj Krishna (1967).
[22]*Ibid.*
[23]Chandra (1973).
[24]Dandekar and Rath (1971). Some of the rural poor may have access
to payments in kind or be able to undertake some form of food-gathering.

the inability of the Government ever to get hold of a sizable proportion of the marketed supply of foodgrains. According to Raj Krishna, the proportion acquired by the Government did not exceed 8 per cent of sales between 1951 and 1965.[25] The situation has since got worse. Less has been procured proportionally in recent years out of a larger total output than was done during the worst drought years of 1965-67, ending in the reversal of the Government's decision to nationalize the grain trade in 1974.[26] Promulgation of non-enforceable procurement prices and quotas has simply had no effect on prices or procurement, while the periodic zonal restrictions on the movement of foodgrains from surplus areas have led to an atrophy of surplus grain in surplus states.[27] Here, we have a good example of the characteristic tendency of the Government to try to manipulate the outcome of an economic process without being able to influence the major forces behind that outcome.

For the non-agricultural sector, the Government has tried to operate two distinct types of control, both of which can be said to belong to the type that bypasses the price mechanism. First, the Government has tried, from time to time, to control the allocation of certain scarce industrial inputs, such as cement or steel. This has been done through an elaborate system of controls and licences. For while the Government levies an excise duty on, say, domestic steel, the main object of that tax is not to bring supply into balance with demand.[28] Secondly, the Government has tried to control the growth, composition and concentration of industrial capacity through a system of industrial and import licensing.

An example of how the first type of control operates in practice has been provided in the report of the Committee on Steel Prices.[29] The rationale of the control policy was to ensure the availability of steel to priority users, regulate the amount of steel being devoted to non-priority uses, control prices of different categories of steel, and enable producer firms to plan optimal production pro-

[25] Raj Krishna (1967), p. 114.

[26] Raj Krishna (1967); a more recent work on the public distribution schemes for foodgrains is the one by Gulati and Krishnan (1975).

[27] Bardhan, K. (1966); Raj (1966).

[28] It has been argued that the main effect of the excise duty on steel is to reduce domestic demand and lead to excess capacity and low profits.

[29] India, Ministry of Steel, Raj Committee (1963).

grammes.[30] The Government had tried to ensure this by a very detailed licensing and allocation procedure on the one hand and a channelling of requests for steel to particular producers on the other. In effect, the procedure was not successful for a variety of reasons. There was no co-ordination of decision-taking at any level. A failure to define priority uses with any precision defeated the main purpose of the controls, which was to ensure that certain key sectors got their requirements of steel. Attempts to enforce control across the economy led to administrative delays and the inability either to grant licences on time or to enable producers to plan economic 'runs' for producing particular types of steel. In addition, inability to control the re-marketing of steel by some of the initial licensees led to a failure to control prices.

This is a classic example of the tendency of the Government to undertake unnecessarily wide and detailed controls that its administrative capacity cannot handle, in pursuit of a mirage of complete equity, instead of concentrating the scarce administrative skills in ensuring that a certain clearly defined 'core' of industries or investments were not denied an adequate supply of inputs. This tendency merely mirrors at the micro-level the inability of the planners to define their objectives in any operationally meaningful manner at the macro-level.[31]

The instrument of control that has probably had the most impact on the pattern of development of the economy is the system of industrial licensing introduced under the Industries (Development and Regulation) Act of 1951. To say that it has had the most impact is not to say that it has had the effect intended by the Government. There are now a number of studies relating to the operation of industrial licensing and import controls in India,[32] and it is not necessary for us to go into the matter in great detail. The policy framework for the control of industrial development was laid down in the industrial policy resolutions of 1948 and 1956, as part of the Government's policy towards a socialist pattern of development. Broadly speaking, the policy

[30]*Op. cit.*, Ch. II.

[31]On the absence of concepts such as trade-offs, see Ch. 1 above; see also Chaudhuri (1971), pp. 28-29.

[32]Bhagwati and Desai (1970); India, Planning Commission, Hazari Committee (1967); Little, Scitovsky and Scott (1970); Medhora (1968); Srinivasan (1974).

may be said to have had four major objectives: control of growth and the industrial composition of output capacity, foreign exchange saving, control of monopoly and encouragement of smaller industrial units, and control over the location of industry.[33]

While great emphasis is laid on all these objectives, in practice the operation of the policy has probably been most influenced by the need to conserve foreign exchange. As this has been a very real and difficult problem for economic policy in India, it will be as well to bear this point in mind during the following discussion. The system of control that I am about to summarize was operated most fully until the devaluation of the Indian rupee in 1966. Thereafter, there was a period of 'liberalization' of economic policy until the late 1960s, after which the system has tended to revert in some ways to the old mode.[34]

The industrial policy resolutions classified industries into three major groups: those which were to be the monopoly of the public sector, those where further expansions of capacity were to be in the public sector and those which were open to the private sector. In fact, industries have sometimes tended to move in and out of these categories, to reflect the exigencies of the times. All planned investments above a certain limit had to be licensed; this refers mainly to expansion of capacity or creation of new capacity, although the introduction of new products and planned changes in location also came under the licensing system. The industry for which the new capacity was sought had to be one which was marked for expansion in the relevant plan, the current balance between supply and demand had to justify the creation of new capacity and the project itself had to be 'economically viable'.

If an industrial licence was granted and the project involved any outlay of foreign exchange, it overlapped into the area of operation of foreign exchange control. The project then had to be granted an import licence. In order to qualify for allocation of foreign exchange, the project had to be cleared by the Directorate General of Technical Development from the 'indigenous angle'. This is to say the DGTD had to certify that the required imports were not available from domestic suppliers. In addition, if any foreign collaboration was involved, the terms of that colla-

---

[33]Bhagwati and Desai (1970), p. 249f; Srinivasan (1974).
[34]Srinivasan (1974).

boration had to be in accordance with Government policy on foreign private investment or technology transfer. If domestic capital had to be raised, that in turn had to be approved for the company seeking the licence.

All these controls were operated by the Industrial Licensing Committee, the Import Licence Committee, the Foreign Collaboration Committee and the Capital Issues Committee and also involved the DGTD for 'indigenous angle clearance'. Although much of the personnel of the committee was the same, for most of the period they met separately as the application went through the various stages of clearance. Needless to say, it was an involved and time-consuming process.

In order to work effectively, such a system of detailed controls requires a clear set of criteria on the basis of which proposals can be ranked, accurate technical information relating to the project and its alternatives, and administrative efficiency in processing of applications. In practice, none of these has been adequately forthcoming. The planners have hardly ever laid down any but the broadest criteria for choosing between projects. Adequate technological information has not been available on time. In this respect, the work of the DGTD leaves much to be desired. A great deal of responsibility rests on the recommendation of that body as to the availability of domestic substitutes. In fact, its technical information is regarded by many as being neither comprehensive nor up-to-date. Moreover, in interpreting the 'clearance from the indigenous angle', it has often taken note of the mere theoretical availability of a particular component or equipment, without taking account of its suitability, availability or competitiveness in terms of price. The elaborate committee structure has also turned out to be too cumbersome a mechanism for handling large numbers of applications.[35]

More specifically, the following criticisms have been laid against the licensing procedure:

1. The lack of any clear guidelines has led to applications being treated on a more or less *ad hoc* basis. There have been no clear or consistent criteria of social profitability against which projects can be measured.

2. There have been long delays in the process of approving or

[35]Chaudhuri, A. (1972).

rejecting applications. This has led to the creation of uncertainty and long gestation lags in the building of new capacity, with a consequent slowing down in the growth of industrial output.

3. No systematic rules have been followed to take account of the objective of locational dispersion of industry. In a great many cases the ultimate location of a particular industrial project has been determined, not in terms of economic feasibility but of the political necessity of awarding some projects to particular regions.

4. The system has not succeeded in controlling the growth of monopoly and reducing the concentration of economic power in industry. Because the licensing procedure is both highly centralized and specialized, it gives a large firm certain built-in advantages in playing the system. It can afford the time and resources needed to file applications and undertake the necessary 'lobbying' to get them through. In addition, large firms have widely used smaller subsidiaries to get licences they have not taken up, in order to foreclose certain sectors to new entrants. They are also known to have bought up small firms with licences to prevent their exploitation. It must be said, in fairness to the procedure, that exactly the opposite claim has also been made against the Government. That is to say an undue concern with the problem of monopoly has prevented an economically sensible expansion of the industrial sector, by holding back the expansion of firms that could utilize economies of scale.[36] Unfortunately, there are few detailed studies of industrial development in India that can be used to evaluate these criticisms.

5. Lastly, and perhaps the most important, the licensing procedure has not enabled the Government to economize on the use of imports but has had quite perverse effects. In order to develop this criticism fully, it has to be remembered that one of the major objectives of the licensing procedure, in fact, was to control the demand for imports in the economy. Throughout this period, there was excess demand for imports in the economy and the Government used a method of direct control rather than frequent devaluations to balance the external account.[37] Industrial licensing and

[36]This is the view associated, for example, with the World Bank and some of the aid agencies.

[37]The one example of the use of devaluation is that of June 1966. As explained in Srinivasan (1974), that policy was chiefly one of bringing some form of order into a state of confusion caused by the existence of a number

import licensing often operated together, and more often than not the best chance of securing an industrial licence was to show that the licensee had access to foreign exchange in the form of foreign collaborations or credit. It is true that the import licensing procedure was more comprehensive, in that it also included the demand for imports for use as current inputs. However, an industrial licence which sanctioned the use of capital imports and an import licence which sanctioned the use of imports of current inputs interacted to have a particular effect on industrial development. The fact that imports were in short supply gave successful licensees access to imports which carried a considerable import premium in the economy. The fact that such premiums could be obtained often led to applications for industrial licences, not so much to increase capacity as to obtain more imports, because the current input allocation for imports was related to the registered capacity of the user. The import premium attached to such imports acted as a hidden subsidy to the user and thus discriminated in his favour against producers who used domestic inputs that did not carry such a premium. Moreover, the fact that the assurance of a source of foreign exchange was often a critical factor in obtaining a licence often favoured projects involving capital-intensive techniques, because they were most often of the kinds that were supplied by foreign firms, who could also supply a foreign credit. In both ways, the net effect was to encourage rather than discourage the use of scarce foreign exchange. Moreover, the use of this system to keep a balance between supply of and demand for foreign resources in the presence of an overvalued foreign exchange also acted as a tax on exports.

6. Because the import premium mentioned in the previous paragraph accrued to the importer and not the Government, it is also said that the licensing system led to a loss of Government

---

of administrative practices that had led to a *de facto* devaluation of the rupee. It is argued by both Bhagwati and Desai (1970) and Srinivasan (1974) that the devaluation was partially successful. A careful study by Nayyar (1974) shows that the effective rate of devaluation varied from commodity to commodity and was quite low. Moreover, there is little evidence that the devaluation had any significant effect on the size of exports. However, the devaluation also coincided with a severe drought and a widespread industrial recession, so that it is difficult to evaluate its precise effects.

revenue, at least potentially.[38]

All these criticisms have been profusely, if not always rigorously documented in the works cited above and there are not many
documentations of the success of such a policy. It would not be
easy to defiend the system as it was actually operated. However,
one or two points need to be made in its favour. If one rejected
the extreme view that no direct controls were necessary and that
the price mechanism could be left to balance both the internal
and the external sectors, then obviously some system of control
had to be operated. The objection to the policy that was pursued
is really that the Government was neither consistent in the criteria
it followed nor did it devise a system that it had the capacity to
operate efficiently. Here again the system was too detailed and
required interference on a scale which was quite beyond the
capacity of the Government to implement efficiently. Again, in
its predilection for making the best the enemy of the good, it
did not consider an alternative of promoting the effective development of a core of industries or investment projects, paying less
attention to any distortions that might have developed elsewhere
in less important sectors. Even so, not all the difficulties were
entirely of its own making. Not all the critics have appreciated
that the mechanism of aid administration followed by official aid
donors added greatly to the problems of the Government. Thus,
the elaborate licensing of current imports arose out of the need to
budget for the disbursement of tied, bilateral aid.

We have so far concentrated on non-price controls as instruments of policy used by the Government. In addition, the Government has also used a system of taxes, especially import tariffs and
export subsidies, the latter especially during the last ten years or
so.[39] As import tariffs have been used in conjunction with quota
restrictions and export subsidies with such incentives as import
entitlement schemes, they cannot be regarded as pure forms of
price incentives or disincentives. In a detailed study of exchange
controls, Bhagwati and Srinivasan have tried to evaluate the effect
of these controls. In their view, tariff policy has led to a misallocation of resources through the creation of substantial unplanned
subsidization and penalizing of various sectors. The nominal

[38]Srinivasan (1974).
[39]Srinivasan (1974); Nayyar (1974).

rates of tariff have differed widely from the effective rates of tariff and the joint operations of the import and export incentives have led to the creation of substantial divergences in the domestic resource costs of producing different commodities.

As Srinivasan points out, the limitations of such studies are well known and such findings by themselves may not constitute overwhelming criticisms of economic policy. In any case, it is easier to criticize the effects of particular policies with the benefit of hindsight than to administer such policies with imperfect knowledge in a changing world. A dynamic, growing economy can carry the costs of misallocation of resources as inescapable costs of growth and change. However, in the context of an economy which has persistently performed below expectations and which has failed to achieve most of the major objectives that were being aimed at, it is difficult to escape the conclusion that both the economic strategy and the chosen instruments of economic control have largely failed to tackle the problems facing the economy.

CHAPTER ELEVEN

Conclusions

I have attempted in this book to present a somewhat complicated, some might even say confused, set of developments that the Indian economy has undergone in the last 20 or 25 years. Unfortunately, there are not even at the end some clear conclusions, an unambiguous set of right and wrong answers and policies, that can be set before the reader. There are very good reasons for such an unsatisfactory state of affairs and little is to be gained by glossing over the difficulties that face us in the interpretation of economic events in India.

One reason is that the case of India is somewhat unique in the annals of developing countries, in terms of her size, heterogeneity and the juxtaposition of the traditional and the modern in her economic structure. Not a great deal is to be achieved by trying to read her future in terms of prewar Russia or postwar Taiwan or Hong Kong, while she is set apart from China by a completely different social and political system.

Secondly, our factual knowledge of various aspects of economic life in India is still very fragmented. Quite often, we have had to note the very dissimilar conclusions about particular economic developments in India that have been reached by different, equally distinguished economists. While this is often to be explained by differences in areas and methods of study, it does not make the problem of generalizing about the Indian economy any easier. If at present we get contradictory messages from the past, the problem of anticipating the future is even more daunting. All too often, prophets of gloom and glory have changed roles at a turn of the monsoon. It would, therefore, be wise not to be too categorical in our prognostications.

Thirdly, the reality of events in India *is* complex. Quite often, one has a firm conclusion about, say, the population problem or the failure or success of the 'green revolution', that dissolves in one's hands as one begins to look into the contradictory details of the situation. Moreover, we have to bear in mind that we are today observing a situation that has, as a backdrop to it, very long-term developments that are gradually influencing the basic forces of production in the economy. It does not follow that, because they are largely ignored by policy makers and commentators alike, factors such as deforestation or soil erosion or the classical extension of cultivation on to marginal land have less explanatory power than the more familiar categories of the economists.[1]

In spite of these difficulties, I shall attempt to restate, in a few words, my particular assessment of Indian economic performance. To what degree has the Government, in its attempts to steer the economy, been successful in promoting economic progress over the last quarter of a century? To what extent has it failed to meet its objectives? What have been the major constraints on the development of the Indian economy? To answer these questions, it is essential to return to the distinction that I laid down at the beginning, between the behaviour of the economy as an aggregate and the fortunes and misfortunes of its component parts. Any attempt to evaluate the performance of the Indian economy must be made at these two levels.

Addressing myself to the problem of the overall performance of the economy, I have argued that the years 1965-67 should be viewed as a watershed. Before that period, the economy grew at a modest but fairly steady rate. Output expanded more rapidly than did employment, even if we bear in mind some of the conceptual problems that arise in giving a precise meaning to 'employment' in a poor, underdeveloped country. The share of investment in national income rose, somewhat outpacing the growth of domestic savings. Hence, a growing and unforeseen dependence on foreign aid to finance part of that investment and, especially, its high import content. The economy did best in the industrial sector. Both large-scale and small-scale industrial output expanded rapidly; there was considerable gross import substitution; the

[1]For an interesting discussion of the effects of population growth in India, see Cassen (1973).

economy built up, almost from nothing, a very useful capital goods producing sector, which is in my view, quite a remarkable technical achievement for a poor country. Agricultural output was pushed along a rising trend line, not so much by any fundamental changes in its production base as by the happy configuration of a number of independent factors. These were, first and foremost, some favourable monsoons; and then an expansion of acreage and the completion of a number of major irrigation projects. The common factor in all these was that they were in the nature of once-for-all improvements, which could not be expected to bail out the economy in the years to come.

This tale of mixed blessings came to a surprisingly shattering end during the drought years of 1965-67. Severe though the droughts were, during 1967-68 the economy showed every sign of recovery. As the previous pages have tried to make clear, such a recovery never came, for which one must cite causes that are more economic and social rather than metereological. Except for that part of foodgrains production which consists of wheat, all the other major series of economic performance, real national income, *per capita* availability of foodgrains and industrial production, all show signs of either stagnation or significant deceleration. Only population and the price level show remarkably vigorous growth. Moreover, in 1965 say, one could regard the onset of the droughts as a temporary setback, from which one expected a confident recovery. Today, the future of economic progress in India has been called into doubt in a way which could not have been foreseen in the mid 1960s.

Of the various interest groups that make up the society, I have chosen particularly to concentrate on that part of the population, numbering some hundreds of millions, that is designated as the 'poor'. Everyone is agreed that it is the poor whose welfare should concern us most. The planners have throughout laid much emphasis on improving the standard of living of this section of the population. I have tried to answer the questions—what constitutes poverty in the Indian context and who are the 'poor'? I have also tried to ask the question, what does the economic performance we have witnessed in these years mean to the poor; what has it done for them? Our detailed knowledge of poverty in India does not extend beyond the 1960s. The very recent developments have to be pieced together against a background of faltering agricultural production and rising prices of food and other essentials. What we have discovered is uniformly gloomy, without even the glimmer of a false dawn somewhere way back in the mid 1960s when things suddenly worsened. For what we have found is that even in those days, when the overall rate of economic growth was not unsatisfactory, very little of the fruits of growth came the way of the poor. Since then, the deceleration in the growth of the economy has not improved matters for the poor. Given the subsequent growth of population, stagnation in the *per capita* availability of basic wage-goods and the cumulative rise in food and other prices, that would be a fairly safe inference to draw.

If we pose the question, how has this state of affairs come to pass, we shall be posing two distinct but related problems. One relates to the overall performance of the economy; the other to those aspects of growth which are of particular concern to the poor. Given the fact that the poor in India make up a very large number and are on some counts measured as being almost half the total population, we would not expect to maintain a watertight division between these two aspects of the question. However, as I have endeavoured to show, the significance of particular economic strategies and policies differs according to who we envisage to be the beneficiaries of such policies. That is to say whether we think in terms of benefits accruing to an abstraction, the Indian economy stretching into the timeless future or of identifiable groups of population, alive and being born, who will live or starve or die within the lifespan of our generation or the next.

To return to the question of economic growth, in the early years, and more especially since the inception of the second five-year plan, the basic constraint on the growth of the economy was perceived to lie in a scarcity of capital. The view was held that an increase in productivity and in employment both required a substantial increase in the capital stock of the economy. From this starting point, it was a fairly easy slide into the logic of the Mahalanobis model, where the objective was to maximize the share of investment in the capital goods producing sector, in order to maximize the rate of growth of consumption over time rather than the current level of consumption.[2]

[2]On the Mahalanobis strategy, see pp. 214-20 above.

In my view, there has been a persistent tendency in discussions on Indian economic development to give the Mahalanobis strategy far less credit than it deserves. The view that investment had a key role to play in Indian economic development, that the share of investment in national income had to be raised, were substantially correct. Moreover, given the size of the economy and the low degree of 'openness' of the economy, something of the stress on investment towards creating output capacity rather than immediate output was also inevitable. This concentration of investment gave a certain impetus to the growth of the modern industrial sector in India, which was very substantial by all accounts during the periods of the second and third five-year plans.

However, there are a number of reasons why this strategy proved to be abortive There is, of course, the fact that it gave too little recognition to the problems of agricultural development. This, in an economy where almost half of total output originated in agriculture. However, even within the narrow compass of industrial development, the strategy contained within itself the seeds of its failure. The most basic flaw in it was, perhaps, the failure to realize that a policy, formulated initially in a centrally planned economy, might not work in quite the same fashion in a mixed economy, where only a small part of total activity would be within the direct control of the Government. Especially, the critically important need for financing a given flow of investment was ignored.[3] The result was a failure to reach investment targets according to any order of priority and a diversion of resources away from certain strategic sectors towards less essential consumer goods and their inputs and towards construction. Even in the public sector, there was a diversion of resources away from development expenditure towards non-development expenditure.[4]

Why did public investment fail to generate its own savings? The answer to this question is a somewhat complex one. It lies partly in the very long gestation periods of some public investment projects. While this may in some ways have acted as a rationing device for scarce savings, it also pushed back the period at which the projects began to produce a stream of marketable output. It

[3]On the performance of the economy, see Chs. 3 and 4 and the references cited there.
[4]See pp. 86-7 above.

also lies in part on the low levels of operational efficiency in some public sector industries. Both these factors reduced the ability of the public sector to generate a reinvestible surplus.

However, influences on the side of demand also helped to tighten the savings constraint. Public sector industry was typically capital-intensive, the rate of profit being highly sensitive to the degree of utilization of capacity. For a heavy industry strategy to be self-financing, it was essential to maintain a high rate of growth of overall demand in the economy. However, it was not possible to maintain a high rate of growth of demand, consistent with internal and external stability, without a concomitant increase in the rate of supply of wage-goods. This in turn implied a rapid and sustained rate of growth of output in that sector which is the chief producer of wage-goods in the economy, that is to say agriculture.

The failure to sustain a rate of growth of agricultural production, especially of foodgrains production, consistent with the rate of growth of population *and* a high rate of growth of aggregate demand, provides at once an insight into a number of problems. Given that agriculture produces the lion's share of output it explains, if one likes, in a purely statistical sense, the failure to achieve and sustain a high rate of growth of total output. Moreover, even given the structural independence of the agricultural and the non-agricultural sectors for most of our period, it provides an explanation of how a failure to achieve a high rate of growth of wage-goods production can act as a constraint on the rate of growth of the non-agricultural sector. Here also lies the way to the resolution of an apparent paradox, that in an underdeveloped economy with a substantial amount of underutilized labour, labour absorption becomes a problem. In a mixed economy, more productive employment requires more consumable wage-goods.

The question why Indian agriculture has not performed better is a highly controversial one, as I have tried to indicate in an earlier chapter.[5] The answer that I have tried to provide, which is not entirely an adequate one, runs along these lines. Prior to the discovery of the high-yielding varieties of foodgrains, agricultural production was taking place close to a technological frontier, once the possibilities of extension of total acreage were substan-

[5]See Chapter 5 *passim.*

tially used up. At that time, I did not think that the provision of additional resources by themselves would lead to a large increase in total foodgrains production. No doubt, some improvements could have been achieved by more investment in minor irrigation or more production of fertilizers. The point is that with traditional varieties, larger inputs of water or fertilizers would not have been highly profitable.

The explanation of the behaviour of agricultural production after the introduction of high-yielding varieties must run along different lines. As we know, the technological breakthrough was partial. The new varieties have been most successful for wheat, less for rice and bajra and almost non-existent for pulses and cash crops such as cotton. There is evidence, however, that even for wheat and rice the actual increase in yields has been very much smaller than the potential yield, largely due to the limited spread of the new varieties and agricultural practices, both between and within the different states.

The limited impact of the technology can be traced directly to the way in which the Government has tried to implement it. One of the most critical factors in the adoption of the new technology is the availability of water. The policy of concentrating an expensive package to areas of assured irrigation, instead of investing in cheaper forms of minor irrigation over wider areas, has simultaneously had two effects. One has been to ensure that the higher-yielding seeds could, at best, be used over only one-third of the total cultivable area. The other is to ensure that within that area only the larger, rich farmers could profit from the new development. This is a major reason why a potentially promising technological breakthrough has yielded such meagre fruits.

This brings us to the question why, in spite of the concern shown for the poor in the writing of the plans, so little has been done to improve their standards of living. I have pointed out earlier that the emphasis throughout had been put upon the overall growth of the economy as the major vehicle for the removal of poverty. This was in contrast to any strategy of redistribution of incomes and assets from the rich to the poor, except for land redistribution where an agreement in principle was sabotaged by the practice of non-implementation by the state government. Why is it that the strategy of alleviating poverty through the filtering-down effects of the growth process ran into the ground?

Part of the answer lies in the fact that the growth that was in fact achieved was very much more modest than had been hoped for. The Indian case is not a good example of the consequences of sacrificing distribution for growth. But even if the economy had been on target, so to speak, it is still unlikely that much improvement would have been made to the lot of the poor. The Mahalanobis strategy implied, in any case, that the incremental incomes going towards consumption would tend to be small in the early years. If the poor were to be made less poor, it was essential to ensure that a large part of the incremental output did in fact accrue to the poorer sections of the population. Here, Government policy ignored certain basic structural character-istics of the Indian economy.

In India, the bulk of the poor consists of those in the rural sectors who own no land or too little land to grow their own sub-sistence requirements and those in the urban sector who are either unemployed or are severely underemployed in low productivity occupations. For peasants with, say, less than two acres, the only way to improve their standard of living is either to provide them with more land or to provide them with resources and a techno-logy to increase the output per acre up to their subsistence re-quirements The non-implementation of land reform and the embodiment of the new technology in the form of a package that can only be afforded by the richer peasants, together put paid to their lot.

As for the rest—the major part of the poor in India who do not grow their own food, in the rural and the urban sector—an increase in real consumption requires initially an increase in their purchasing power. This in turn requires an increase in employment opportunities as well as wages. As I have tried to show, employ-ment in India has grown even less rapidly than output, while real wages have grown very little if at all. However, not even an increase in money incomes would have been sufficient to increase the real incomes of the poor. The consumption of the poor is highly concentrated on a very narrow range of goods. These are primarily foodgrains, and then other basic necessities which com-pete in one way or another with foodgrains for scarce land. As a very large part of the poor buy these goods against wages, that is to say against payment for the supply of labour, these I have called 'wage-goods'. Where wage-goods are in short supply, the poor cannot compete successfully with those with higher incomes, who also consume these goods.[6]

An increase in the real consumption of the poor in India thus requires, as of necessity, a sustained increase in the production of wage-goods. The failure of economic policy to either identify the wage-goods constraint or give adequate attention to the allocation of resources to increasing the production of wage-goods, must be reckoned one of the major shortcomings of Indian economic strategy. In the face of the oft-reiterated desire to abolish poverty, it is also a failure that is very hard to understand.

It follows, of course, that if a breakthrough had been achieved in the production of wage-goods, especially after 1965-67, this expansion of the agricultural sector would also have helped to sustain growth in the industrial sector, through its effects on levels of demand. A successful policy to improve the standards of living of some hundreds of millions of people would have produced and sustained growth in the economy as a byproduct. On the other hand, to aim at sustained growth without a successful resolution of the wage-goods constraint was to aim at a chimera.

I do not wish to minimize some of the difficulties that have faced the Government during these years. There have been some years of very severe drought, which affected agricultural output adversely. There have been wars with Pakistan and China, which saddled the economy with very heavy defence expenditure. There has been the heavy absorption of resources into relief expenditure on famines or on refugees from Bangla Desh. Lately, there have been severe pressures on the balance of payments as a result of rising oil prices, world inflation and decline in foreign aid. These last forces have yet to work their way through the system, so that we cannot now be sure how they will affect the ability of the economy to cope with its grinding problems. However, it would be quite wrong to dismiss the Indian economy as being merely accident-prone. Economic policy in India has not made the best

---

[6]The marginal propensity to consume on the part of the richer sections is obviously low. The point is that the total supply of foodgrains may not be sufficient to satisfy the total demands of the relatively better-off population, which they have the means to satisfy to the full, as well as the additional demands that would ensue from the poor, if their purchasing powers were allowed to increase.

of a bad job. It appears, rather, to have made a hard task un-
manageable.

I have argued above that, plainly speaking, things have got
worse since 1965-67, when there was every prospect that they would
get better. Except for wheat, agricultural output has not been expanding more rapidly. There has been continued industrial stagnation since the recession of 1967. The overall effect has been a very
sharp decline in the rate of growth of the economy. Moreover,
the one major achievement of economic policy of the earlier years,
that of relative price stability, has gone by the board. If the state
of the poor showed little improvement until the late 1960s, it would
be difficult to argue that they have fared better in the recent years
of rising food prices. The situation has been made worse by the
commonly shared view that the failure of the economy is due
to an overemphasis on investment, while the major problems have
been a low level of investment and a low share of the wage-
goods sector in the composition of investment. The wrong diagnosis has led on the one hand to various makeshift measures to
increase consumption, without any effective policy either to
increase total supply or reduce the purchasing power of higher
income groups. On the other hand, a falling level of development
expenditure has saddled the economy with larger burdens of underutilized capacity.

The continued severity of the problem of poverty in India points
to what is perhaps a more fundamental shortcoming in the formulation of economic policy in India. That is the predilection of
the planners to talk in terms of general solutions to general problems, formulated in all-embracing categories. The poor are to be
made less poor, through growth, development and socialism. I
have tried to argue for a different approach, which consists in
trying to establish the nature of a problem precisely, in terms of
its structural components.[7] To illustrate the point, with reference
to the problem of poverty, it is essential to identify who precisely
are the poor and what their poverty consists in. This has been
discussed at some length in Chapters 7 and 8 above. One then
has to form some idea of the magnitude of poverty, of how many
of the poor there are, by how much it is expected to raise their

---

[7]There is, of course, nothing original in this formulation. Similar views
have been expressed by many economists in recent years.

standards of living, what the resource cost of such a programme is and where those resources will come from. It is only after some 25 years that such questions are even being asked by the planners, and even then in highly aggregative terms.[8] Such an approach identifies the critical need to increase the supply of foodgrains production and its corollary, adequate production and distribution of the necessary inputs. The second set of questions will relate to how the consumer goods that are produced are actually distributed to the poor in a market economy. This raises questions of the inter-relationship between allocation of resources, income distribution and patterns of demand, which have had no place in Indian planning strategy.

It will be objected that these criticisms are too academic and ignore the fact that India is a poor country. While it is true that to wish for everyone to become better off in India is to beg the question, it is difficult to believe that the failure to improve the lot of even the bottom 5 or 10 per cent of the population, in terms of basic foodstuffs, health or education, is really constrained by an overall lack of resources. It is to a much greater extent a question of how the problem is seen and how priorities are fixed and enforced within the economy.

[8]India, Planning Commission (1973).

Bibliographical References

Note: The following abbreviations have been used.

CPU (Lok Sabha) Committee on Public Undertakings
EPW Economic and Political Weekly
IJAE Indian Journal of Agricultural Economics
JISAS Journal of the Indian Society of Agricultural Statistics
PEO (Planning Commission) Programme Evaluation Organization
PPD (Planning Commission) Perspective Planning Division
UP University Press
Gokhale Inst. Gokhale Institute of Politics and Economics
Where reference is made to more than one issue of a serial publication
in a particular context, the publication is referred to thus: *Economic Survey*
(annual). Where a specific issue is cited, it is referred to thus: *Economic
Survey* (1970).

Agricultural Economics Research Centre, University of Delhi (1971).
Primary Education in Rural India: Participation and Wastage. (Tata-
McGraw Hill, Delhi).

Akroyd, W. (1951). 'The Nutritive Value of Indian Foods and the Planning
of Satisfactory Diets', *Health Bulletin*, No. 23

Alavi, H. ('973). 'The State in Post-Colonial Societies: Pakistan and
Bangla Desh', in Gough and Sharma, *op. cit.*

Alavi, H. (1975). 'India and the Colonial Mode of Production', *EPW* Special
No., July.

Alexander, S.S. (1952). 'Effects of a Devaluation on a Trade Balance', *IMF
Staff Papers*, April.

Appu, P.S. (1974). 'The Bamboo Tubewell: A Low Cost Device for Ex-
ploiting Ground Water', *EPW*, June.

Atkinson, A.B. (1970). 'On the Measurement of Inequality', *Journal of Economic Theory*, Vol. 2.

Bagchi, Amaresh (1974). 'Rendistribution Role of Taxation in India', in
Srinivasan and Bardhan, *op. cit.*

Bagchi, Amiya K. (1970). 'Long-term Constraints to India's Industrial Growth 1951-1968', in Robinson and Kidron, *op. cit.*

Bagchi, Amiya K. (1972). *Private Investment in India, 1900-1939*, Cambridge UP.

Bailey, F.G. (1957). *Caste and the Economic Frontier*, Manchester UP.

Banerji, D. (1972). 'Prospects for Controlling Population in India', *EPW*, October.

Banerji, D. (1973). 'Health Behaviour of Rural Population: Impact of Rural Health Services', *EPW*, December.

Baranson, J. (1967). *Manufacturing Problems in India*. Syracuse UP.

Bardhan, K. (1966). 'Do Foodgrains Imports Affect Prices?', *EPW*, November.

Bardhan, P. (1970) 'On the Minimum Level of Living of the Rural Poor', *Indian Economic Review*, April.

Bardhan, P. (1970a). 'The Green Revolution and Agricultural Labourers', *EPW*, July.

Bardhan, P. (1973). 'Size, Productivity and Returns to Scale: An Analysis of Farm Level Data on Indian Agriculture', *Journal of Political Economy*, November-December.

Bardhan, P. (1973a). *The Pattern of Income Distribution in India; A Review*, (mimeo), IBRD. (A revised version reprinted in Srinivasan and Bardhan, *op. cit.*)

Bardhan, P. and Bardhan, K. (1971). 'Price Response of Marketed Surplus of Foodgrains', *Oxford Economic Papers*, July.

Beckerman, W. (1968). *National Income Analysis*, Weidenfeld and Nicolson, London.

Berg, Alan (1973). *The Nutrition Factor*, Brookings, Washington.

Beteille, A. (1974). *Caste, Class, and Power*, California UP.

Beteille, A. (1974). *Studies in Agrarian Social Structure*, Oxford UP.

Bettelheim, C. (1968). *India Independent*, MacGibbon and Kee, London.

Bhaduri, A. (1973). 'Agricultural Backwardness and Semi-Feudalism', *Economic Journal*, March.

Bhagwati, J.N. (1962). 'On how to Decide what to Import and what to Produce', *Oxford Economic Papers*, February.

Bhagwati, J.N. (1970). 'The Tying of Aid', in Bhagwati, J. and Eckhaus, R.S. (eds.), *Foreign Aid*, Penguin, Harmondsworth.

Bhagwati, J.N. and Chakravarty, S. (1969). 'Contributions to Indian Economic Analysis: A Survey', *American Economic Review*, Supplement, September.

Bhagwati, J.N. and Desai, Padma (1970). *Planning for Industrialization: India's Trade and Industrialization Policies, 1950-66*, Oxford UP.

Bharadwaj, K. (1974). *Production Conditions in Indian Agriculture*, Cambridge UP.

Bhatty, I.Z. (1974). 'Inequality and Poverty in Rural India', *Sankhya (Indian Journal of Statistics)*, Series C, parts 2 and 4, vol. 36, reprinted in Srinivasan and Bardhan, *op. cit.*

Billings, M. and Singh, A. (1969). 'Labour and the Green Revolution: The Experience in Punjab', *EPW*, December.

Blyn, G. (1966). *Agricultural Trends in India, 1891-1947: Output, Availability and Productivity?*, Pennsylvania UP.

Bose, D.K. (1974). 'A Note on Stagflation' (mimeo), Indian Statistical Institute.

Boserup, E. (1972). 'Food Supply and Population Growth in Developing Countries', in Islam, N. (ed.), *Agricultural Policy in Developing Countries*, Macmillan, London.

Brahmanand, P. and Vakil, C.N. (1956). *Planning for an Expanding Economy*, Vora, Bombay.

Brown, Dorris D. (1971). *Agricultural Development in India's Districts*, Harvard UP.

Buchanan, D. (1934). *The Development of Capitalist Enterprise in India*, Frank Cass, London.

Byres, T.J. (1972). 'The Dialectic of India's Green Revolution', *South Asian Review*, January.

Cantor, S.M. and Associates (1973). *The Tamil Nadu Nutrition Study*, Haverford, Pennsylvania.

Cassen, R. (1973). 'Population, Development and the Distribution of Income', IDS Communication Series, No. 107.

Cassen, R. (1974). 'Realistic Paths to Reduced Fertility' (mimeo), IDS working paper, No. 13.

Chakravarty, S. (1971). 'Some Aspects of Economic Growth in India, 1950-1967', in Maddison, A. (ed.), *Myrdal's Asian Drama*, Ciriec, Lige.

Chakravarty, S. and Maiti, P. (1974). 'A Note on Current Inflation' (mimeo) Indian Statistical Institute.

Chandra, N.K. (1973). 'Western Imperialism and India Today', *EPW*, February.

Chattopadhyay, P. (1972). 'On the Question of the Mode of Production in Agriculture', *EPW*, March.

Chattopadhyay, P. (1973). 'Some Trends in India's Economic Development', in Gough and Sharma, *op. cit.*

Chaudhuri, A. (1972). 'Industrial Licensing Policy and Prevention of Concentration of Economic Power in India: A Critical Review', *Arthavijnana*, December.

Chaudhuri, P. (ed.) (1971). *Aspects of Indian Economic Development*, Allen and Unwin, London.

Chaudhuri, P. (ed.) (1972). *Readings in Indian Agricultural Development*, Allen and Unwin, London.

Chaudhuri, P. (1974). 'The Impact of Aid on the Indian Economy, 1950-70' (mimeo).

Chaudhuri, P. (1975). 'East European Aid to India', *World Development*, May.

Chaudri, D.P. (1968). 'Education and Agricultural Productivity in India' (mimeo), Delhi.

Chelliah, R.J. (1960). *Fiscal Policy in Under-developed Countries*, Allen and Unwin, London.

Chelliah, R.J. (1971). 'Trends in Taxation in Developing Countries', *IMF Staff Papers*, July.

Chelliah, R.J., Bass, H.J. and Kelley, M.R. (1975). 'Tax Ratio and Tax Effort in Developing Countries 1969-71', *IME Staff Papers*, March.

Chenery, H.B. (1960). 'Patterns of Industrial Growth', *American Economic Review*, September.

Chenery, H.B. (1961). 'Comparative Advantage and Development Policy', *American Economic Review*, March.

Chenery, H.B., Alluwalia, M., Bell, C., Duloy, J. and Jolly, R. (1974). *Redistribution with Growth*, Oxford UP.

Chopra, K. (1972). *Tractorization and its Effect on the Agrarian Economy of the Punjab* (mimeo), USAID, New Delhi.

Clay, E.J. (1974). *Innovation, Inequality and Rural Planning: The Economics of Tubewell Irrigation in Bihar;* thesis submitted for D. Phil degree at University of Sussex.

Coale, A. and Hoover, E.M. (1958). *Population Growth and Economic Development in Low-Income Countries: A study of India's Prospects*, Princeton UP.

Cohen, B.I. (1964). 'The Stagnation of Indian Exports, 1951-61', *Quarterly Journal of Economics*, November.

Cummings, R W. and Ray, S.K (1969). '1968-69 Crop: Relative Contribution of Weather and New Technology', *EPW*, September.

Dandekar, V.M. and Rath, N. (1971). *Poverty in India*, Economic and Political Weekly, Bombay.

Dandekar, V.M. and Khundanpur, G.J. (1957). *The Working of the Bombay Tenancy Act, 1948*, Gokhale Inst., Poona

Dantwala, M L. (1967) 'Incentives and Disincentives in Indian Agriculture', *IJAE*, April-June.

Dantwala, M.L. (1972). 'Preface' to Indian Society of Agricultural Economics, *op. cit.*

Dastane, N.G. (1969). 'New Concepts in Irrigation—Necessary Changes for New Strategy', *EPW*, March.

Datar, A.L. (1972). *India's Economic Relations with the USSR and Eastern Europe 1953-1969*, Cambridge UP.

Desai, B.M. (1972). 'Analysis of Consumer Expenditure Pattern in India', Cornell University, Dept. of Agricultural Economics, Occasional Paper No. 54.

Desai, D.K. (1969, 1971a). 'Intensive Agricultural District Programme: Analysis of Results', *EPW*, June, reprinted in Chaudhuri, *op. cit.*

Desai, Padma (1972). *The Bokaro Steel Plant*, North Holland, Amsterdam.

Dhar, P.N. and Lydall, H. (1961). *The Role of Small Enterprises in India's Economic Development*, Asia, Bombay.

Dharm Narain (1961). *Distribution of Marketed Surplus of Agricultural Product by Size-level of Holding in India 1950-51*, Asia, Bombay.

Dharm Narain (1965). *The Impact of Price Movements on Areas under Selected Crops 1900-39*, Cambridge UP.

Dharm Narain (1972). 'Growth and Imbalance in Indian Agriculture', *JISAS*, June.

Dharm Narain and Joshi, P.C. (1969). 'Magnitude of Agricultural Tenancy', *EPW*, September.

Domar, E. (1957). 'A Soviet Model of Growth', in Domar, E., *Essays in the Theory of Growth*, Oxford UP, New York.

Dunning, J. (ed.) (1971). *The Multinational Enterprise*, Allen and Unwin, London.

Emmanuel, A. (1974). 'Myths of Development vs. Myths of Underdevelopment', *New Left Review*, May-June.

Enke, S. (1966). 'The Economic Aspects of Slowing Population Growth', *Economic Journal*, March.

Epstein, S. (1962). *Economic Development and Social Change in South India*, Manchester UP.

Eshag, E. (1968). 'Study on the Excess Cost of Tied Economic Aid Given to Iran', UNCTAD, 2nd Session, Proceedings, Vol. IV, New Delhi.

Fel'dman, G.A. (1964). 'On the Theory of Growth Rates of National Income', I and II, in Spulber, N. (ed.), *Foundations of Soviet Strategy for Economic Growth*, Indiana UP.

Food and Agricultural Organization (1967). *Agricultural Commodities: Projections for 1975 and 1985*, Vol. II, FAO, Rome.

Frankel, F.R. (1971). *India's Green Revolution: Economic Gains and Political Costs*, California UP.

Gadgil, D.R. (1945, 1952). *Poona: A Socio-Economic Survey*, 2 vols., Gokhale Inst., Poona.

Gadgil, D.R. (1972). *Planning and Economic Policy in India*, Gokhale Inst., Poona.

Galbraith, J.K. (1957). *American Capitalism; the Concept of Countervailing Powers*, Hamish Hamilton, London.

Gandhi, V. (1966). *Tax Bu den on Indian Agriculture*, Harvard Law School.

Ganshof, F.L. and Verhulst, A. (1971). 'France, the Low Countries, and Western Germany' in Ch. VII, Sec. 1, in M.M. Postan (ed.), *op. cit.*

Geertz, C. (1970). *Agricultural Involution*, California UP.

Ghandhi, J.K. (1972). *The Capital Market in India* (unpublished).

Gopalan, C., Rama Sastri, B.V. and Balasubramanian, S.C. (1971). *The Nutritive Value of Indian Foods*, Indian Council of Medical Research, Hyderabad.

Gopalan, C., Balasubramanian, S.C., Rama Sastri, B.V. and Rao, K.V. (1971a). *The Diet Atlas of India*, ICMR, Hyderabad.

Gopalan, C. and Vijaya Raghavan, K. (1971). *The Nutrition Atlas of India*, ICMR, Hyderabad.

Gough, J. (1971). 'Agricultural Wages in the Punjab', *EPW*, March.

Gough, K. (1955). 'The Social Structure of a Tanjore Village', in Srinivas, M.N., *India's Villages*, Asia, Bombay.

Gough, K. and Sharma, H. (1973). *Imperialism and Revolution in South Asia*, Monthly Review Press, New York.

Griffin, K. (1970). 'Foreign Capital, Domestic Saving and Economic Development', *Oxford Bulletin of Economics and Statistics*, May.

Griffin, K. (1974). *The Political Economy of Agrarian Change*, Macmillan, London.

Gulati, I.S. and Krishnan, T.N. (1975). 'Public Distribution and Procurement of Foodgrains: A Proposal', *EPW*, May.

Gupta, A.P. (1975). 'The Rich, the Poor and the Taxes They Pay in India' (mimeo), ILO World Employment Programme, Research Working Paper No. 12.

Hanson, A.H. (1966). *The Process of Planning*, Oxford UP.

Haq, Mahabub ul (1963). *The Strategy of Economic Planning*, Oxford UP.

Haq, Mahabub ul (1967). 'Tied Credits—A Quantitative Analysis', in Adler, J. (ed.), *Capital Movements and Economic Development*, Macmillan, London.

Harcourt, G.C. (1972). *Some Cambridge Controversies in the Theory of Capital*, Cambridge UP.

Harris, D. (1969). 'Price Behaviour in India: An Examination of Professor Raj's Hypothesis', *Indian Economic Review*, Vol. IV, No. 2.

Hazari, R.K. (1966). *The Structure of the Corporate Private Sector*, Asia, Bombay.

Hazari, R.K. and Ojha, A.N. (1970). 'The Public Sector in India', in Robinson and Kidron, *op. cit.*

Hopper, W.D. (1965). 'Allocative Efficiency in a Traditional Indian Agriculture', *Journal of Farm Economics*, August.

Hopper, W.D. and Freeman, W.H. (1969). 'From Unsteady Infancy to Vigorous Adolescence: Rice Development', *EPW*, March.

India

Ministry of Agriculture (1973). *An Introduction to the Agricultural Census Operations in India, 1970-71.*

Ministry of Food and Agriculture (annual) *Indian Agriculture in Brief.*

Ministry of Food and Agriculture (annual) *Estimates of Area and Production of Principal Crops in India.*

Ministry of Food and Agriculture (1968). *Growth Rates in Agriculture, 1949-50 to 1964-65.*

Ministry of Food and Agriculture (1971). *Modernizing Traditional Agriculture*, Vols. I and II.

Ministry of Food and Agriculture (1958). *Area, Production and Average Yield per Acre of Principal Crops in India 1949-50 to 1957-58.*

Ministry of Finance (annual) *Economic Survey.*

Ministry of Finance (annual) *Pocketbook of Economic Information.*

Ministry of Finance (1971). *Direct Taxes Enquiry Committee, Final Report (Wanchoo Committee).*

Ministry of Finance (1972). *Report of the Committee on Taxation of Agricultural Wealth and Income (Raj Committee).*

Bureau of Public Enterprises (annual) *A Handbook of Information on Public Sector Enterprises.*

Ministry of Irrigation and Power (1972). *Report of the Irrigation Commission*, Vol. I.

Ministry of Labour and Employment, Labour Bureau (1960). *Agricultural Labour in India, Report of Second Enquiry*, Vol. I.

Ministry of Labour and Employment, Labour Bureau (1968). *Agricultural Labour in India—A Compendium of Basic Facts.*

Lok Sabha Estimates Committee 3rd Lok Sabha (1964). *Rural Works Programme* (55th Report).

Lok Sabha Estimates Committee 4th Lok Sabha (1967). *Utilization of External Assistance* (11th Report).

Lok Sabha Estimates Committee 4th Lok Sabha (1968). *Fertilizers* (49th Report).

Lok Sabha Committee on Public Undertakings 3rd Lok Sabha (1965). *Fertilizer Corporation of India* (6th Repot).

Lok Sabha Committee on Public Undertakings 3rd Lok Sabha (1965a). *Rourkela Steel Plant* (11th Report).

Lok Sabha Committee on Public Undertakings 3rd Lok Sabha (1966). *Indian Drugs and Pharmaceuticals Ltd.* (22nd Report).

Lok Sabha Committee on Public Undertakings 3rd Lok Sabha (1966a). *Durgapur Steel Plant* (29th Report).

Lok Sabha Committee on Public Undertakings 3rd Lok Sabha (1966b). *Bhilai Steel Plant* (30th Report).

Lok Sabha Committee on Public Undertakings 4th Lok Sabha (1968). *Heavy Electricals (India) Ltd.* (12th Report).

Lok Sabha Committee on Public Undertakings 4th Lok Sabha (1968a). *Heavy Engineering Corporation Ltd.* (14th Report).

Lok Sabha Committee on Public Undertakings 4th Lok Sabha (1968b). *Indian Drugs and Pharmaceuticals* (30th Report).

Lok Sabha Committee on Public Undertakings 4th Lok Sabha (1968-69). *Hindustan Steel Ltd.* (31st Report).

Planning Commission (1952). *First Five Year Plan.*

Planning Commission (1956). *Second Five Year Plan.*

Planning Commission (1961). *Third Five Year Plan.*

Planning Commission (1966). *Fourth Five Year Plan.*

Planning Commission (1969). *Fourth Five Year Plan 1969-74.*

Planning Commission (1973). *Approach to the Fifth Plan 1974-79.*

Planning Commission (1974). *Draft Fifth Five Year Plan,* Vols. I and II.

Planning Commission (1957). *Review of the First Five Year Plan.*

Planning Commission (1963). *Third Five Year Plan Progress Report 1961-62.*

Planning Commission (1971). *The Fourth Plan Mid-Term Appraisal,* Vols. I and II.

Planning Commission (n.d.). *Report of the Task Force on Nutrition* (mimeo).

Perspective Planning Division (1966). *Draft Fourth Plan: Material and Financial Balances.*

Perspective Planning Division (1974). 'Perspective of Development 1961-1976: Implications for Planning for a Minimum Level of Living', in Srinivasan and Bardhan, *op. cit.*

Programme Evaluation Organization (1967, 1968). *Regional Variations in Social Development and Levels of Living,* Vols. I and II.

Programme Evaluation Organization (1969). *Report on Evaluation of Consolidation of Holdings Programme.*

Programme Evaluation Organization (1970). *Family Planning Programme in India: An Evaluation.*

Programme Evaluation Organization (1970). *Evaluation Study of Post Stage II C.D. Blocks.*

Programme Evaluation Organization (1964, 1969). *Report of the Committee on Distribution of Income and Levels of Living,* parts I and II (*Mahalanobis Committee*).

Programme Evaluation Organization (1967). *Report of the Committee on Industrial Planning and Licensing Policy* (*Hazari Committee*)

Programme Evaluation Organization (1970). *Report of the Committee on Unemployment Estimates* (*Dantwala Committee*).

Office of the Registrar General, Vital Statistics Division (1971). *Infant Mortality in India.*

Office of the Registrar General, Vital Statistics Division (1972). *Sample Registration of Births and Deaths in India.*

Office of the Registrar General, Vital Statistics Division (1972a). *Measures of Fertility and Mortality in India.*

Registrar General and Census Commissioner (1971). *Census of India: Provisional Population Tables.*

Ministry of Steel and Heavy Industries (1963). *Report of Steel Control* (*Raj Committee*).

Indian Society of Agricultural Economics (1966). *Indian Journal of Agricultural Economics—Selected Readings*, ISAE, Bombay.

Indian Society of Agricultural Economics (1972). *Comparative Experience of Agricultural Development in Developing Countries of Asia and the Far East since World War II*, ISAE, Bombay.

International Bank for Reconstruction and Development (1972). *World Bank Atlas*, IBRD, Washington.

International Labour Organization (1970). *Towards Full Employment*, ILO, Geneva.

International Labour Organization (1971). *Matching Employment Opportunities and Expectations*, ILO, Geneva.

International Labour Organization (1972). *Employment, Incomes and Equality*, ILO, Geneva.

Januzzi, F. Thomasson (1970). 'Land Reform in Bihar, India: The Agrarian Structure in Bihar, in USAID, *op. cit.*

Johl, S.S. (1975). 'Gains of the Green Revolution: How they have been shared in Punjab', *Journal of Development Studies*, April.

Jose, A.V. (1974). 'Trends in Real Wage Rates of Agricultural Labourers', *EPW*, March.

Joshi, P.C. (1971). 'Land Reform and Agrarian Change in India and Pakistan since 1947' in Dutta, R. and Joshi, P.C. (eds.) *Studies in Asian Social Development*, No. 1, Tata-McGraw Hill, Delhi.

Journal of Development Studies (1972). Special Issue on *Development Indicators* (N. Bastor ed.), April.

Journal of Development Studies (1972). Special Issue on *Technology* (C. Cooper ed.), October.

Joy, J.L. (1971). 'Economic Aspects of Food and Nutrition Planning', IDS Communication Series, No. 101.

Kaldor, N. (1955-56). 'Alternative Theories of Distribution', *Review of Economic Studies*

Kanwar, J.S. (1969). 'From Protective to Productive Irrigation', *EPW*, March.

Kapoor, A. (1970). *International Business Negotiations: A Study in India*, New York UP.

Khusro, A.M. (1964). 'Returns to Scale in Indian Agriculture', *IJAE*, October-December.

Khusro, A.M. (ed.) (1968). *Readings in Agricultural Development*, Allied, Calcutta.

Khusro, A.M. (1973). *Economics of Land Reform and Farm Size in India*, Macmillan, Delhi.

Kidron, M. (1965). *Foreign Investments in India*, Oxford UP.

Kosambi, D.D. (1972). *The Culture and Civilization of Ancient India in Historical Outline*, Vikas, Delhi.

Krishna, Raj (1959). 'Agrarian Reform: The Debate on Ceilings', *Economic Development and Cultural Change*, January.

Krishna, Raj (1963). 'Farm-Supply Response in India-Pakistan; A Case-study of the Punjab Region', *Economic Journal*, September.

Krishna, Raj (1967, 1972). 'Government Operations in Foodgrains', *EPW*, September; reprinted in Chaudhuri, *op. cit.*

Krishna, Raj (1973). 'Unemployment in India', *IJAE*, January-March.

Krishnamurthy, J. (1973). 'Working Force in 1971: Unilluminating "Final" Results', *EPW*, August, Special no. 31-33.

Krishnamurthy, J. (1974). 'Structure of the Working Force of the Indian Union', Fourth European Conference on South Asian Studies, University of Sussex.

Krishnan, T.N. (1965, 1972). 'The Marketed Surplus in Foodgrains', *Economic Weekly*, February, reprinted in Chaudhuri, *op. cit.*

Krueger, A. (1970). *The Benefits and Costs of Import-substitution in India*, Minnesota UP.

Kuznets, S. (1966) *Modern Economic Growth*, Yale UP.

Ladejinsky, W. (1965). *A Study of Tenurial Conditions in Package Districts*, Government of India.

Ladejinsky, W. (1969a). 'The Green Revolution in the Punjab', *EPW*, June.

Ladejinsky, W. (1969b). 'The Green Revolution in Bihar', *EPW*, September.

Ladejinsky, W. (1972). 'Land Ceilings and Land Reform', *EPW*, February.

Ladejinsky, W. (1973). 'How Green is the Indian Green Revolution?', *EPW*, December.

Lal, Deepak (1972). *Wells and Welfare*, *OECD*, Paris.

Lal, Deepak (1975). *Appraising Foreign Investment in Developing Countries*, Heinemann, London.

Lall, S. (1973). 'Transfer Pricing by Multinational Manufacturing Firms', *Oxford University Bulletin of Economics and Statistics*, August.

Lall, S. (1974). 'The International Pharmaceutical Industry and the Less Developed Countries, with special reference to India', *Oxford University Bulletin of Economics and Statistics*, August.

Lefeber, L. (1973). 'Income Distribution and Agricultural Development', in Bhagwati, J. and Eckaus, E. (eds.), *Development and Planning*, Allen and Unwin, London.

Lefeber, L. and Datta-Chaudhuri, M. (1971). *Regional Development: Experiences and Prospects for South and South-east Asia*, UNRISD/Mouton, Paris.

Lewis, J. (1962). *Quiet Crisis in India*, Brookings, Washington.

Lewis, S.R. Jnr. (1968). 'The Effect of Trade Policy on Domestic Relative Prices: Pakistan 1951-65', *American Economic Review*, March.

Leys, C. (1974). 'The Politics of "Redistribution with Growth" ' (mimeo).

Lipton, M. (1967). 'Should Reasonable Farmers Respond to Changes in Prices?', *Modern Asian Studies*, January.

Lipton, M. (1968). 'Strategy for Agriculture: Urban Bias and Rural Planning', in Streeten, P. and Lipton, M. (eds.), *The Crisis of Indian Planning*, Oxford UP.

Lipton, M. (1968a). 'The Theory of the Optimising Peasant', *Journal of Development Studies*, April.

Lipton, M. (1969). 'The Transfer of Resources from Agriculture to Non-Agricultural Activities: The Case of India', IDS Communication series No. 109.

Lipton, M. (1975). 'Urban Bias and Food Policy in Poor Countries', *Food Policy*, November.

Little, I., Scitovsky, T. and Scott, M.F. (1970). *Industry and Trade in Some Developing Countries*, Oxford UP.

Lubell, H. (1974). *Urban Development and Employment: the Prospects of Calcutta*, ILO, Geneva.

MacDougall, G.A.D. (1958). 'The Benefits and Costs of Private Investment from Abroad: A Theoretical Approach', *Economic Record* March.

Macmichael, P., Rhodes, R. and Petras, J. (1974). 'Imperialism and the Contradictions of Development', *New Left Review*, May-June.

Macpherson, W.J. (1972). 'Economic Development in India under the British Crown 1858-1947', in Youngson, A.J. (ed.), *Economic Development in the Long Run*, Allen and Unwin, London.

Mahalanobis, P.C. (1963). *The Approach of Operational Research to Planning in India*, Asia, Bombay.

Mamdani, M. (1972). *The Myth of Population Control*, Monthly Review Press, New York.

Mandelbaum, D. (1974). *Human Fertility in India: Social Components and Policy Perspectives*, California UP.

Mann, Harold (1967). *Social Framework of Agriculture*, Vora, Bombay.

Mann, J.S. (1967). 'The Impact of PL 480 Imports', *Journal of Farm Economics*, February.

Manne, A. and Rudra, A. (1965). 'A Consistency Model of India's Fourth Plan', *Sankhya*, Series B, February.

Mathur, P.N., Valavade, S.P. and Kirloskar, M.V. (1967). 'Optimum Capacity and Imbalance of Capital Structure', *Arthavijnana*, September-December.

Mazumdar, D. (1963). 'On the Economics of Relative Efficiency of Small Farmers, *Economic Weekly*, July.

Medhora, P. (1968). *Industrial Growth since 1950*, Univ. of Bombay.

Mehra, S. (1966, 1972). 'Surplus Labour in Indian Agriculture', *Indian Economic Review*, April; reprinted in Chaudhuri, *op. cit.*

Mencher, J.P. (1975). 'Land Ceilings in Tamil Nadu: Facts and Fiction', *EPW*, February.

Minhas, B.S. (1970). 'Rural Poverty, Land Redistribution and Development', *Indian Economic Review*, April.

Minhas, B.S. (1974). *Planning and the Poor*, S. Chand, Delhi.

Minhas, B.S. and Srinivasan, T.N. (1972). 'The New Agricultural Production Strategy: Some Policy Issues', in Chaudhuri, *op. cit.*

Minhas, B.S. and Vaidyanathan, A. (1965, 1972). 'Growth of Crop Output in India', JISAS; reprinted in Chaudhuri, *op. cit.*

Minhas, B.S. and Vaidyanathan, A. (1969). 'Water Requirements of Crops and Economic Efficiency of Irrigation Water in India' (mimeo), Indian Statistical Institute.

Mitra, A. (1963). 'Tax Burden on Indian Agriculture', in Braibanti, R. and Spengler, J.J., *Administration and Economic Development in India*, Duke UP.

Mitra, A. (1970). 'Population and Foodgrain Output in India: A Note on Disparate Growth Rates', in Robinson and Kidron, *op. cit.*

Mitra, A. (ed.) (1974). *Economic Theory and Planning*, Oxford UP.

Mitra, A. (1977) *Terms of Trade and Class Relations*, Frank Cass, London.

Mitra, A.K. (1974). 'Employment in the Manufacturing Industry—an Analysis of Growth Rate and Trend, 1960-70', *Arthavijnana*, March.

Moore, Barrington (1967). *The Social Origins of Dictatorship and Democracy*, Allen Lane, London.

Morris, Morris D. (1965). *The Emergence of an Industrial Labour Force in India*, California UP.

Morris, Morris D. *et al.* (1969). *The Indian Economy in the Nineteenth Century*, Hindusthan Pubns., Delhi.

Morris-Jones, W.H. (1967). *The Government and Politics of India*, Hutchinson, London.

Mukherjee, M. (1969). *The National Income of India: Trends and Structure*, Statistical Publishing House, Calcutta.

Myrdal, G. (1968). *Asian Drama*, 3 vols., Allen Lane, London.

Nair, P.R. Gopinathan (1974). 'Decline in Birth-rate in Kerala: A Hypothesis about the Inter-relationship between Demographic Variables, Health Services and Education', *EPW*, February.

National Council of Applied Economic Research (1971). *Foreign Technology and Investment*, NCAER, New Delhi.

National Council of Applied Economic Research (1972). *Household Income, Saving and Consumer Expenditure*, NCAER, New Delhi.

National Council of Applied Economic Research (1973). *Impact of Mechanization in Agriculture on Employment*, NCAER, New Delhi.

Nayyar, D. (1976). *India's Exports and Export Policies in the 1960s*, Cambridge UP.

Nayyar, D. (1975). 'India's Trade with the Socialist Countries', *World Development*, May.

Ohkawa, K. and Rosovsky, H. (1960). 'The Role of Agriculture in Modern Japanese Development', *Economic Development and Cultural Change*, October.

Ohlin, G. (1966). *Foreign Aid Policies Reconsidered*, OECD, Paris.

Ojha. P.D. (1970). 'A Configuration of Indian Poverty: Inequality and Levels of Living', *Reserve Bank of India Bulletin*, January.

Panikar, P.G.K. (1972). 'Economics of Nutrition', *EPW*, February.

Papanek, G. (1972). 'The Effect of Aid and other Resource Transfers on Savings and Growth in Less Developed Countries', *Economic Journal*, September.

Parikh, A. (1969). 'Complementarity between Irrigation and Fertilizer in Indian Agriculture', *IJAE*, July-September.

Parikh, K. and Srinivasan, T.N. (1974). 'Optimum Requirements of Fertilizers' (mimeo), Indian Statistical Institute.

Parthasarathy, G. and Suryanarayanan, Raju (1971). 'Andhra Pradesh (Andhra Area) Tenancy (Amendment) Act, 1970: A Critical Review', *EPW*, March.

Passinetti, L. (1961-62). 'Rate of profit and income distribution in relation to the rate of economic growth', *Review of Economic Studies*, October.

Patel, I.G. (1969). 'The Strategy of Indian Planning', in Rao, C.R. (ed.), *Essays in Econometrics and Planning*, Pergamon, Oxford.

Patel, S.J. (1959). 'Export Prospects and Economic Growth: India', *Economic Journal*, September.

Patnaik, P. (1972). 'Imperialism and the Growth of Indian Capitalism', in Owen, R. and Sutcliffe, B., *Studies in the Theory of Imperialism*, Longmans, London.

Patnaik. P. (1972a). 'The Disproportionality Crisis and Cyclical Growth: A Theoretical Note', *EPW*, February.

Patnaik, Utsa (1971). 'Capitalist Development in Agriculture', *EPW*, September and December.

Penrose, E. (1973). 'International Patenting and the Less Developed Countries', *Economic Journal*, September.

Postan, M.M. (1971). 'England', Ch. VII, Sec. 7, in Postan (ed.), *op. cit.*

Postan, M.M. (ed.) (1971). Cambridge Economic History of Europe, Vol. I, *Agrarian Life of the Middle Ages*, Cambridge UP.

Preobrazhensky, E. (1965). *The New Economics*, Oxford UP.

Rahman, Anisur (1968). 'Foreign Capital and Domestic Savings', *Review of Economics and Statistics*, February.

Raj, K.N. (1948). *Monetary Policy of the Reserve Bank of India*, National Information & Pubns. Ltd., Bombay.

Raj, K.N. (1959). 'Employment and Unemployment in the Indian Economy', *Economic Development and Cultural Change*, January.

Raj, K.N. (1962). 'The Marginal Rate of Saving in the Indian Economy', *Oxford Economic Papers*, February.

Raj, K.N. (1965). *Indian Economic Growth: Performance and Prospects*, Allied, Calcutta.

Raj, K.N. (1966, 1972). 'Price Behaviour in India, 1949-66: An Explanatory Hypothesis', *Indian Economic Review*, October; reprinted in Chaudhuri, *op. cit.*

Raj, K.N. (1966a). 'Regional Variations in Foodgrains Prices', *EPW*, August.

Raj, K.N. (1967). 'Fourth Plan and Future Economic Policy', *EPW*, March.

Raj, K.N. (1967a). 'The Role of the "Machine Tools Sector" in Economic Growth', in Feinstein, C.H. (ed.), *Socialism, Capitalism and Economic Growth*, Cambridge UP.

Raj, K.N. (1970). 'Some Issues Concerning Investment and Saving in the Indian Economy', in Robinson and Kidron, *op. cit.*

Raj, K.N. (1972). 'Mechanization of Agriculture in India and Sri Lanka', *International Labour Review*, July-December.

Raj, K.N. (1973). 'Approach to the Fifth Plan', *EPW*, February.

Raj, K.N. and Sen, A.K. (1961). 'Alternative Patterns of Growth under Conditions of Stagnant Export Earnings', *Oxford Economic Papers*, February.

Rajaraman, Indira (1975). 'Poverty, Inequality and Economic Growth: Rural Punjab, 1960-61—1970-71', *Journal of Development Studies*, July.

Randhawa, M.S. (1974). *Green Revolution· A Case-study of Punjab*, Vikas, Delhi.

Rao, C.H. Hanumantha (1965, 1968). 'Agricultural Growth and Stagnation in India', *Economic Weekly*, February, reprinted in Khusro, *op. cit.*

Rao, C.H. Hanumantha (1966). 'Alternative Explanations of the Inverse Relationship between Farm Size and Output per Acre in India', *Indian Economic Review*, October.

Rao, C.H. Hanumantha (1975). *Technological Change and the Distribution of Gains in Indian Agriculture*, Macmillan, Delhi.

Rao, C.R. (ed.) (1972). *Data Base of the Indian Economy*, Vol. 1, Statistical Publishing Society, Calcutta.

Rao, V.K.R.V. (1952). 'Investment, Income and the Multiplier in an Under-developed Economy', *Indian Economic Review*, February.

Rao, V.K.R.V. (1953). 'Some Reflections on the Comparability of Real National Income of Industrial and Underdeveloped Countries', *Income and Wealth*, Series III, Bowes and Bowes, Cambridge.

Rao, V.K.R.V. and Desai, P. (1965). *Greater Delhi*, Asia, Bombay.

Rath, N. and Patvardhan, V.S. (1967). *Impact of Assistance under PL 480 in the Indian Economy*, Asia, Bombay.

Reddaway, W.B. (1962). *The Development of the Indian Economy*, Allen and Unwin, London.

Reserve Bank of India (1968). *Foreign Collaboration in Indian Industry*, RBI, Bombay.

Reserve Bank of India (1968). 'Time Lags in the Implementation of Development Projects', *RBI Bulletin*, March.

Reserve Bank of India (1974). 'Survey of Financial and Technical Collaboration in Indian Industry, 1964-70: Main Findings' in *RBI Bulletin*, June.

Reserve Bank of India (1962, 1966, 1972, 1973). 'Finances of Branches of

Foreign Companies and Foreign-controlled Rupee Companies', *RBI Bulletin*, March, July, May, October.

Robinson, E.A.G. (1970, 1971). 'Economic Progress in India', *Three Banks Review*, March; reprinted in Chaudhuri, *op. cit.*

Robinson, E.A.G. and Kidron, M. (eds.) (1970). *Economic Development in South Asia*, Macmillan, London.

Rodgers, G.R. (1973). 'Effects of Public Works on Rural Poverty', *EPW*, February.

Rosovsky, H. (1968). 'Rumbles in the Ricefields: Professor Nakamura vs. the Official Statistics', *Journal of Asian Studies*, February.

Rudra, A. (1969). 'Big Farmers of Punjab: Second Instalment of Results' *EPW*, December.

Rudra, A. (1971). 'Capitalist Development in Agriculture: A Reply', *EPW*, November.

Rudra, A. (1973). 'Direct Estimation of Surplus Labour in Agriculture', *EPW*, February.

Rudra, A. (1974). 'Minimum Level of Living—A Statistical Examination', in Srinivasan and Bardhan, *op. cit.*

Rudra, A. (1974a). 'Usefulness of Plan Models: An Assessment based on Indian Experience', in Mitra, *op. cit.*

Rudra, A., Majid, A. and Talib, B.D. (1969). 'Big Farmers of Punjab: Some Preliminary Findings of a Sample Survey', *EPW*, September.

Satyanarayana, Y. (1972). 'Impact of the Government of India's Licensing Policy on Industrial Output' (mimeo), USAID, New Delhi.

Schebeck, E.M. (1969). 'An Analysis of Capital Flows between Agricultural and Non-agricultural Sectors of India' (mimeo), IBRD.

Schulter, M. (1971). 'Differential Rates of Adoption of the New Seed varieties in India: The Problem of the Small Farmer', Cornell Univ.

Schultz, T.W. (1964). *Transforming Traditional Agriculture*, Dept. of Agriculture, Yale UP.

Seers, D. (1952-53). 'Role of National Income Estimates in the Statistical Policy of an Under-developed Area', *Review of Economic Studies*, Vol. XX.

Seers, D. (1972). 'What are we Trying to Measure?', IDS Communication Series No. 106R.

Sen, A.K. (1960). 'Choice of Techniques', Blackwell, Oxford.

Sen, A.K. (1964). 'Size of Holdings and Productivity', *Economic Weekly*, February.

Sen, A.K. (1966). 'Peasants and Dualism with or without Surplus Labour', *Journal of Political Economy*, October.

Sen, A.K. (1973). *On Economic Inequality*, Oxford UP.

Sen, A.K. (1973a). 'Poverty, Inequality and Unemployment: Some Conceptual Issues in Measurement', *EPW*, August.

Sen, A.K. (1973b). 'Dimensions of Unemployment in India', Indian Statistical Institute.

Sen, A.K. (1975). *Employment, Technology and Development*, Oxford UP.

Sen, S.N. (1960). *The City of Calcutta: A Socio-economic Survey*, Bookland, Calcutta.

Sen, S.R. (1967). 'Growth and Instability in Indian Agriculture', *JISAS*, June.

Shetty, S.L. (1971). 'An Inter-sectoral Analysis of Taxable Capacity and Tax Burden', *IJAE*, July-September.

Shirokov, G.K. (1973). *Industrialization of India*, Progress, Moscow.

Shukla, T. (1965). *Capital Formation in Indian Agriculture*, Vora, Bombay.

Simmons, G.B. (1971). *Indian Investment in Family Planning*, Population Council, New York.

Singh, Manmohan (1964). *India's Export Trends and Prospects for Self-sustained Growth*, Oxford UP.

Singh, Tarlok (1974). *India's Development Experience*, Macmillan, London.

Sovani, N. (1951). *Social Survey of Kolhapur City*, Gokhale Inst, Poona.

Spate, O.H.K. and Learmonth, A.T.A. (1967). *India and Pakistan: Land, People and Economy*, Methuen, London.

Srinivasan, T.N. (1972). 'The Green Revolution or the Wheat Revolution?' in Indian Society of Agricultural Economics, *op. cit.*

Srinivasan, T.N. (1974). *Foreign Trade Regime and Economic Development of India* (mimeo), Indian Statistical Institute.

Srinivasan, T.N. (1974a). 'Income Distribution: A Survey of Policy Aspects', in Srinivasan and Bardhan, *op. cit.*

Srinivasan, T.N. and Bardhan, P.K. (eds.) (1974). *Poverty and Income Distribution in India*, Statistical Publishing Society, Calcutta.

Srinivasan, T.N., Radhakrishnan, P.N. and Vaidyanathan, A. (1974). 'Data on Distribution of Consumption Expenditure in India: An Evaluation', in Srinivasan and Bardhan, *op. cit.*

Stewart, F. and Streeten, P. (1971). 'Conflicts between Output and Employment Objectives in Developing Countries', *Oxford Economic Papers*, July.

Streeten, P. (1972). *Frontiers of Development Studies*, Macmillan, London.

Sukhatme, P.V. (1965). *Feeding India's Growing Millions*, Asia, Bombay.

Sukhatme, P.V. (1971). 'The Present Pattern of Production and Availability of Food in Asia', IDS Communication Series No. 101.

Sukhatme, P.V. (1972). 'Protein Strategy and Agricultural Development', *IJAE*, January-March.

Tanzer, M. (1969). *The Political Economy of International Oil and the Underdeveloped Countries*, Temple Smith, London.

Tendulkar, S.D. (1971). 'Inter-action between Domestic and Foreign Resources in Economic Growth', in Chenery, H.B. (ed.), *Studies in Development Planning*, Harvard UP.

Tendulkar, S.D. (1974). 'Planning for Growth, Redistribution and Self-reliance in the Fifth Five Year Plan', *EPW*, Vol. IX, January.

Thamarajakshi, R. (1969, 1972). 'Inter-sectoral Terms of Trade and Marketed Surplus of Agricultural Produce, 1951-2 to 1965-6', *EPW*, June; reprinted in Chaudhuri, *op. cit.*

Thorner, A. and Thorner, D. (1962). *Land and Labour in India*, Asia, Bombay.

Thorner, D. (1954). *Agrarian Prospect in India*, Univ. of Delhi.

Townsend, P. (ed.) (1970). *The Concept of Poverty*, Heinemann, London.

USAID (1970). *Spring Review of Land Reform*, Vol. 1, country papers: *Land Reform in India*, Washington.

USAID (1972). *Economic and Social Indications: India*, New Delhi.

UNO (1975). *Poverty, Unemployment and Development: A Case Study of Selected Issues with Reference to Kerala*, New York.

US Department of Agriculture (1973). *Agricultural Development and Farm Employment in India*, Foreign Agricultural Economic Report No. 84, Washington.

Vaidyanathan, A. (1974). 'Some Aspects of Inequalities in Living Standards in Rural India', in Srinivasan and Bardhan, *op. cit.*

Vaidyanathan, A. (1974a). 'On the New Economics of Poverty', in Mitra, A. (ed.), *op. cit.*

Vaitsos, C.V. (1974). *Inter-country Income Distribution and Transnational Enterprises*, Oxford UP.

Viner, J. (1957). *International Trade and Economic Development*, Oxford UP.

Vyas, V.S. (1973). 'Regional Imbalances in Foodgrains Production in the Last Decade: Some Preliminary Results', *EPW*, December.

Walters, A.A. (ed.) (1973). *Money and Banking*, Penguin, Harmondsworth.

Warren, Bill (1973). 'Imperialism and Capitalist Industrialization', *New Left Review*, September-October.

Warriner, Doreen (1969). *Land Reform in Principle and Practice*, Oxford UP.

Weisskopf, T.E. (1972). 'Dependence and Imperialism in India' (mimeo).

Weisskopf, T.E. (1975). 'China and India: A Comparative Survey of Performance in Economic Development', *EPW*, February, Annual no.

Wharton, C.R. (1969). 'Green Revolution: Cornucopia or Pandora's Box?' *Foreign Affairs*, April.

Wunderlich, G. (1970). 'Land Reforms in India', in USAID, *op. cit.*

Wyon, J.B., and Gordon, J.E. (1971), *The Khanna Study*, Harvard UP

Subject Index

Author Index